THE
post-behavioral era
perspectives on political science

THE
post-behavioral era
perspectives on political science

Edited by

GEORGE J. GRAHAM, JR.
Vanderbilt University

and

GEORGE W. CAREY
Georgetown University

DAVID McKAY COMPANY, INC.
NEW YORK

Cover Design by Saul Schnurman
Cover Photo: Hedrich-Blessing

To *Carmen Michelle* and *Michelle Marie*

Preface

In the fall of 1969, a panel was held at the Southern Political Science Association Conference in Miami on the general question: What should political scientists be doing? Lewis Lipsitz and George J. Graham, Jr., presented papers (included in this anthology) on the topic. The differences at least one author felt would develop did not. More important, the differences among individuals over the basic purpose of political science did not seem too great once positions were formally articulated. While involved in a discussion pursuant to the panel, the idea for this book emerged.

The purpose of the book, discussed more fully in the Introduction, is to bring together diverse personal commitments to political science in a fashion that will facilitate meaningful discourse. Once positions are seriously stated, discussion tends to be positive and constructive because the underlying agreements among the disputants become apparent.

The editors thank Robert C. Grady of Eastern Michigan University, Scarlett G. Graham of The University of Chicago, and Edward B. Portis of Vanderbilt University for critically reading portions of the book. We also thank Elizabeth R. McKee and Mildred White for typing final copy of the manuscript. The gracious assistance of Edward Artinian, senior editor at David McKay, is acknowledged and appreciated.

Contributors

Christian Bay, The University of Alberta
George W. Carey, Georgetown University
Dante Germino, The University of Virginia
George J. Graham, Jr., Vanderbilt University
Henry S. Kariel, The University of Hawaii
E. W. Kelley, The University of Chicago
Avery Leiserson, Vanderbilt University
Lewis Lipsitz, The University of North Carolina at Chapel Hill
Theodore J. Lowi, Cornell University
Eugene J. Meehan, The University of Missouri at St. Louis
Jorgen Rasmussen, Vanderbilt University
Ellis Sandoz, East Texas State University
Leo Strauss, St. John's College at Annapolis
Thomas Landon Thorson, Indiana University at South Bend

Contents

PREFACE. vii

INTRODUCTION: Political Science—What Next?   1

PART ONE: Political Science and "The
Discipline"

Introduction   7

1. THEODORE J. LOWI, The Politics of Higher
    Education: Political Science as a Case Study . . .   11

2. GEORGE W. CAREY, Beyond Parochialism in
    Political Science   37

3. EUGENE J. MEEHAN, What Should Political
    Scientists Be Doing?   54

4. JORGEN RASMUSSEN, "Once You've Made a
    Revolution, Everything's the Same":
    Comparative Politics   71

5. CHRISTIAN BAY, Thoughts on the Purposes of
    Political Science Education   88

PART TWO: Political Science and Action

Introduction 103

6. GEORGE J. GRAHAM, JR., Reason and
    Change in the Political Order 107

7. HENRY S. KARIEL, Possibilities 124

8. AVERY LEISERSON, Realism and Commitment
    in Political Theory 144

9.   LEWIS LIPSITZ, Vulture, Mantis, and Seal:
     Proposals for Political Scientists 171

10.   E. W. KELLEY, Political Science as Science
     and Common Sense 192

     PART THREE: Political Science and Political
     Philosophy

     Introduction 213

11.   LEO STRAUSS, Political Philosophy and the
     Crisis of Our Time 217

12.   DANTE GERMINO, Two Conceptions of Political
     Philosophy 243

13.   THOMAS LANDON THORSON, The Biological
     Foundations of Political Science: Reflections on
     the Post-Behavioral Era 258

14.   ELLIS SANDOZ, The Philosophical Science of
     Politics Beyond Behavioralism 285

Introduction:
Political Science—What Next?

AN ANTHOLOGY usually requires extensive justification. In the present case we think it does not. As the discipline of political science continues to undergo efforts to define or redefine itself in rather immodest degrees, the reverberations touch every student of politics from the undergraduate taking his first course to the president of the American Political Science Association. Much of the continuing debate has been negative—individuals condemning each other for grievous errors, oversights, lack of sophistication and/or training, denseness, shallowness, soft-mindedness, and so on. The list could be extended to little avail. The reason for this volume is found in the need for a set of diverse, *positive* evaluations of to what we can, if properly motivated, aspire as a discipline.

In justifying their own prescriptions, the essayists incorporate the specification of weaknesses in the present structures and conditions of the discipline. But even when negating certain practices, their focus remains on the potential for developing political science. The statements breathe fresh life into the situation of stale negativism often expressed among groups within the discipline. The options presented are personal perceptions of pathways toward a more meaningful joint effort by political scholars. Since all prescriptions are also personal convictions, the biases they include specify, in support of their perspective, suggestions affecting teaching and research, action and theory. The reader is asked to consider all the arguments

1

before forming his own final response. Each author has attempted to support his case; the reader is judge and jury.

Neither editor, and probably no contributor, believes the choice of perspective is merely a matter of taste. The issues involved run deep. Moral commitments, metaphysics, and conceptions of possibilities are clearly at the heart of the matter. The central theme is "What should political scientists be doing?" The responses presented are examples of, and reasons for, pursuing specific forms of analysis of political reality; positions held for factional reasons—the politics of the social organization of American political science—are set aside for the more demanding purpose of justifying why a position should be pursued.

The advantage of studying the internal views of others who are, after all, colleagues, becomes apparent. The major consideration of the editors was to bring together representative perspectives on political science that would permit the new student of politics an opportunity of surveying the discipline's nuances together, to assess the options, and to get beyond the number of perspectives that inevitably develop within a single department. Indeed, we wanted statements about personal orientations and commitments that are often gleaned by students only through personal interaction and discussions with political scientists.

The contributors' statements present their "personal" perspectives on political science. They go beyond common assessments of the scope of political science because they are prescriptive: they say what the authors think important about their own activities. The ground rules are perhaps best clarified by quoting from the standard portion of the letters originally sent to each contributor:

> Because of the importance of the present divisiveness within political science, and because of the lack of discussion of the issues involved in a fashion which will readily facilitate consideration of the options and alternatives which confront the discipline [the editors] believe that it will improve the quality and level of deliberation to bring together the various sides of the arguments in a single volume. The editors differ widely in their own perspectives on political science and hope to bring together, fairly, all of the competing perspectives. We both feel that your own orientation and response to the question "What should political scientists be doing?" would be an important contribution to our anthology.

There are very few ground rules to be imposed upon the essays for the anthology. This is to permit each contributor as much latitude as is possible in presenting his own thoughts on the problems confronting the discipline and his suggestions for what we should be doing. The theme identified by the title provides the basic linkage of the essays. The contributors vary from the extreme of neo-positivists to moral activists (of several varieties). In essence, the hope is that the contributor will respond to the theme as fully as he can in about twenty pages.

Some of the questions which we hope will hold the attention of the contributors are: What is the proper relationship between the discipline and political knowledge? (What is the proper form of political knowledge, its proper objectives, and its practical consequences?) What is the proper relationship between political scientist *qua* scholar and political action? (What is the proper formal relationship? Informal relationship?) What is the proper relationship of the Association and political action? What is the proper way to determine *what* subject matters deserve the attention of political scientists? How is this decision related to political action? What are your impressions of the divisions within the discipline and how significant are these divisions? You may be interested in pursuing the consequences of these divisions and the proper means for handling the present difficulties. How do the divisions relate to the discipline's objectives?

The questions are wide-ranging. Clearly, they cannot all be handled in an essay of the length we suggest. Some would not be relevant to a single essayist. They do, we think, indicate some of the issues which will be important when collectively viewing the various essays on what political science ought to be doing.

The responses compose this anthology. Interestingly, the authors speak to common problems and, therefore, to each other. Emphases vary, but the fit of the essays is a product of the issues in hand rather than editorial juggling. It speaks well of the discipline that a selectively diverse set of political scientists, speaking to each other and to common problems, enhance as well their discourse with the neophyte.

The selection of contributors ranges widely in political and methodological orientations as well as in their primary research interests. The responses were somewhat surprising because, in spite of their differences, the essays converge in their emphasis. The common agreements among the scholars provide appropriate departures for analysis. The apparent state of flux in political science is perhaps less chaotic than we expected. Different directions are advocated for the post-behavioral period, but the diversity seems stimulating rather than stultifying.

The essays have been placed into three general categories which seemed to grow quite naturally from the issues that attracted the authors' interests. Most essays at least touch on all three categories, but the main themes of each essay fit best one of the issues. The *first* is the general issue of the discipline itself. Questions are raised about how we should collectively act as a profession. The *second* is the relationship of political science and action. The difficult relationship between activity as a political scientist in pursuit of knowledge and as a citizen is investigated. The *third* is the relationship of the discipline and political philosophy. The impact of philosophical stances on political science is discussed both as a position from which to evaluate the discipline and as a subject providing the key to the meaning of the discipline. The separation of these basic questions, and the discussions of them, make clear the interrelationships of the underlying issues.

Part One: Political Science and "The Discipline"

Introduction

POLITICAL SCIENTISTS have a built-in concern over the nature of their professional organization. Research and teaching are both greatly affected by the styles of analysis, assumptions, and predispositions of the associated scholars of politics. The impact of the discipline touches all political scientists not only by means of its effect on professional training, but also by its effect on control over publication in journals, referees of book manuscripts, and funding of research. The central element in this is the American Political Science Association. The organization's leadership, formal and informal, is to a great extent the focal point for analysis of political science as a discipline.

It is important to note, and is discussed specifically in the essays by Theodore J. Lowi and George W. Carey, that the Association's leadership is not, or need not be, monolithic. The fact that the essays in this section are written by "successful" political scientists invalidates any such charge. The presupposition behind each essay is that certain important questions must be answered, and evaluative criteria developed, for improving the quality and the character of political science. Not surprisingly, the response to the presupposition brings forth generically different answers. The answers, however, share this in common: The work of a discipline ought neither to be treated as the inconsequential, random pursuit of fleeting interest nor be measured by mere criteria of acceptance by others on the basis of the prevailing, perhaps fleeting, orthodoxy. The significant consensus is the request—the plea—to be significant on our own ground, the ground established by the scholar.

If the consensus is clear, the diversity becomes all the more important because it is externalized as specific proposals about proper direction which can be discussed in lowered voices; that is, issues and positions are defended in a manner which leads to meaningful discussion. The positions presented are often in direct opposition to each other. The positions of Lowi and Eugene J. Meehan on the issue of the proper relationship of the discipline and actual application are, at first blush, irreconcilable. The radical rationalist position of Lowi and the social engineering perspective espoused by Meehan hit head-on. But the agreement that the issue is critical and must be resolved makes the confrontation constructive.

The five essays in this section, then, are arguments concerning the goals and standards the authors believe ought to be adopted by the discipline's members. They are normative prescriptions and must be evaluated in normative terms. The proposals affect different dimensions of research and teaching, but all generally touch on an agenda for the American Political Science Association; that is, they are shared concerns which require for their resolution a common response.

Lowi's essay assesses the formal association of political scholars both from the perspective of the impact of the Caucus for a New Political Science and from the larger perspective of the relationship of the university and society. His analysis of the Caucus is an outsider's view by a previous insider—Lowi having once been a leader within their organization. The linkage of the Caucus to the Association, in light of Lowi's analysis of the relationship of universities and societies, permits him to assess the future of political scholarship either as free or as coopted into a technocratic system, depending upon the willingness of the discipline to reassert commitment to mind over action.

The perspective of Carey is more characteristic of analysis concerning "what went wrong" and how to reinstitute freedom for certain scholarly pursuits that do not fit the behavioral commitments of most political scientists. His argument is that behavioral analysts were quick to adopt value-free positions in analysis "professionally," but that their values affected clearly their own research and, more critically, the discipline as a whole. This schizoid position of value-free scholar and valuing individual was instrumental to the inability of most political scientists to grasp the impact of new demands recently developing among the younger members of the discipline. His proposal is for a more catholic orientation, paradoxically involving what can be termed an academic "apartheid." Different departments and journals should be available for all important orientations.

Meehan's essay is directed at the theme of fact-value analysis, espousing firmer standards for what research deserves rigorous scientific analysis, although he remains in favor of rigorous scientific analysis. His proposals cut both against scientific political study *qua* scientific political study and against analysis of values without science. He argues for useful science and against research and education that has no meaningful impact on human existence. His strongly instrumentalist view of science links science and action.

Jorgen Rasmussen's argument echoes some of this disaffection with science as science. His essay focuses on the field of comparative politics and its development since Roy Macridis's 1955 report on the unscientific state of comparative political research. Rasmussen's research has been heavily empirical, so his argument must be read as a challenge to the value of what has developed from contemporary comparative research independent of whether science itself is at stake. This leads him to the underlying question: Can better research be pursued with one's focus on political subjects, employing science, or with one's focus on science, applied to political subjects? His conclusion is for the former, marking along the way the fact that theory (and even traditional political theory questions) ought to be the major focus.

The final essay in the section is Christian Bay's discussion of political science education. His approach to the question is critical because it states that the goals or purposes that affect teaching are instrumental to research. Indeed, he begins by pushing the question to the level of the "purpose of politics." This purpose, promoting a more just society committed to optimal security and freedom for all human beings, is applied in assaying prescriptions for the university in general and the discipline in particular. Bay's argument accepts science, but quickly adds that much more is required of political scholars, especially because of the potential effects of education on students and society.

.1. The Politics of Higher Education: Political Science as a Case Study

THEODORE J. LOWI

*"We have met the enemy
and he is us."*
—*"Pogo"*

IT WAS inevitable that political science would feel the impact of the Great Disorder of the 1960s. This was not the Great Depression. In the 1960s the hard times were political, governmental. Government could not be used to restore confidence. Government itself was the problem. It was going to be difficult, if not impossible, to use politics to correct political problems. Rarely is a cure constituted by more of the disease.

Political disorder does not favor political scientists; it deranges their theories and cracks their time-honored assumptions. But the shortcomings of political science during this period are not to be found in the poor advice political scientists gave to authorities. Quite the contrary; probably more political scientists than ever before got into positions where they could offer advice aplenty. The somber fact of the matter was that, on most of the fundamental questions underlying disorder, the discipline of political science simply did not have anything to say one way or the other. To a great number of people the impression began to grow that political science had defined these questions as irrelevant.

THE POLITICIZATION OF POLITICAL SCIENCE

As a consequence, political science entered into something of a crisis of its own between 1967 and 1970. It was probably not a crisis of major proportion, but at least it involved a widely shared sense that the profession was at a crossroads and that many professional alternatives, including the status quo itself, had become calculated risks.

The character, scale, and intensity of the crisis inside political science can be directly assessed by studying the single most important insurgent movement ever to emerge inside the profession: the Caucus for a New Political Science. Until the 1960s political science had been a stable profession. Fashions did change, but usually through unplanned developments within the profession or by virtue of changes in the outside world, accelerated by changing fashions among governmental and philanthropic grantsmen. For example, allowing for a certain amount of lag, professional fashions were shaped by whether a Democrat or a Republican majority held Washington. For a time after World War II, public administration and national government were dominant. During the Republican 1950s, when Washington access was reduced, the most exciting work was done in urban politics. Congressional studies revived for the same reasons. Comparative studies also expanded, thanks to the failure of foreign aid programs outside Western Europe and the area crash programs of large foundations. But these changes were unplanned and unorganized, governed more by opportunity than by choice. Even the "behavioral revolution" of the early 1950s was carried off without any organization.

All of this puts the Caucus for a New Political Science in a special place. It was, and is, an organized insurgency. It produced a mailing list, officers, bylaws, and a rather distinct consciousness, part of which is expressed in an actual platform. For these reasons, the Caucus is worth studying. Its program and activities between 1967 and 1970 define clearly enough the alternatives the profession is likely to face in the 1970s.

Beyond this, the Caucus as an organization raises in a most fundamental way the whole question of what any learned society is all about, what its relations are and should be to the intellectual and cultural life of a nation, and what its ultimate impact is and should be on the society at large. And these questions are intensified because it is a social science that is at issue.

The Caucus—its emergence, its successes, and its gradual dissolution—provides an excellent case study through which to evaluate political science in particular and the politics of higher education in general. The account of such a complex event by one of the participants involves many opportunities for distortion. Yet, even the distortions will be productive if they contribute to the analysis of the challenges facing an important learned society.[1] The case of the Caucus is important only insofar as it raised larger issues.

The Caucus: Insurgency in Search of Purpose

The Caucus for a New Political Science was formed during the American Political Science Association Meetings of 1967 in Chicago. The Caucus was the final and inevitable intersection of a rather large number of currents of dissatisfaction arising out of America's failures in the war on Vietnam, the war on poverty, and the war on race discrimination. The insurgency was made up of a large number of Left activists whose attentions turned toward the discipline of political science following such embarrassments as the discovery in 1966 that certain APSA officials had been for years involved professionally with the Central Intelligence Agency. They were joined eventually by a number of less activistic professors who had become increasingly dissatisfied with the way political science had come to define itself away from so many of the most pressing political subjects of the day.

The emerging leadership of the Caucus presented the APSA Business Meeting of 1967 with probably the ugliest confrontation in the history of the profession. During the course of that confronta-

---

[1]For an account written from an almost diametrically opposed point of view, see Alan Wolfe, "Unthinking about the Thinkable: Reflections on the Failure of the Caucus for a New Political Science," *Politics and Society* 1, no. 3 (May 1970): 393–406. Wolfe was also a participant, a member along with myself of the Caucus Executive Committee. Wolfe's article was published four months after the first draft of this paper. My account of the Caucus history was not changed in a single particular as a result of Wolfe's article, yet there is a surprising amount of agreement between us on what happened and why. Our interpretations differ largely because Wolfe was a leader of the faction aimed at converting the learned society into an interest group, and I was a highly vocal member of a smaller faction intent on keeping that from happening by attacking the Caucus and the Association.

tion a number of specific grievances came to light. But months were to pass before the intellectual base of the Caucus became clear. There was a New Left participatory orientation among many of the members. There was a strong sense among many that political science as a profession should be condemned for being aloof to war and discrimination; and there was an even stronger sense that political scientists as citizens should be condemned for their unwillingness to sign petitions and to commit themselves to important social changes. But there were also dissenters within the Caucus on these major points. It seems clear that the only issue on which there was probably no dissent was the concern of the Caucus about the intellectual biases that had come to be built into the contemporary profession of political science. Political science, so the Caucus argued, had developed a number of blind and unquestioned ideological biases that followed almost inevitably from the prevailing definition of political science as a behavioral science, that followed almost directly from the dominant belief that facts could and should be separated entirely from values, and that followed from the criterion that rigor always comes before relevance in questions of good political science. Many people of various ideological viewpoints and various attitudes toward the profession felt the weight of these commitments. Expressions of dissatisfaction about the prevailing journals in political science were voiced by many people who would never go along with the Caucus. However, the Caucus through many of its major spokesmen put the issue on a much broader and important basis. Their statement was not merely that the standards were unfair to many perfectly good political scientists. They went on to argue that these standards involved ideological commitments that needed severe reexamination and criticism. Their critique implied that the learned society was not neutral, as required by its constitution. Their criticisms argued quite the contrary, that neutrality, particularly with the peculiar kind of scientific commitment that prevailed in political science, amounted to a corporate commitment that had to be exposed and perhaps reversed.

In summary, there were two elements to the revolt represented by the Caucus. One was concerned with the question of scientific pseudo-neutrality and was at bottom an intellectual revolt. The other was concerned with organizational non-neutrality, and was obviously a question of organizational revolt.

Intellectual revolt dominated the concerns of the founders of the Caucus and was the basis for a broad distribution of ideologies on the first Caucus Executive Committee. The bylaws of the Caucus stated as its purpose, "Whereas the APSA ... has consistently failed to study, in a radically critical spirit, either the great crises of the day or the inherent weaknesses of the American political system, be it resolved that this Caucus promote a new concern in the Association for our great social crises. ... Be it resolved that one of the primary concerns of the Caucus be to stimulate research in areas of political science that are of crucial importance and that have been thus far ignored."

A year later the official concerns of the Caucus were still with the question of relevant political science *research*. Nevertheless, there had been a clear shift of emphasis, as expressed by the first Caucus newsletter following the 1968 Meetings: "In sum, the result of the events of the convention are that we have become a membership organization. ... We intend to put on another program of Caucus panels at next year's APSA convention, we will establish some kind of Caucus publication, and we are still in the process of defining what precisely our role in the profession shall be."

By April 1969, and probably well before that point, the Caucus had come to something of a clarification of the second element in its revolt, and once that clarification was made, the resolution between these two conflicting purposes was on its way to being made. In its Manifesto of April 1969, the Executive Committee established the following major goals: "(1) encourage and support new modes of political thought and action, social and intellectual criticism ... (including the development of panels and research projects, re-examination of criteria for teaching, research, appointments and promotion in universities, and establishing publication programs); and (2) *reform the APSA*—... especially its bureaucratic and un-democratic organization, its academic irrelevancy, and its establishmentarian political orientation ... [emphasis added]." In a separate paragraph in the same document, the Executive Committee defined as the "purpose" of the Caucus "the creation of a political science which is guided not towards the indoctrination of men and the directives of science, but the enlistment of science in the cause of man; and thus a political science which can serve the poor, oppressed, and underdeveloped peoples at home and abroad in their struggles against the established hierarchies, elites, and institutional forms of manipulation. . .."

Those in the Caucus who favored organizational revolt over intellectual revolt had probably been in the majority all along. These urges had at first been overshadowed, but once the alternative of organizational revolt within the Association became defined clearly, it became somehow impossible for the leadership of the Caucus to work against it. Other members who favored intellectual revolt in any form but opposed stress on organizational reform began to drop out of the Caucus altogether. Consequently the policies of the Caucus became increasingly organizational. Many individual members of the Caucus continued to write reviews and articles suggesting that intellectual revolt was still very much alive. As a collective organization, however, there is no question about what aspects of their interests dominated. For example, the Caucus decided for its second and for its third national Meetings to spend most of its energies organizing separate panels. In doing this, it rejected a frequently offered proposal to abandon the panels and to infiltrate the regular panels with what one member called "intellectual goon squads." The purpose of these infiltrators was to read each paper with unusual care, and then to raise all of the questions about the purpose and implications of the paper that were implied by the general criticisms of the Caucus against the APSA. This way, the Caucus would organizationally bring its intellectual charges against those who most needed to hear them, whereas in the separate Caucus panels the Caucus message tended to be heard only by those who were already inclined to agree with it.

A second important decision reflecting the emergence of organizational revolt was the decision to reject over $7,000 offered by a foundation for purposes of establishing a journal. In a related decision the Executive Committee sternly rejected a proposal to publish Caucus panel and other papers in one or more anthologies, the royalties from which were to be devoted to other Caucus causes. Several Executive Committee members even rebuked the publisher, whose senior editor was present. A year or so later, after my resignation, the Committee apparently relented, for at least one such volume was published, by the same persevering publisher. Or perhaps the Caucus did not relent: the editors of this volume received the royalties on their own personal account.

However, the most important manifestation of the development of the Caucus's purpose was a decision during its second year of operation to offer a full slate of insurgent candidates for all official elective positions in the Association. Alternatives that were voted down included the offering of a limited number of insurgent candidates as members of the Executive Council in order to expand the scope of interest and awareness in Council decisions. The other rejected alternative was that of deliberately and explicitly refusing to accept any official APSA positions in order to preserve the critical effectiveness of the Caucus as an organization of political scientists in revolt.

By the end of the second year of the life of the Caucus, the offering of insurgent slate and the campaign for the Presidency came to be the dominating interest of most Caucus members. Between that campaign and the organization and processing of the Caucus panels, there was neither time nor financing for the furtherance of the collective effort at intellectual revolt.

The culmination of these tendencies was the development of a platform to which all Caucus candidates for Association offices would be pledged. In the tradition of good old-fashioned oligarchy, the Caucus Platform Committee drew up a draft platform in June 1969, which was approved by the Executive Committee and did not change in general purpose during the 1969 and 1970 campaigns. It began with a charge that the profession had devoted its energies primarily to supporting the status quo, at home and abroad. It proceeded then to recognize that the APSA, "more than any other single force, can be used to shape the nature and direction of political science in America." It then proposed to redirect the energies and expertise of the discipline so as to encourage on a corporate and collective basis the development of a new political science among the individual members of the profession.

The main implication through all of this was that there was nothing at all wrong with the fact that the APSA might have been guilty for many years of collectively encouraging individual research along lines that had important social and intellectual biases. The only thing wrong was that the biases were not the ones with which the typical Caucus member had complete sympathy. The intention of the Caucus, as spelled out in the letter and spirit of its platforms, was simply to take over the Association in order to have it serve a different set of masters. The improvement would be that, under Caucus rule, the Association would serve the new masters explicitly and unashamedly rather than the old masters covertly and unconsciously.

Most striking of all was the very act of pledging Caucus candidates to the platform. An essential function of a learned society is to protect its members from political suppression. This is the foundation of academic freedom. And this concern for political suppression has never been more strongly or explicitly expressed than by members of the Caucus on behalf of the new radical dissenters. Yet, during recent years of increasing political suppression, no organization has been more clearly guilty of political suppression than the Caucus. It approached two distinguished scholars—Christian Bay and Hans Morgenthau—and offered them the nomination for president of the APSA on condition that they pledge themselves to a platform. This was probably the clearest example of political suppression to be found in the entire history of the Association.

Following the campaign of 1970, in which Professor Morgenthau did spectacularly well against the victorious regular candidate, Morgenthau objected to one letter of criticism in which he was misquoted as having said he and the Caucus will "try to win control in the APSA because it has avoided the real political issues of the day." Every version of the Caucus platform beginning in June of 1969 implies precisely that, however. It implies that every collective device used consciously and unconsciously by the APSA for purposes of preserving the status quo would, upon Caucus victory, be used for some other kind of collective purpose. Mr. Morgenthau pledged himself to that goal when he accepted the nomination, and in doing so he added his immense distinction and his great reputation for individuality to the almost totally organization-oriented Caucus. In so doing, he had helped to convert the Caucus for a New Political Science into the Caucus for a New Political Science Association.

The Association Response: Brothers under a Thin Skin

The elders of the Association were more than eager to respond to the Caucus. After surviving the uncivil and embarrassing attack by Caucus leaders in the 1967 Business Meeting, the president-elect, David Easton, and many of his colleagues entered into a serious and sincere investigation of the personalities of the Caucus leadership and the basis of their complaints. In all of his travels, the president-elect devoted a tremendous proportion of his time to this particular research. He conscientiously sought out reasons why so many political scientists were unhappy with the Association, and he probably sifted through a trememdous number of proposals for how to respond to these charges.

Eventually a pattern of response was worked out. It was not merely a product of the president-elect; it was probably the most natural and comfortable thing for a large organization of any sort to do. To summarize, the Association sought to develop all of those responses that would satisfy the largest number of Caucus members while at the same time minimizing the impact of the Caucus on the Association.

Primarily this was done by providing a large number of organizational responses to the intellectual *and* the organizational onslaught of the Caucus. It was done very early during the first year of the Caucus by facilitating discussions of what it was the Caucus wanted from the Association. Detailed, lengthy, and friendly discussions ensued regarding the question of Caucus panels at the 1968 Meetings. It is doubtful whether any of the APSA officials ever seriously resisted the demand for separate panels. Once agreement was reached, the complicated problem of organizing the panels, plus the problem of reaching potential members, occupied most of the time and energies of the Caucus during its first year of existence. And this provided the necessary breathing space for the Association.

The success of the first Caucus panels, coupled with the successful introduction of turmoil once again at the 1968 Business Meetings, pushed the Association to further adjustments. All of these adjustments were organizational. Almost as a matter of course, the Association approved the Caucus's request for separate panels for the 1969 Meetings. In addition to this it expressed its willingness to cooperate with the Caucus in use of the Association mailing list and the pages of the new journal, *PS*. Next, the Council of the Association approved the formation of several new, high-level policy committees, whose membership would include Caucus members—although not as official representatives of the Caucus. The new committees included the Constitutional Revision Committee, Committee on the Status of Blacks in the Political Science Profession, Committee on Journals, Committee on the Status of Women in the Political Science Profession, Committee on Political Science in the Secondary Schools, Editorial Board of *PS*, Committee on Finance, Committee on Professional Ethics, Committee on Scientific Information Exchange, Committee to Review the Graduate Record Examination, Committee on Procedures and Agenda, Committee on Academic Freedom, Committee on Undergraduate Instruction, and Committee for an Exploratory Study of Graduate Education in Political Science. Each was given a budget, and each entered into its new responsibilities with all the enthusiasm of people sensing a state of crisis. Within the year the Association was facing a financial crisis as a consequence, but the sense of participation and change was exuding throughout the length and breadth of the profession.

The Association also entertained a number of business and procedural reforms rather than await the development of a whole new constitution. The most important of these was the adoption, over the objection of the Caucus, of a new rule that, in the event of a contest for the election of any Association officer, the election would be removed from the Business Meeting and would be conducted by mail ballot to the entire individual membership. An effort to provide the same procedure for contested resolutions was tabled and referred to the Constitutional Revision Committee. These measures were aimed at making certain that the Business Meeting would be a forum but could never be dominated by any insurgent faction.

Another important organizational response was the founding of the new journal, *PS*. It was founded as a forum for the expression of concerns about political science as a profession. As a measure of the energies that were turning toward matters of internal organization, *PS* expanded from a modest and unimpressive 50-page newsletter to a flashy journal reaching 200 pages in some issues, and containing a variety of articles submitted and occasionally commissioned by the new *PS* Editorial Board.

In none of these matters was there any real intellectual confrontation between the regular organization and insurgents. During this period a few good critical review articles and books were written by Caucus members, and occasionally there were hurt responses by those who felt the criticisms applied to them. Moreover, the Caucus panels at the annual Meetings were very often more lively and productive than the regular panels. But collectively, the interactions between the Caucus and the Establishment were organizational and incremental.

This suggests a still larger and more significant pattern. Since both tendencies—organizational revolt and intellectual revolt—were present from the beginning in the Caucus, it seems fair to say that *the Association's response contributed to the final confirmation of the Caucus as an organizational revolt.* The official and unofficial responses of the Association seemed to be motivated by a desire to avoid direct intellectual confrontation. And since the very essence of the Association, both as a professional organization and as a learned society, was being questioned by the Caucus, it seems clear that separate panels and various devices of proportional representation were the worst responses the Association could have devised. It is irrelevant that the Caucus demanded separate panels. The response of the Association to these demands is in a sense the clearest confirmation of many of the charges being made by the Caucus against it. That is, the Association was guilty of cynically adopting a pluralistic and incrementalist response, in which the majority does not consult its own standards and its own ideology but simply waits to see what demands will be made on it. And the consequent conservatism of the neutral or realistic approach to politics has been clear. The confrontations were redefined into disagregable issues; those issues were then compromised and the costs and gains parceled out, a little for everyone. The seriousness of the original confrontation was soon destroyed.

As a consequence, the Caucus and the Association grew more and more alike. Both turned out to be organizations seeking the same kinds of goals. This is why an incremental approach became possible. The Association could go on behaving like an interest group— it could merely adopt some, but by no means all, of the Caucus's interests. The Association could have its internship programs—so long as the list of nominees was properly balanced. The Association could go on seeking to expand its treasury with the means of making collective rewards—so long as a few Caucus causes and symbols were also rewarded.

The difference between the Association and the Caucus came to be nothing more than one of defining which Establishments shall be served. And the answer was: all Establishments, to varying degrees, depending on the amount of influence a given coalition could exert. The question of having a learned society, and what is required to sustain it, was quietly laid to rest. No one officially seemed to recognize the possibility that the Association and the Caucus had become, to defenders of learned societies, one and the same enemy.

A POLITICS OF HIGHER EDUCATION

Why did the rebels allow themselves to be so diverted from their original goals? Why did their goals so easily become translated into organizational reform? Why did the Association and the Caucus grow more and more alike? Why, in effect, did both come to be the same kind of enemy against the future of the Association as a learned society?

Part of the explanation lies in the fact that the Association has been politicized in recent years on a scale probably unprecedented in the history of political science as a discipline. Nonetheless, it is the response to this politicization and not the fact of politicization that explains the problem. In a sense, influential members of the Association allowed the politicization to have its most harmful possible effect by treating the Association as though it were a political system rather than a learned society. All of this derives from a basic confusion over whether politics is a vocation or profession, or whether politics is a subject of study. Philosophically, this amounts to confusion or guilt over the separation of thought from action.

If political science is either a profession or a vocation, then the Association is an ordinary professional interest group and ought to be expected to behave as such, both as regards the outside world and with regard to the rights and duties of individual members and the services to be rendered to them. Thus, if political science is either a profession *or* a vocation, we can expect to look at the Association of political scientists as a political system of sorts. But however meaningful this view may be, it amounts to the introduction of a very important but unexamined major premise. This premise is that the members of the profession are actors and that the Association is an actor on their behalf within the larger political system. This is the major premise shared by both the Caucus and by most of the senior members of the Association.

This development is not an inevitable result of the history of the discipline of political science or of the Association that has emerged to service it. In fact, the recent responses of the Caucus and the Association to each other are unhealthy and dysfunctional, if viewed in the context of the development of learned societies and higher education rather than the artificial context of "political science as a political system."

In order to put these issues in this more appropriate context, it is first necessary simply to look at political science as a subject. Political Science is a subject of long standing, and it is one that has been distinguished from other subjects of study for quite a long time. It possesses an identifiable body of materials, usually called "organized knowledge." These materials are very disparate and heterogeneous both in subject matter and quality. And it is impossible to draw a precise line to separate what is in and what is outside the subject. But it is a definable subject, even if the boundaries are unclear and permissive.

As with most other important subjects, political science came to be organized. Early in this century, it had taken on an identity as a department within the major colleges and universities. Some of the larger departments produced people who were stamped and qualified in the subject of political science, and as their numbers grew and their self-conception established itself, they became a discipline. Then, in order to advance the subject and protect the members, the discipline found itself organized as an Association.

This happened in other disciplines as well, and it is still happening through the establishment of new disciplines and the subdivision of old ones. There is no mystery about the process, and there is also no difficulty in defining the advantages and the disadvantages of the development.

The primary advantage was the uplifting of the social status of the subject and of the persons dedicated to its study. A correlative advantage was that the concept of the discipline, and the organization of the discipline, helped produce true academic freedom and helped defend it once it came to be established. The existence of separate and organized disciplines, coupled with the identification of the professor as a person who belongs to a discipline even as he is located in a specific institution in order to teach, is quite evidently the means by which the academic revolution was institutionalized in the United States.

The major disadvantage of this development lies in the tendency of anything, once defined and organized, to resist redefinition and reorganization. Disciplinary lines tend to change only across generations. Disciplinary organizations can, like any other organizations, suffer the old ailment called "displacement of goals." Perhaps the most important manifestation of inertia in academic disciplines is the tendency for prevailing fashions to be defined as standards of excellence. When a discipline is organized, these prevailing fashions *qua* standards become a means of systematically shaping the character of the discipline itself and thence reducing the autonomy of individual members. But insofar as disciplines facilitate the exchange of information, changes in the criteria of excellence can be made, perhaps in periods shorter than a generation. It is quite clear, for example, that fashions and standards in political science changed more than once between the Great Depression and the postwar period, once again, if not more than once, during the behavioral 1950s, and are undergoing another as yet undefined transformation at present.

Higher Education and Social Classes

These developments can perhaps be best understood within the context of the general development of higher education in the United States. Table 1 is a schematic summary of the major developments. Each "educational norm" represents a period of time within which a certain outlook or general set of criteria dominated the organization of universities and defined, for those in it at least, the "Nature of the University." The third column is intended to suggest that the universities and the subjects being taught therein were always inextricably tied in with society. This is not to suggest that the particular social class or interest dictated the type of university or in any other way "caused" a particular educational norm to come into being. The relationship through most of the history of higher education was

Table 1.   Educational Systems and Class Interests

Educational Norm	Educational Ethic	Social Interest Represented	Form of Social Integration
Classical education (classic Church education)	Consumer ethic: "knowledge for its own sake" (knowledge for personal discipline)	aristocracy	community
Liberal arts education	Consumer ethic: "Renaissance man," "genteel erudition"	old bourgeoisie	fraternity
Disciplinary education	Producer ethic: "the Ph.D.," "the major"	new middle classes– professional salariat	society
Practical education	Training ethic:* "A & M," "experience"	working classes	estate
Technocratic education	Problem-solving ethic: "the multiversity," "service"	regimes	corps

*The recent revival of training schools is a curious one, containing a mix of junior colleges and radical "free universities" as well as courses inside four-year colleges. It also includes some courses specifically designed for black studies; however, the growing emphasis in black studies programs on consciousness and cultural nationalism is actually a liberal arts norm and is already dominated by the black middle classes. What, after all, is traditional liberal arts but "white studies"?

rather one between a service agency and its clientele. A certain kind of university will take root and prosper if it has a social base; specific standards and self-conceptions will change in their importance as social interests rise and fall in scale, resources, and demands. Symbiosis is a better word than service.[2]

But this relationship obtains only for the first four of the five educational norms identified in the table. There is something very

[2]As will become apparent, the table is not intended to imply that each norm and ethic disappears as another arises to take its place. In the modern university, all of these coexist, but the dominant one is the one that counts.

special about the fifth category, the "technocratic education." Here service no longer means a symbiotic or functional relationship between a particular educational activity and some social aggregate. The technocratic system means service in a direct, institutional, and deliberate sense. It means service as a matter of conscious policy, as in a master-servant relationship. It is a contractual relationship between a group of decision makers in the university and a group of decision makers in any non-university establishment—a government, a business, an organized class, or any other social structure stable enough to have a regime to act on its behalf.[3]

Universities have always performed some services of the master-servant type. But traditionally these have been resisted and feared; they were taken on in full awareness that compromise was necessary for survival, and they were usually kept separate from the institution in their own schools or in institutes attached to the university. The best example would be the agricultural extensions and other services within agricultural schools otherwise run along departmental lines. Other services of this sort have cropped up during the 1950s and 1960s—on a scale that has made service activity for the first time a threat to the university.

The fourth and final column on the table further emphasizes the sociopolitical importance of each educational norm, for here we see that even individual relationships—"campus life"—tended to be shaped by the prevailing university–social-class ties. In the aristocratic system, for example, there was an ideal of *community* association among persons who had their superiority of learning and standing in common. This university was merely an expression of the society, and standing in the one generally was derived from standing in the other. Students were more often than not of a standing higher than their professors—and hence had influence on the hiring and firing of faculty. But the point is that the university was in and of the community, had no particular identity except in those terms, and tried to justify itself as the holder of the cultural heritage.

These integrated associations, based on the narrow base of high status and higher learning, must have been altered only slowly; but, fast or slow, the increased heterogeneity of class composition meant

---

[3] *The Politics of Disorder* (New York: Basic Books, 1971), chap. 6. The first three columns of Table 1 were also drawn from that source, although their purpose differed there.

new interests that must ultimately change the university in some fundamental ways. At this second stage, the integration of society and university through learning could still be found, but the scale and intimacy of relationships between university and society were reduced. There would never again be a relationship between the *whole* campus and the *entire* upper-class structure of the society at large. Distinctions among students in the middle-class university were clear and could be severe—as is seen most concretely by the exclusiveness of the aristrocratic secret societies in the Ivy League colleges. Students adjusted to this heterogeneity by finding persons of their own kind, as is suggested by the very notion of *fraternities*. Fraternities grew in size, many distinctions among fraternities emerged, and class awareness inside colleges and universities probably intensified.

As far as the higher learning apparatus was concerned, however, the major impact of this kind of heterogeneity among the privileged classes was probably the loosening and weakening of ties *between faculty and students*. Students developed their identifications among themselves and with their careers in the society at large. The average student no longer held social standing higher than his professors; he no longer held any direct influence over their hiring and firing. The association between students and faculty came to be more formal and distant, despite the fact that all students and faculty continued to be recruited from comparably high social strata.

The emergence of the disciplinary norm clearly constitutes a third revolution in the history of higher education. It was associated with, or took root in, a very significant expansion of the class origins of the student body and the faculty. The doors to the *new middle classes* were flung wide open. And that meant the newer ethnic minorities, except blacks. In general these were what Robert Dahl would call the "ex-plebes," persons whose families had already experienced a certain amount of social mobility and turned their children to college as a fulfillment of the American Dream. By the end of World War II one even began to see Jews on Ivy League faculties.

Aside from its symbolic value, the most important result of this development was the weakening of all effort to carry general class statuses into campus life. This was slow to come but was accelerated after World War II with the GI bill and eventually the universalization of educational opportunity. Concretely, this meant much greater individualization among students. Fraternities grew in number and size until traditional class, ethnic, and religious distinctions among them came to mean less and less. They were already weakening as a social force on many campuses before the universities began officially to attack them and to require elimination of all explicit efforts to maintain ties to the general social status system. Fraternities and sororities became small dormitories where, as in larger dormitories, cliques came to be the prevailing pattern of interaction. The student body was developing its own forms, less and less derivative of, or predictable by, one's extra-college life.

Perhaps of still greater importance, there was the rise of *alienation*, both as a fact and as a matter of concern. Beginning in the 1920s, the "problem" of campus life in the larger universities and colleges emerged, but it was solved for a long time by intercollegiate athletics and other kinds of "campus spirit." In full association with that phenomenon is the rise of more deliberate administration of social life by the university itself. Student unions, counseling, and many other such devices have been employed. In more recent years, students have provided for their own solutions in various forms of communal living, withdrawal, and drugs.

But out of all these patterns attendant to the spread of the university to the "middle masses," the most important is the *severing of the university from the society at large.* The university became its own society. Neither faculty nor the typical student was a mere extension of some outside social class. Few faculty were discernible members of any social classes at all. But even where they were, the greater social reality for them was their own profession, their own vocational career, and the organized discipline within which their career was defined.

And with affluence, the real character of the faculty began to emerge. Large numbers of faculty proved themselves extremely mobile. And those who were not geographically mobile often proved their weak association with their local campus by their pattern of professional activities. This was particularly true in the large universities engaged in graduate teaching. The exceptions were the professors in the smaller colleges, but that is associated with the continued dominance of the classical or the liberal arts norm and the maintenance of close societal ties in general (see Table 1).

The significance of this severing is profound. This is the process by which a real measure of academic freedom ultimately came to the universities. Consider the interaction of only three of the factors in the process: (1) the adoption of the Ph.D. and of the disciplinary pattern associated with it; (2) the emergence of an enormous "middle mass" of a student body to whom a disciplinary education was valuable; and (3) a campus social structure that had been broken loose from established social-class moorings. These three factors alone could have produced the fluid situation within which a professoriat established its autonomous position in the society. In a sense, the professoriat became a class in and of itself. This class position was institutionalized and given organizational muscle by the many and various disciplines into which the professoriat organized. The disciplines have helped maintain a fairly clear separation between the professors and their university structures as well as between professors and nonprofessorial persons of comparable standing in society at large. Through the discipline, in brief, there is an actual social interest in academic freedom—a vested interest, one that is organized better than most. Through the discipline, academic freedom is not merely a cultural value highly prized in the society at large. It is in fact, concretized in many organizations.

The Technocratization of the Intelligentsia

It is within this larger context that the technocratization of the universities and the intelligentsia is seen in all its importance. First, the technocratic norm involves a return to a direct tie between the university and the society at large. But there is a difference. With technocratization, the university enmeshes itself with regimes. This means purposive social action, master-servant relationships, rather than merely the older functional relationship expressing the needs of a given social class. This is new. It is not a mere return to face-to-face relationships, involving endogamous marriage, the repetition and reinforcement of general social norms, the old fluid whole-person, "old boy" relationships. Rather, technocratization forges a connection between the university and society along vocational and subject-matter lines. Technocratization takes the organized disciplines and turns them toward a direct problem-solving and policy-oriented *relationship* to the society.

Technocratization, superficially, seems a good deal more democratic than the other forms of education. Lower-class persons can enjoy expanded access to the disciplines and yet have higher horizons of ambition than they can enjoy by entering technical institutes, community colleges, trade schools, and the like. But this vanishes with further evaluation.

Perhaps the best way to evaluate technocratization is to consider briefly the French administrative concept, the *corps*. There is nothing quite like it in the United States, but there are some functional equivalents to it, and the French pattern is probably nothing more than an advanced version of the direction toward which technocratization will ultimately lead American higher education.

The *corps* is the primary channel of recruitment, promotion, and status in the French civil service.[4] Government jobs are classified, and people are assigned responsibilities accordingly, in classic bureaucratic fashion. But the *upper* levels are limited almost entirely to those who entered the ministry by route of proper training. "Proper training" is not defined by official job-oriented skills one might acquire in any university or by on-the-job training, or released time, night school, or correspondence. "Proper training" *exclusively* means schooling in a *specifically designated* university.

These universities are euphemistically called the *Grande Écoles*, but they are essentially high-powered graduate trade schools. They were set up outside the traditional university system to meet the needs of the growing bureaucracies in the nineteenth century. More recently some of these schools also serve the large private bureaucracies.

The needs of government have dominated the curriculum of the *Grandes Écoles*. The mutual influence, the intimacy of the ties, can be seen concretely in the way each *corps* is based directly in a *Grande École* whose student output is suitable primarily for such governmental functions. For example, one of the oldest and most important of French ministires is Public Works. Its highest personnel are dominated by the very old and prestigious *Corps des Ponts et Chaussées* (bridges and roads). In turn, this *corps* is fed by one of the

---

[4]The five major *Corps Administratifs* are *Corps Techniques, Corps de Controle Administratif, Grands Corps, Corps d'Administration Centrale,* and *Corps des Services Exterieurs.*

Grandes Écoles which bears the same name. Another of the *Grandes Écoles* takes its name and function from the ministry that handles post and telegraph, customs, and excises. Each of the so-called *Grandes Écoles Scientifiques* is organized to train and direct students toward the functions of a specific technical ministry.

The limitations of this sort of thing were most dramatically expressed during the student manifestations of May 1968. Clearly one of the significant causes of these uprisings, and one of the primary elements in the rhetoric of revolt, was the technocratization of higher education in France. And significantly, the leadership emerged at Nanterre, which was the one university where students could take academic social science courses and, in a sense, "major" in a social science. This adjustment in the university at Nanterre simply served to emphasize the general problem in France, because these courses in the curriculum at Nanterre could not lead to certification in relevant terms. For certification and for entry into the major professional institutions, the examinations continued to stress either the classical subjects or the more technocratic aspects of modern subjects.

The United States has not gone such a distance toward technocratization and central control of higher education. But significant examples can be found of organized ties between an institute and a governmental agency or other public or semi-public function. The Forest Service is an important instance of an intimate interrelation between an agency and one or two dominant schools of forestry. Perhaps the classic example is the military academies and the armed services. On a smaller scale, two or three universities in Washington have attempted to staff the middle echelons of the State Department and many of its agencies. Several schools of public affairs, the most notable being the Maxwell School of Syracuse University, have attempted to perform the functions of Sciences Politiques and École Nationale d'Administration (ENA) but the number of autonomous governments in the United States has served to interfere with any dominating relationship on a national scale. Nonetheless, there are new and recent efforts to fashion more effective schools of public affairs which will at least provide a large proportion of the upper administrators in Washington and the state governments.

The *corps* pattern will probably never come to dominate the discipline of political science as such. But the concept of the *corps* captures a contemporary tendency in any and all disciplines, and it is a tendency that is being accentuated by the Caucus and by the Association. It is accentuated by many of their positive plans and compromises, but more important, it is accentuated by the fact that neither organization is making an effort to fight strong influences in this direction coming from governments, foundations, and many public-spirited individuals. Technocratization in all forms is a fundamental need for a government and an industrial sociey that is already technocratized. It would be inevitable for responsible policy makers to encourage and demand technocratic services from all sources. And these demands and incentives will be too great for universities to resist, unless vigorous disciplines exert influence in the opposite direction. Even at The University of Chicago, that most academic of academic institutions, it became official policy in 1971 to try to found a school of public affairs that would have the power to grant terminal M.A. and Ph.D. degrees in subjects and techniques of practical problem-solving importance.

Thought Versus Action in Political Science

It is sadly ironic, but no less true, that political science does not recognize the fundamental change that technocratization brings to its relationship to learning and to society. Problem solving is inherently conservative. The technocratic education focuses on real social problems and puts the scholar into an intimate functional relationship with those who are interested in the problem. Here is a basis for a high degree of consonance between the scholar and the policy maker. As earlier observed, "service" no longer implies merely a general functional relationship, but comes to mean a conscious institutional rendering of services; and this has particular bearing on political science. To help the policy maker solve problems is to make the conduct of his responsibilities a good deal more comfortable. And the problem and the solution are made more legitimate by virtue of the academic help rendered him. But most importantly, *it means that the intellectual agenda of the discipline is set by the needs of the clientele, not by the inner logic of political science.*

Technocratization is conservative in still another way. It brings the discipline into *mesh* with society in a way that is directly sub-versive to the academic purpose. Setting the agenda according to clientele needs produces parallelisms of concepts and hypotheses that in turn lead either to ideological parallelisms or to differences of opinion that are basically incremental. An academic political scien-tist should be asking: Does society behave like my model? The hardheaded, technocratic, and practical political scientist would ask rather: Does the model behave like society? "Power corrupts," it is said, and when said it usually refers to the corruption of vanity and self-indulgence. Technocratization involves a power that also corrupts, but this power corrupts in a culturally more important sense. It involves a corruption of the intellect, of the purpose of academic freedom. It involves the academic with the immediate and the concrete; corruption means a blurring of the difference be-tween theory and rationalization.

Political scientists are concerned of late about their relationship, especially as teachers, to society. But the tendency is to look only at substantive attitudes and how these are distributed among individ-uals in the profession. In some quarters there is concern for Left-wing bias, in other quarters the opposite. Self-studies usually reveal that political scientists are generally to the slight left of the society at large, but less so than sociologists. Self-studies find a growing dissatisfaction with U.S. foreign policy and a tendency by a small but growing minority to sign petitions and engage in older forms of political action.[5]

These substantive attitudes are being stressed more frequently in recent years, but all of this has simply been ground into the mill of incremental adjustment. Since the structural features of the disci-pline itself are not brought into the center of the context, assessment of the impact of political science leads to mere concern for dis-tributing the attitudes properly; it turns on specific persons or on types of persons who receive the honors or on who teaches what to whom, etc.

All of this is superficial in comparison to the institutional rela-tionships with the outside world and the conceptual apparatus

[5]The best of these are being done by Professors Everett C. Ladd and S. M. Lipset. See, for example, their "The Politics of American Political Scientists," *PS* 4, no. 2 (Spring 1971): 135–144.

through which the discipline associates with the outside world. Political science, or any other discipline, is radical or conservative by virtue of its conceptual apparatus rather than by virtue of the distributions of individuals and substantive attitudes. It is radical insofar as it is out of mesh with society, rather than insofar as the individual member of the discipline may feel or act in a personally radical way about certain social issues.

That is, the radical influence is historic and institutional. It is built into the independence of the discipline. It comes from theory, not from practice—thought, not action. It comes from the assumption that there is an order and meaning in society that can be discovered by good theory and good empirical rigor in relation to theory. It comes from building new insights on established insights through logic, rather than building one insight on another through experience.

These factors constitute the essence of a learned discipline, and they also fly directly in the face of most of the recent reforms and demands for reform. Most important, they fly in the face of those who would wipe out the distinction between thought and action. It not only opposes the fusion of those two, it proposes also, at least for some role players in the society, that theory is much more practical than action. It militates against the notion that all forms of organizational neutrality are conservative: organizational neutrality can be conservative when the reality of the organization is one of being in mesh with society. But organizational neutrality is not at all conservative when that neutrality is based on the traditional practice of being *out of mesh*—autonomous, alienated.

For example, if political scientists in hundreds of colleges, teaching thousands or hundreds of thousands of students, produce concepts and propositions that are virtually incomprehensible to persons outside academia, they are not merely confusing the citizenry. If the theories are energetic and relevant, they are creating a generation of students who simply do not think like their older policy makers. This is deeply radical. In more respectable terms, it institutionalizes a capacity for social change. Each new generation promises to spring from different roots, and radicalism has to do with roots. These students will not be necessarily radical in the sense of being dedicated to cutting out the old roots. The important thing is that the capacity to deal critically with the roots of the polity is a capacity without which political science would indeed be nothing but a handmaiden.

Thus, a political science dedicated to better solutions to society's problems cannot in the long run be radical *or* science, because it will be too closely tied to the very regimes whose roots it must constantly question. There is danger in realism. There is danger in problem solving. There is certainly danger in setting up an entire curriculum that stresses problem solving. There is danger in defining science as nothing more than a collection of rigorously stated individual hypotheses aimed at manipulating the real world. There is danger in these because each one tends to reduce the autonomy of political science as a learned society. We need look no further than public administration to find a mature example. Each of these dangers is a virtue of technocratization that tends to reduce the alienation and the detachment of political science from the society which sustains it. There are many dangers because most of the tendencies in a mass democracy are generally toward the reduction of detached and alienated institutions in favor of a society in which all institutions are in mesh.

Thus, neither the autonomy nor the radicalism of political science can come from political science taken merely as a profession with a large trade union representating and serving it. In fact, autonomy and radicalism are simply two different ways of looking at the same thing, two different ways of capturing the ideal relationship between a learned society and its larger social context; and only by de-emphasizing the professional aspects and by shedding the superficial notion of political engagement—that is, by objecting to the tendencies among the members of the Establishment as well as the proposals and criticisms of the dominant faction of the Caucus— and by returning to a more fundamental concept of a learned society, can political science establish and strengthen its proper relationship to the society. By doing so it also maintains its academic freedom, and solves most of the problems concerning the relationship between individual members and the collective Association. The politics of political science was captured brilliantly by the original thrusts of the Caucus and was then lost sight of in the ensuing battle between the Caucus and the Association over who should control the committees and the budget of the Association. As a consequence, nobody is really minding the store, because the Caucus sought primarily to force the Association to continue doing what it has been doing but on an expanded basis in order to add the unrepresented interests. The Caucus and the Association have become one and the same thing. "You can serve your interests, but only so long as you will let us use the Association to serve ours."

These developments should be a matter of intense concern to political scientists. But political science is only a single case, and these developments affect all organized disciplines. Political science merely illustrates the relationship between the learned societies and the universities and shows how that relationship is vital to the maintenance of academic freedom in general. Pressures are on, inside and outside the universities, to convert every aspect of American culture into a series of service stations, putting everything into mesh. It is probably a general tendency in mass democracies to take on elements of totalitarianism, particularly with regard to the democratization of excellence. But the problem will not be one in which governments and capitalists, or the militant students, will forcibly occupy the universities and the learned societies. Rather, the change toward technocratization and the loss of academic autonomy will more likely come from voluntary actions on the part of the guilt-ridden academicians themselves. Their therapy is not compromise with these forces but a better understanding of what it is they are prepared to defend.[6]

[6]This essay was written more than a year before I was made aware of RANN, Research Applied to National Needs, the National Science Foundation's new rubric for handling social science grants. The heat, as anticipated above, is now unmistakably on; and so is the scramble among political scientists to get in on the boondogle.

.2. Beyond Parochialism in Political Science

GEORGE W. CAREY

THIS PAPER is written with the conviction that a full understanding and appreciation of the present state of the profession and the direction it will take in the foreseeable future necessitate an examination of the theoretical foundations of both liberalism and behavioralism, doctrines that have exercised a decisive influence on political science in the relatively recent past and, for reasons we will spell out, promise to shape the future of the discipline.

Some years ago (we need not fix a precise date, though most would say it was a post-World War II phenomenon), the profession took an abrupt turn in the direction of behavioralism. Two developments in the profession are associated with this abrupt change. First, attention was lavished upon statistical techniques and methods of social research, partly to the exclusion of substantive materials. This can be seen today in virtually all the major subdivisions of political science—American government, international relations, comparative government, and even Constitutional law. Second, and I believe those who lived through the era of change would substantiate this, the feeling existed that political scientists, in order to understand political systems, had to move beyond inquiry into formal institutions and procedures. The techniques and findings of other disciplines (notably economics, sociology, and psychology) found their way into the discipline; indeed, as we see today, many of our most highly praised books are those which employ an interdisciplinary approach.

The impact of these developments was so great that it was commonplace to hear many "middle-aged" political scientists talk about "retooling" so that they would be equipped to comprehend the latest findings and developments in the field. A totally new vocabulary blossomed forth and the holdouts, those who felt that these developments were nothing more than a passing fancy, were warned that in a decade they would not be able to understand articles published in the *American Political Science Review*. This prophecy has finally come to pass, or just about.

Along with this there were other, perhaps more significant, evidences of change in the profession. Political science departments across the country eagerly sought after those trained in the behavioral persuasion so that the new methods and approaches could be incorporated into their undergraduate and graduate curricula. This, of course, meant that there had to be some degree of curriculum reform in order to accommodate this change of emphasis. (One such "reform" with which many are familiar is the elimination of the second language requirement for the Ph.D. degree and substitution of a suitable "research" tool, usually statistics.) At some schools the curriculum reform, accompanied by a corresponding change of personnel, was drastic. A belief seemed to prevail in some quarters that the behavioral approach could even absorb those areas of study with which political scientists with more traditional approaches had been concerned.

These and like changes have been characterized as a "revolution." This characterization seems accurate for the term revolution certainly implies rapid and basic change. And this, of course, is what occurred. What is interesting to note (and we shall have more to say about this later) is that at first the "revolutionary" operational base in the profession was relatively small. Occasionally one will find reference to the "Chicago school" of the 1930s which probably laid the pre-World War II foundations for the subsequent revolution.[1] We have yet to give full credit to the "Yale school" of the 1950s and 1960s, in so many ways the modern counterpart of the Chicago school. Its products, much like the disciples of Christ, went forth

---

[1]The Chicago group probably represented the first "school." Of course there were individual efforts and statements which preceded the Chicago school regarding the utility and need for emphasis on the behavioral approach. In this connection see Charles E. Merriam's presidential address of 1925.

with an uncommon zeal to spread the word about the need for change in the discipline, and their success has been nothing short of phenomenal for they have, within a relatively short period of time, gained powerful allies. Indeed, today most of our prestigious departments are dominated by those of behavioral persuasion. And, if we look to the "heroes" of the profession, say, those who have served as presidents of the Association in the last ten or fifteen years, we find abundant evidence to support the contention that those who led the revolution have been duly honored, accorded the highest honorary position the profession can bestow.

Let us take up the matter of why the profession underwent such a rapid metamorphosis.

We can well imagine, and not without good reason, that the prestige of the principal institutions responsible for the new political science lent a great deal of weight to the movement. This is probably true. Over time we would expect graduates from these and equally prestigious schools to have an impact on the profession, the more so given a high degree of uniformity of approach—the fact, that is, that these departments represented a school of thought in which its graduates were trained and immersed. This does not account for the rapidity of the change that took place in the profession as a whole, however. Obviously, it would take time, and a good deal of it, to make such a significant impress on the profession unless, as suggested above, there was a very high degree of receptivity to the new approaches on the part of the general profession.

Another plausible explanation is that outside factors began to work on the profession. Universities could provide only limited resources for scholars who needed time and money to pursue their interests. Hence the need to look elsewhere. These outside sources of funding, so the argument runs, were quite receptive to the study of political behavior, particularly the major foundations (e.g., Ford and Carnegie) and the Social Science Research Council. And, of course, governmental funds to the profession have largely been used to sponsor projects of behavioral bent.[2]

---

[2] I well recall the consternation of some of my colleagues because the National Science Foundation did not until a relatively recent date acknowledge political science to be a science and, accordingly, would not give research grants to political scientists. The grounds for consternation apparently no longer exist; still another indication of the extent of the revolution.

We can grant so much to this line of argument. In important respects the discipline was not able to call its shots. The concentration of resources outside the profession, both private and public, facilitated rapidity of change in the profession. More than this, the resources available to the traditionalists, say, those interested in traditional political thought, were relatively scant in comparison.

Nevertheless, this explanation, while valid to some extent, is partially question-begging. Why did those sympathetic to the so-called revolution in political science gain a more receptive hearing from outside sources? Initially it might be argued that this support was designed to correct an imbalance in the profession, to provide greater opportunities for those who felt that political science should become more scientific. However, if this explanation were sound, the rapidity of the change that resulted in the dominance of the behavioralists would then logically lead the foundations and other outside sources of revenue to correct the imbalances they had created. This has not been the case. Rather, what has resulted is an intramural fight between behavioralists over the outside funds available. This is interesting in itself because it helps explain why the issue of the proper orientation of the discipline is seldom framed in strategic terms: the competition among different schools of behavioralism, largely technical and tactical in nature, has served to divert our attention from the major issue: Are we doing what we should be doing? Instead, the question has become: Are we doing what we are doing well, no matter whether we should be doing it or not?

Still another factor has to do with the "clubbishness" of some of its leading proponents. Put another way, it is possible to argue that a hard core of loyal and dedicated individuals, perceiving the need for a change of emphasis in political science, did whatever they could to advance each other's career so that the sum result was the establishment of an elite with the power to redirect the focus of the discipline. Stated in such a blunt manner, one could well equate the revolutionaries in our profession with the activities of Communist cell groups. This clearly is not the case. The contention, however, is more subtle than this and is not completely without foundation. Beyond any question there are "in" groups within the profession, and once members of any such groups gain positions of authority within the higher councils of the Association, they are in a position not only to advance the reputation of others but also, directly or indirectly, to determine what articles are suitable for publication, who will and who will not be appointed to high prestige committees within the Association, who will and will not assume positions of authority within the Association (e.g., who will be our program chairman, who will serve on our Council).[3] And just as in state and national politics the faithful are rewarded, so too can this process operate within the profession.

The question is, of course, whether any one "in" group has managed to gain such dominance within the Association. Certainly if this were the case we would have every reason to anticipate a "snowball" effect simply because the dominant group by rewarding those with the same views and approaches could perpetuate itself in power within the higher circles of the Association. And this is what we have witnessed to a great degree with the behavioral revolution. But while it is true that perpetuation of control is relatively easy, we must ask: What accounted for the relatively rapid ascendance of behavioralism? How and why did such control pass into the hands of the behavioralists in the first place? Again the best explanation we can offer is the high degree of receptivity to behavioralism that must have existed among rank-and-file political scientists.

These explanations do not account for the rapid success of the behavioral revolution. Rather, all of them lead us to assert that the profession was "ripe" for the revolution and quite willing to move in new directions. But what we have called receptivity does help us to understand. What, then, accounts for this receptivity? Here, again, we run into difficulties. Allow me to show their dimensions at some length.

Many, if not most, incoming graduate students are required to take a course that deals in some fashion with the scope and methods of political science. The title of the course varies from institution to institution, but the goals are essentially the same: Give the incoming student some idea of the subject matter of political science, the various approaches used, and some appreciation of the ongoing

---

[3]As neophytes in the profession will soon learn, there are many "clubs" formed on many bases of loyalty and friendship. Graduate students of the same school and vintage frequently are clubbish. So, too, are students of the great teachers (e.g., Strauss, Voegelin, and Hyneman) apt to form clubs based on common experiences, knowledge, and approach.

disputes in the discipline both with respect to the proper object of study and the best techniques available. Now, given the character of the behavioral revolution, we should certainly expect a relatively precise definition or statement of what political science is, its proper objects of study, and its goals. However, I think it fair to say that this is precisely what the student does *not* gain from his studies. In sum, it seems that a revolution occurred without any clear statement on the part of the behavioral wing of the profession concerning the goals or purposes of the revolution. This is to be seen in their own writings. In the mid-1950s we were told that the "authoritative allocation of values" should be our central focus of concern. At the same time others focused on interest groups and their activities. For others the formula came down to the simple matter of "who gets what, when, why, and how." For still others the study of "power" and "influence" served as integrating concepts.

   In large measure these and like efforts were prompted by the behavioral revolution in order to provide an orientation amid the changes in the profession; to provide us, so to speak, guidelines that would better enable us to absorb and organize the various approaches and findings within the discipline. But such efforts were doomed from the outset for a number of interrelated reasons. We can easily imagine that one way to mark out the legitimate boundaries of political science or to discover its central concerns would be to utilize the *descriptive* approach; to examine exhaustively what acknowledged political scientists had been doing and then try to find some element common to all. But this approach runs into the same difficulties that Ludwig Wittegenstein notes with respect to finding the "essence" of "games."

Consider for example the proceedings that we call "games." I mean board-games, card-games, ball-games, Olympic games, and so on. What is common to them all?—Don't say: "There *must* be something common, or they would not be called 'games'"—but *look and see* whether there is anything common to all. —For if you look at them you will not see something that is common to *all*, but similarities, relationships, and a whole series of them at that. To repeat: don't think, but look! —Look for example at board-games, with their multifarious relationships. Now pass to card-games; here you find many correspondences with the first group, but many common features drop out, and others appear. When we pass next to ball-games, much that is common is retained, but much is lost. —Are they all "amusing"? Compare chess with noughts and crosses. Or is there always winning and losing, or competition between players? Think of patience. In ball-games there is winning and losing; but when a child throws his ball at the wall and catches it again, this feature has disappeared. Look at the parts played by skill and luck; and the difference between skill in chess and skill in tennis. Think now of games like ring-a-ring-a-roses; here is the element of amusement, but how many other characteristic features have disappeared! And we can go through many, many other groups of games in the same way; can see how similarities crop up and disappear.[4]

Moreover, from the revolutionaries' point of view, the descriptive approach by its very nature could scarcely serve their purposes because they sought to change the focus or boundaries of the discipline that had previously been generally accepted.

For these reasons, those endeavoring to find the essence of political science had to use, at least to some degree, a *prescriptive* approach. This meant that certain enterprises in political science either had to be totally discarded because they would not fit very well within the prescriptive boundaries or they had to be considered as tangential or distinctly secondary to the prescribed concerns. And this is precisely why we have had, and continue to have, bitter controversy within the profession; certain groups of scholars, most notably those in the field of political theory or political philosophy, were all but read out of the discipline with the prescriptive formulations devised by the behavioralists. In this connection, it was not at all unusual to hear a confirmed behavioralist argue with the fervor of a true believer that courses in the history of political thought ought to be dropped from the curriculum. Although there is no measure of how widespread this belief was or what influence it had, we can surmise that it was fairly strong. Indeed, the fact that few, if any, of our graduate schools are today adequately staffed to provide a student interested in this field a well-rounded background is evidence of this. The same cannot be said of the other major fields such as American politics, comparative government, or international relations—fields that have largely become the domain of the student of behavior.

Other difficulties of both a practical and theoretical nature arose

[4]From his *Philosophical Investigations* reproduced in *The Age of Analysis*, ed. Morton White (New York: New American Library, 1955), pp. 230–31.

with respect to this prescriptive approach. For obvious reasons the prescribers could not go too far in their whittling; that is, the shucking of the traditional areas of concern. Otherwise they would certainly have opened themselves up to the charge that they were in fact establishing a new discipline. And the need of such a discipline would have been difficult, if not impossible, to justify, particularly since the new approach relied so heavily on other established disciplines. Not surprisingly, therefore, the new political science was presented in such a fashion as to provide an "umbrella" under which many of the traditional writings and approaches could fit. If, for example, we were to take the proposition that political science ought to concern itself with who gets what, when, why, and how, the writings of Aristotle, Plato, and most other classical theorists are relevant to this concern. But note, and this is important, the writings are relevant only to the extent that they deal with these questions and are read with this formulation in mind. Put otherwise, the behavioralists as much as told us that the classics are best read through the eyes of modern political science with the preoccupations of the moderns on the mind of the reader, not through the eyes of the author or his contemporaries. We can only speculate concerning the degree to which the teachings of traditional literature have been distorted because of this.

Let us look at this matter from another angle. All formulations offered by those seeking to reorient the study of politics are broad and inevitably lead one into difficulties of one kind or another. Is the proper object of our study "groups?" Very well. What constitutes a group? What philosopher has not at one time or another dealt with groups, no matter how defined? Is our study the authoritative allocation of values? Well, then, how far do we stretch this? Does it extend to parental authority over the child? Does it extend, say, to the toilet training of individuals? I shan't belabor the point. The formulations offered us by the moderns, even in their most prescriptive form, by themselves are of little help to those who wish to establish some sense of priorities. True, we know that there is a sense of priorities manifest among the revolutionaries: they would prefer a less descriptive approach; greater utilization of data which explore the "informal" rather than "formal" explanation of what transpires within a political system; greater precision, quantitatively speaking, when describing the behavior of individuals and institutions; and, inter alia, greater knowledge about what contributes to an individual's behavior within the state. But what the behavioralist did by defining political science in such broad terms was to (1) incorporate (outwardly at least) many of the more traditional concerns and problems; and, more important (2) legitimize, without regard to their relevance or worth, inquiries far outside the boundaries of traditional political science.

We have before us now two facts of some interest. First, it is conceded on all sides that a revolution did take place in the profession. Second, this revolution took place despite the fact that its goals, aims, or purposes were never clearly defined. With this in mind let us return to our previous question: Why was the Association membership so receptive to behavioralism? Certainly factors other than those we have cited (and others we can readily imagine) were responsible, the more so as the goals of behavioralism were somewhat vague but still called for drastic reorientation.

One possible answer which, given current developments in the profession (see below), is to be found in another development of similar proportions that had its origins at some point in the 1930s. We refer here to the increasing acceptance within the profession of the doctrines, principles, and tenets of political liberalism. We can say with certainty that by 1940 a very large majority of political scientists embraced most of the tenets of the liberal ethic, both in terms of specific policies and general theory. This distinct movement to the Left probably was the outgrowth of the 1929 depression, though it can be argued that the depression just accelerated a movement already begun. But no matter when, where, why, or what, the Association is today oriented toward liberalism, perhaps even more so than it was in the 1940s and 1950s.[5]

To link behavioralism with liberalism is not easy, even though by all outward evidences most behavioralists accept liberalism, and most liberals accept behavioralism. Clearly we are dealing with a concomitant relationship, but to argue cause and effect in the sense indicated above (that is, that liberal orientation prepares one to readily accept behaviorism) is difficult. Despite this, there are many reasons involving both specifics and theory that would tend, at least, to establish a linkage between the two which could very well account for the receptivity of behavioralism in the profession.

---

[5]The discourteous reception accorded presidential candidate Barry Goldwater at the 1964 Chicago APSA convention should serve to dispel any doubts on this score.

At the practical level consider the following:

1. The acceptance of a doctrine as broad as liberalism manifests the extent of common belief and shared values that must have existed among political scientists concerning what has been done and what ought to be done in the realm of politics. Now this commonality of belief is of significance largely because those with shared beliefs, who, moreover, argue their relative positions within the bounds of these beliefs, are apt to seek consensus and move as a group once consensus is achieved. It certainly is not unreasonable to suggest that these conditions provided the prerequisites for rapid change.

2. Insofar as one accepts the speculation that the depression and its aftermath had a profound influence on the profession, then we can assume that there would not only be agreement about what *should* be done to alleviate the crisis but also a tolerance toward diversity of opinion concerning the best means to the goal. Of even greater importance, however, was the realization that agreement on a goal, even when sanctioned by the authority of the government, was not enough to secure its achievement. Certainly there must have been a growing awareness during the 1930s that there is a great disparity between the announced objective of public policy and that which is actually achieved. Hence a tendency to look beyond formal governmental pronouncements and processes for an understanding of both the failures and relative successes of announced policy goals. Put otherwise, some "forces" were operative that needed further exploration if we were to understand fully the governmental process, its limitations and capabilities.

3. Finally, the transcendent concerns of liberalism such as freedom, equality, and the dignity of man, touching as they do almost every aspect of human relationships within society, compelled political scientists of this persuasion to widen their concerns. Put another way, far from posing any obstacle to the behavioral revolution, liberalism seemed to demand the expansion of interest and concern that behavioralism could provide.

As much as these and like conditions encouraged the rapid and relatively total receptivity of behavioralism, the basic philosophical and theoretical affinity between behaviorism and liberalism was probably even more significant. Others have dealt with this affinity at great length and we shall content ourselves with a few observations.

The stress upon equality in liberal theory leads us logically to an ethical relativism; that is, to the proposition that ultimate values are beyond proof or disproof, that they are not susceptible to verification as are facts. Indeed, to a great extent, the justification of political democracy (certainly one of the tenets of the liberal creed) rests upon this very foundation: when there is disagreement within a political society about the proper course of action or value or goal to pursue, the only "just" method of resolution is to count everybody equally. Why? Because, in the last analysis, when it comes to matters of values and preferences, one man's view or judgment in such matters is equal to another's. Why? Because within the liberal's theoretical framework to demonstrate the superiority of one value position over another is impossible. Any violation of this "All opinions are equal" doctrine soon involves us with asserting that some values are superior to others, that some people have a better insight into these matters. And, soon or late, we must construct an elaborate justification for holding any such opinion which, on the face of it, is incompatible with liberal tenets because it would of necessity involve the assertion of some degree of inequality among men.[6]

This fact-value dichotomy has had a twofold impact on the course of political science. On the one hand, the liberal premises as much as inform us that most of our classical literature in which we find the central inquiries revolving around such questions as "What is the good state?" "What is the best state?" or "What is Justice?" to be meaningless or, as some positivists would say, "nonsense questions." Consequently we have witnessed a decline in the study of traditional thought (as well as, we should add, an understanding of the relevance of history through which a "feel," understanding, and appreciation of the human condition is derived). Worse still, we have also witnessed a change of approach to the study of traditional theories because, in an effort to avoid eschewing them, behavioralists, with all of their liberal paraphernalia, had to render them

[6]A good deal of relativist thought concerning freedom of thought and speech is traceable to John Stuart Mill's *On Liberty*, particularly chap. 2.

"meaningful." How? Through various devices of transmutation, all of them involving transformation of classical theory to fit the grand design of behavioralism, that is, a translation of classical theory into testable propositions or theories.[7] To the extent that this could not be done (i.e., to the extent that the traditional theorist did not render his theories amenable to the presumed "scientific" mill), the theorists and schools of thought were ignored or even more shamefully ridiculed.[8]

On the other hand, and of equal importance, stress was placed on the accumulation of facts—hard-core data, testable propositions, systems and methods of measurement, with the end in mind of describing things as they are. Although never quite sure that data collected through this rigorous scientific method might be of use to those engaged in constructing normative theory or to politicians who have to make critical decisions, the behavioralist could take refuge behind a façade that he was not, and could not be, engaged in any exploration into the "should" or "ought." At best he could only point out the relative costs of pursuing one policy vs. others. While, of course, this might have an eventual impact on the decision, the behavioralist presumably operated under the ethical principle that he must confine himself to that which he *knows*, knowledge gained through prescribed procedures. A commandment of liberal theology is: Thou shalt not move from the *is* to the *ought*, from *fact* to *value*, while operating in the capacity of a scientist or behavioralist.

So it is that the scientific approach to the study of politics was aided and abetted by the epistemology of liberal theory—a theory that, as we have taken pains to point out, was outwardly, in its more superficial manifestations, already widely accepted in the profession prior to the revolution. And, to use the vernacular, "rewards" and "payoffs" flowed from this combination, at least for a while. Political scientists could at last claim to be scientists with the end of emulating the pure sciences, chemistry, physics, or astronomy. With this came the veneer of objectivity, a disassociation from value ends

---

[7]The most flagrant example of this I have found in Dahl's manhandling of Madison's theory. See *Preface to Democratic Theory* (Chicago: University of Chicago Press, 1956), chap. 1.

[8]For the most part, the theories of Saint Thomas and Saint Augustine fall into this category.

and commitments save only that of collecting and gathering facts in an effort to build scientific theory which would enable us to understand and predict human behavior.

But, obviously, the liberalism that allowed and gave encouragement to behavioralism has another side to it: its normative and prescriptive side. How often do we hear that there is an unjust distribution of wealth within our society, that our political institutions do not enshrine the value of political equality, that we do not pay due attention to the value of equality in our economic or social policies? As if caught between two schools, much of our behavioral literature (presumably value-free) amounts to little more than the accumulation of some data with the obvious intent of showing the failure of society to meet liberal values. At the very least much of it is directed toward discrediting non-liberals, the majority of whom do not accept the behavioral, and, thus, liberal foundations.[9]

With this in mind we can see why within the profession there always has been a "tension," which only recently has surfaced. As certain leaders of behavioral persuasion put the matter, it comes to this: Political scientists should be more concerned with the challenging issues of their time (rather than in "pure" research). Political scientists ought to speak out on these issues and increasingly make them the focal point of their researches. Moreover, political scientists have an obligation to help decision makers by making available the immense knowledge procured through their scientific researches. The crises of our times, in sum, demand that we (i.e., political scientists who describe themselves as behavioralists) veer off the straight, narrow, and demanding path of pure science for failure to do so might well have catastrophic results for our nation and society.[10]

There are at least three things to note about this formulation.

[9]Examples of this are to be found in T. W. Adorno's *The Authoritarian Personality* (New York: Harper, 1950); Samuel Stouffer's *Communism, Conformity, and Civil Liberties* (Garden City, N.Y.: Doubleday, 1955); and Herbert McClosky's "Conservatism and Personality," *American Political Science Review* 52 (March 1958): 27–45. They represent only three of the most transparent efforts along these lines that readily come to attention.

[10]Easton's presidential address (1969) does come, as I see it, to a formulation of this kind.

First, it is not true, as this formulation would have it, that behavioralists in the past have not strayed off the scientific path.[11] What is clear, however, is that they will blatantly do so in the future, rather than trying to conceal their normative assumptions and prescriptions. A second and related point is this: the so-called demand to move beyond behavioralism comes from the ideological Left in the profession who, rightfully enough, have asked the behavioralist wing to drop its pretensions of objectivity and lend their weight directly to the advancement of liberal goals and values. The "rub" is that they must put up a front to their friends of the Left who urge this course of behavior: they must make it clear that heretofore their work has not been normatively oriented for this would cast grave doubts on the credibility of behavioralism and the claims made for it over the past forty years. And third, this formulation allows the behavioralist to save face but, at the same time, accords strategic victory to the vocal Left that would seek to politicize the profession.

From this it is not difficult to see in what general direction the profession is going to move: it will become even more politicized in the years ahead. This will be reflected in written works, curriculum changes (designed to make courses more "relevant" for our contemporary world), and the activities of the Association itself. And we have every reason to expect that this process of politicization will assume a form wherein normative prescriptions are stuffed with the dressing of scientific objectivity. If the telegram of May 7, 1970, signed by eight presidents of the Association to President Nixon concerning our policies in Southeast Asia is any guide, we will find political scientists increasingly invoking the claim that expertise alone enables one to select the proper, best, or "right" course of action.[12]

Of course there are theoretical problems with this. Henceforth the behavioralist will have to pretend that he can bridge the fact-value

[11]On this see Herbert Storing, ed., *Essays on the Scientific Study of Politics* (New York: Holt, Rinehart and Winston, 1962).

[12]See "Communications" section, *American Political Science Review* 64 (June 1970): 589. We quote to illustrate our point: "Those signing the telegram feel that as *professional students* of political science their *special knowledge* permits them to offer *sound* and *objective* advice for easing this crisis [emphasis added]." In the body of the telegram we find the following: "Acting in our individual capacities as *political scientists* who are *devoting their lives to the study of politics* we are *impelled* by the present crisis to offer our *considered professional* advice for the quickest, most effective way of saving lives in Indochina and reducing strife at home [emphasis added]."

gap, that very gap which gave rise to behavioralism in the first place. From this will arise a number of questions: What relevance do behavioral findings have to answering the perennial questions concerning the good and just? How can you presume to know the best course of action or the wisest policy without the knowledge of good? Shouldn't one of your primary tasks be that of informing others how to perceive the good? And wouldn't this logically mean that the profession should, so to speak, turn back the clock or at least reorient its focus toward traditional political philosophy?

These and like questions are enough to indicate that the new behavioral-liberal alliance will be an uneasy one largely because of certain inherent theoretical difficulties. Nevertheless, the very size of the alliance with its relatively high degree of ideological cohesion make it quite improbable that any force inside or outside the profession will be able to prevent its complete domination in the years to come.

A good point of departure for a determination of what direction political science should take is simply to note the damage that has already resulted from this liberal-behavioral domination. The major damage, as I see it, has been the systematic cultivation of a parochialism that has served to stifle diversity of approach and independent thinking.

Evidences of this parochialism are to be found at several levels within the profession. Today, for instance, it is commonly said at both the regional and national meetings that the *American Political Science Review*, the national journal of political scientists, would probably not be able to sustain itself if it were not supported through membership dues. Increasingly one hears that the articles are trivial or just plain boring. And the Association itself is not, so it would appear, relevant to the average political scientist. The various committees of the Association which might perform useful functions are dominated by those of behavioral-liberal persuasion because the top leadership looks largely to their universe of acquaintances when making key appointments or when considering individuals for appointment. This is natural enough. But the process is such that a political scientist *not* in this orbit, no matter what his qualifications or interest in professional concerns, does not even have the opportunity to present his credentials for consideration. This produces, of course, an inbreeding at the highest levels. Moreover, the situation with respect to panels at the national meetings also leaves much to be desired for similar reasons. The major topic areas, the area leaders, and the program chairmen are selected through processes that simply do not accord each interested and qualified individual an equal opportunity to participate. In fact, it would seem, the process is designed to prevent this. The result, however, is a declining interest among the membership in the panels at annual meetings.

How can this parochialism be combatted? The obvious answer is to recognize the diversity that does exist in the profession and to establish the means by which it can express itself. In terms of its government, organization and procedure, the Association needs drastic alteration to achieve this end. Only through decentralization of decision-making authority (e.g., stripping the president of the Association of a good deal of his present powers, ensuring that the nomination procedures to representative bodies, including standing committees, are not controlled by a clique, and providing for greater diversity and wider participation on panels at our annual conventions) does this seem possible. In this regard, there is need for more journals sponsored by the national organization that would provide outlets for those whose approaches to the study of politics are not currently well received. Indeed, an effort could be made to de-fuse what is and what will continue to be a "sore" spot in the profession by instituting a system whereby all manuscripts could be submitted to a central clearing house and would be available to any member of the profession on request. Certainly we have it within our technological capability to provide for a freer flow of written materials than ever before. Beyond any question our present system seems (unnecessarily) to restrict this flow.[13]

At a less formal level certain other changes in the discipline would seem highly desirable. At present, because we have so many universities, it is shameful that political science departments are now fairly standardized in terms of subject offerings and approaches. We should encourage and attempt to develop distinctive departments, each representing a different school of thought or approach to the discipline, particularly in graduate programs. For instance, just as

[13]As of 1963, Alfred De Grazia had many splendid ideas on how to promote the flow of communication through elimination of the rather old-fashioned and costly methods we now use. I wish somebody in a position of authority would contact him on this matter.

there are some departments that in the past were noted for their emphasis on the behavioral approach, so should we move in the direction of consciously building departments that would be similarly distinctive in other areas. If this were achieved, arrangements could even be made between institutions to encourage exchange of students so as to guarantee that they would receive something better than the not-infrequent one-diet dish that has contributed so much to our present plight.

What seems clear is this: Even though the liberal-behavioral wing in the profession is still dominant, the profession and the diversity of its members has grown enormously in the past two decades. This growth, both in terms of numbers and interests, necessitates that we decentralize along the general lines indicated if we are to remain one. To suggest, as many do, that we can and should return to conditions as they were, say, in the 1950s is simply reactionary. Like it or not, we cannot fit back into our baby clothes.

. 3 . *What Should Political Scientists Be Doing?* *

EUGENE J. MEEHAN

To ASK, What should political scientists be doing? is a mistake. In that form, the question suggests that the proper way to select a focus for inquiry is first to identify the properties of something called a "political scientist" and then to infer from the definition the kinds of activities that are appropriate—"political scientists" are treated as natural entities, such as robins or seashells. This way of stating the problem leads to essentialism, to a search for knowledge that is somehow uniquely "political." Methodologically speaking, the search is futile. Worse, it encourages charlatanism to the extent that no honest and competent man can pretend to achieve the essential-ist's objectives, and it leads those already labeled "political scien-tists" to seek for a justification for what they are already doing, or have already decided to do, rather than try to develop a socially significant, self-correcting field of inquiry. No academic discipline, as presently labeled, can be defined adequately in terms of the kinds of phenomena investigated, the methods or techniques employed, or the conceptual apparatus and methodological principles on which it depends. For the most part, individuals are labeled automatically, as a result of university curriculum or place of employment, or the label is self-attached. To know that Jones is a "political scientist" is to know very little of importance about his interests, skills, train-

*Some parts of this essay were used, in modified form, in the last chapter of my *Foundations of Political Analysis: Empirical and Normative* (Homewood, Ill.: Dorsey Press, 1971).

ing, or capacity; even in the physical sciences, performance criteria are identified by specialization within the discipline rather than by department or major field.

The major force presently shaping our beliefs about the kinds of inquiry appropriate for political scientists is, of course, the university department. Unfortunately, university departments are organized for administrative rather than intellectual convenience, hence the sometimes appalling discrepancies between curriculum content and the work actually performed by graduates holding a particular degree. Of course, the large universities are likely to continue to function as day-care centers for middle-class adolescents, and as showcases for man's capacity to amuse, instruct, and titillate his fellow man (thus facilitating the search for activities that appeal to individual taste as well as social need) but faculty and curricula must somehow be organized to provide the kind of training needed to perform particular tasks in society or to deal with particular kinds of phenomena. The commitment to a phenomena-oriented focus has its dangers, given the tendency for any organization to fossilize and resist change and the legendary cowardice of faculties in nonsymbolic enterprises, but it much facilitates the rearrangement of intellectual endeavor. For we can then ask: "What kinds of tasks must be performed in society?" "How can students best be trained to perform them?" "What phenomena are most in need of study?" and "How can they be studied best?" Such questions cannot be answered by reference to guild membership and personal interests, any more than a physician can answer the question: "Why give this drug to this patient?" by referring to his status as a physician or his interest in the outcome. The physician learns to justify his interests by referring to impact on the patient; the social scientist must learn to do likewise.

Meanwhile, methodology provides us with a way of looking at "what is being done" in social science that is extremely useful for critical purposes. For if it cannot legislate the particular objects of social inquiry, it does provide a way of criticizing the objects selected for inquiry, the manner in which they are pursued, and the claims made for the results. Unfortunately, the brief space available will not permit a systematic development of the methodological premises needed for social inquiry, but many of the disagreements that most strongly divide social scientists at the present time relate directly to the purposes that systematic inquiry can fulfill and the means by which those purposes are best achieved, and they could in most cases be resolved if they were driven to the epistemological level. A simple statement of assumptions gives the impression of selecting from a number of equally tenable alternatives, yet accepting a reasoned methodological position necessarily involves rejecting for cause the available alternatives. The fact is that a "live and let live" attitude toward the methodological foundations of inquiry is inexcusable; good reasons can be given for accepting some methodological premises and rejecting others—reasons that a competent critic would be forced to accept. For that reason, the breakdown of communications between methodologists and social scientists, or more precisely, the failure to establish such lines of communication, has created a situation in social science analogous to the circumstances in which a physician could continue to treat a particular disease by a method known to be unproductive, or even injurious, without drawing criticism from his peers. By ignoring our capacity to judge the quality of the methodological assumptions employed in inquiry, social scientists have been able to avoid testing their ideas against evidence, or to hold the view that conflicting evidence is not sufficient cause for abandoning a belief. The result is endless argument that cannot be resolved because the assumptions of the protagonists do not intersect—without agreement at the methodological level, men can only indulge in pseudo-arguments, utterly incapable of generating the kind of impasse that would require change for resolution.

The point of departure for my own approach to inquiry is the human need to cope with the external environment (which includes other humans, of course) using human capacities to create instruments for achieving human needs and purposes. For survival is predicated on man's capacity to anticipate events in the environment, to control events in the environment, and to make choices from among the alternative situation states that can be achieved in the environment through human intervention. That in turn requires man to make and justify propositions asserting what is the case, what can be expected under given circumstances, and what should be preferred in particular situations. Man must organize what he perceives and use it to forecast changes in the environment, to explain changes in ways that allow intervention to inhibit or further them, and to express preferences or make value judgments. Analytically, these are the primary goals of inquiry, social or physical, though they may not be exhaustive.

The crux of man's intellectual dilemma is the need to justify, support, or test propositions about the environment, whatever their form. Assuming that information about the environment comes only through the sensory apparatus (empiricism), it follows that all propositions about the external world refer solely to man's perceptions, not to "reality." Hence they cannot be justified by their correspondence to "reality"—the latter cannot be known by man. Propositions that claim to assert what is the case, then, can be justified by reference to observation (and inference from observation), and various means can be devised for strengthening the justification. However, there is no reason to follow Berkeley and deny the external world altogether. Instead, the naturalist's assumption that there is *something* independent of the observer that serves as a constraint on human behavior becomes an important element in the strategy needed to criticize or support knowledge claims.

Although propositions of fact can be supported by observations, those that incorporate expectations about the future, or that express preferences among available alternatives, cannot. That is the heart of the induction problem, in both empirical and normative inquiry. It follows that neither type of proposition can be supported without referring to some external factor or purpose. That is, two assumptions are needed to bridge the gap between observation and choice or expectation: instrumentalism—the doctrine that concepts, explanations, value judgments, and so on are tools created by man for dealing with the environment; and pragmatism—the belief that the quality of the instrument is measured by its use in the environment to achieve purpose. That is, in a world in which man necessarily begins *in medias res*, and necessarily lives with the consequences of his own beliefs and values, intellectual tools can be criticized in terms of their utility in dealing with the environment, and ultimately in terms of their impact on the human population. Tools that have no purpose are not tools. The intrinsic properties of tools, their authors or sponsors, their past history, and the location where they were conceived, are irrelevant to their quality. In normative inquiry, human purposes are construed as tools for the betterment of human life, and evaluated by comparison with other purposes that might have been pursued in the same situation with different effect. Living with the results of accepting a purpose serves to test the purpose. The structure of human knowledge is unavoidably relativistic, whether the goal is justifiable expectations or prescription. There is no "general" or universal standard for criticizing all tools, no single map that will serve the purposes of every map user. The infinite regress is avoided by selecting a focus in time and pursuing the regress only far enough to control the factors that influence the selected focus to an acceptable degree.

Briefly, then, explanations and forecasts are the instruments man uses to organize his perceptions of the environment so as to produce testable expectations about the environment; value judgments are the tools that provide man with known and therefore corrigible grounds for choosing among the available alternatives in some concrete situation. Both types of instrument can be refined and improved over time on pragmatic grounds. As Norton Long has pointed out, "We are not bemused by the fact that a hammer is an instrument devised in action for the purposes of action, and improved in action for purposes of action that themselves improve with the improved possibilities the hammer's improvement opens up."[1] By stipulating purposes, the available means for achieving them can be subjected to cost analysis; by stabilizing the patterns used to cope with the environment, the variety of purposes that can be entertained in a given situation can be compared and reasons sought for choosing among them. At the very least, man can take known actions or standards to the environment to test the consequences of their use. The apparent circularity of the process can be converted into an ascending spiral over time, in principle as in practice, by referring to human experience gained by acting on expectations and living with the consequences of particular choices.

The prime implication of this conception of inquiry, and the point that most strongly conflicts with current practice in social science, is the need for purpose with reference to the environment. We must accept Karl Marx's dictum to the effect that philosophers should not only seek to describe or explain the world, they must want to change it. Systematic inquiry springs from, indeed cannot exist without, a desire to modify the environment; it consists in a search for dimensions of the environment that need changing and for the most

[1]In "Foreword" to Meehan, *Foundations of Political Analysis*, p. x.

efficient (least costly in normative terms) means of achieving such changes. The principal tasks of social science are social criticism and social engineering. In both areas, social scientists have thus far failed miserably, or failed even to try. For the most part, they have fled from policy making, eyed social criticism with distaste, and studiously refused to accept the principle that inquiry should be directed to the solution of human problems—thereby leaving the field to determined minorities with fewer scruples and even less capacity for reasoned judgment, though with a better instinct for the social jugular. Lacking purposes, there has been no adequate basis for deciding curriculum content, training faculty, rewarding or punishing performance, or structuring the administration of academic affairs. In place of useful knowledge, social science has tended to produce little cults of true believers with their spheres of influence, symbols, and priesthood. Within the cult, procedures for manipulating the symbols of the guild are agreed, and criteria of performance (*within* the church, of course) are established. The result is scholasticism, giving the illusion of argument but minimally committed to the development of knowledge and skills that relate to reasoned pursuit of reasoned goals in the external environment. There are exceptions, certainly, but they are all too rare. Social science, as it now stands, is the best available argument for its own destruction.

While the principal goals of social science are social criticism and social engineering, a division of labor could be expected to hold within the total enterprise, but the justification for particular inquiries must lie in their relation to the overall structure and not in the particular interests of the inquirer. We need to identify the conditions in society that can and should be altered (or maintained), determine the available alternatives and find means of assessing their respective costs, develop priority structures for allocating resources to deal with them, and create the tools that can bring them about as efficiently as possible. The goal is simply maximization of reasoned control over the environment, including its human dimension. It involves the substitution of prediction (expectations based on known patterns of reasoning) for prophesy (expectations conjured from whole cloth without reasoning); it substitutes a search for reasoned and testable intervention strategies for prayer, ritual, and ceremonial; it suggests conscious calculation of costs and consequences rather than dependence on pious hope and good intentions. I assume as a matter of course that DDT or some acceptable substitute is more likely to reduce the damage caused by a plague of locusts than damning with bell, book, and candle; that nothing in this world is free of costs, and that man must find means of calculating them; and that action not based on organized calculations of this kind is mere shadow-boxing and not a product of thought.

The old argument about the relation between facts and values, and the role that each plays in social inquiry, is merely a red herring and can be ignored. The logical distinction between the two kinds of propositions is immutable; that much we owe to David Hume. The distinction serves to prevent justification of *either* normative or explanatory propositions by reference to observations and formal logic alone—though there is no implication that such propositions are, therefore, utterly unrelated to observation. The structures and processes by which explanations are developed and tested and improved are no different from those used to develop, test, and improve value judgments. And it is analytically impossible for *any* inquirer to concentrate on either factual or normative questions to the exclusion of the other, whatever the locus of inquiry and whatever the inquirer's own conception of what he is doing. The division of labor may lead to work in which one component is obvious and the other suppressed, and it has always been the prerogative of the ignorant and naive to believe that their own conception of what is being done defines both the limits of reality and the limits of their own responsibilities. That does not change the analytic situation one whit. Evasion of the normative dimension of inquiry is analytically impossible; it is attained at the practical level by accepting a value structure from someone else—knowingly or not. And normative judgments cannot be made in the absence of explanations, for there would then be nothing to compare, nothing to choose from. Choices always and necessarily refer to the future and the future is always and necessarily a projection from the past or present based on an explanation or theory. And explanation alone is not enough, for without a basis for choosing and improving choice, man is doomed. Even the "act" of doing nothing is a choice whose costs must be calculated and weighed against alternatives.

If inquiry necessarily involves both explanatory and normative dimensions, an adequate criticism of any particular inquiry will also involve both dimensions. For example, the man (or woman, granting equal time) who does a superb job of investigating a trivial event deserves censure just as much, and perhaps more, than the man whose phenomenon is important but whose procedures are faulty. And at a more significant level, social science must develop the capacity to criticize normative argument as well as descriptions and explanations. Regretfully, there are few opportunities for useful borrowing. The philosophers have for far too long been permitted merely to assert their own competence in normative affairs. So long as they did not poach on the province of the empirically oriented, the latter returned the favor, and in truth, neither side has paid very much attention to the other in the last two decades. But the fact is that the traditional philosophers have made an awful mess of normative inquiry without being subjected to criticism, despite the amount of destruction that has taken place in the scientific and epistemological areas of traditional philosophy. The social scientist concerned with value judgment will have to do his own work, in normative as in empirical matters. The questions posed by traditional philosophy bear little relation to the kinds of questions for which social scientists must have answers—most particularly, what reasons can be given for preferring to live in one situation rather than another, where both are attainable and the choice is real. We do not have so much as the basic concepts needed for comparing the impact of human actions on human life, let alone the information needed for preferring the use of one rule of choice to another in a given situation. A conceptual revolution is badly needed in moral philosophy, and the moral philosophers show little sign of producing it, though there are good reasons to suppose that they could be enormously useful if their abilities could be harnessed to a suitable conceptual framework and a meaningful set of questions. A sound historical underpinning for a sociology of values could go a long way toward the development of such a conceptual apparatus.

In this context, the distinction that is sometimes drawn between the "scholar" and the "activist," between the exercise of scholarly skills and giving political advice on policy questions, is overdrawn and misleading. The student or scholar speaks with one tongue, whatever his audience; what he has to say depends on the question posed and the extent of his knowledge. While the scholar may change his mode of presentation to make what he has to say more readily intelligible to a particular audience, he cannot change *what he has to say* without ceasing to be a scholar. The integrity of the enterprise must be maintained at all costs, for without it there can be no enterprise, hence no justification for the privileged position presently occupied by the university in society. Those who propose that different standards of argument, rather than different modes of discourse, may be employed by the scholar as student and the scholar as activist support this form of intellectual schizophrenia by an argument that is inconsistent and contemptible. For it is claimed, at one and the same time, that the man in the street should be the ultimate source of authority in social affairs and that he is incapable of judging complex and intricate arguments and hence must be cozened. But if the premises hold, the conclusion to be drawn, surely, is that either the man in the street ought to have nothing to say about affairs he cannot understand, or those who claim supreme authority in his name must be prepared to take the consequences of their choice. Of course, careful reasoning may lead to the conclusion that the scholar should act in an "unscholarly" way because outcomes that can be justified on scholarly grounds cannot be achieved by scholarly means. Indeed, the scholar could conceivably argue that revolutionary action was essential, and participate in that revolution, on the ground that nothing could be altered without revolution and *any* alternative was preferable to the present situation —a conclusion which seems rather unlikely, all things equal. The essential point, however, is that conclusions are reached by best reasoning possible and criticized in terms of best evidence. The nature of a conclusion does not make it scholarly; that depends on how it was reached.

Given a commitment to social criticism and social engineering, the first need in contemporary society, and not in the United States alone, is for an adequate inventory of existing social conditions. Popular belief to the contrary, there is so little useful information available about the conditions of life of the population that for all practical purposes we begin at rock bottom. The scope of the undertaking is simply enormous, yet without an inventory, talk of reasoned intervention to achieve desired goals is merely fatuous. Planned achievement, analytically at least, is no more than inventory management. And we do not have so much as the basic concepts needed to make the inventory, the concepts that could be used to identify significant differences among men and to discuss the impact of common environmental changes on different classes of persons. Economists are gradually coming to realize, for example, that discussion of the economy in terms of gross national product is almost useless because there may be significant variations in one area that produce little impact in the other. Worse, both the factory that pollutes the river and the work required to cleanse it contribute to GNP—in GNP terms, digging holes and then filling them again is a productive enterprise. Social scientists must learn to move beyond income levels, credentialism based on years of schooling, meaningless job classifications, and income-level definitions of poverty to the use of concepts that will permit us to match social needs to social performance, individual capacities to the opportunity structure, education and training to job performance and life enrichment, and so on. We need indicators that will allow us to weigh the effects of brain damage due to inadequate diet or social ignorance, to balance the absence of medical attention against other dimensions of life, to consider, however rudimentarily, the blighting effect of a total lack of awareness of the quality of culture that man has been able to create. Physicians in the South still argue vociferously about the incidence of worms in young children. Our conceptual apparatus will not manage so much as the physical dimensions of life adequately, ignoring culture, psyche, and the intellect. All of these gaps must be filled in due course, but a beginning is possible, using existing concepts and categories that could serve as a point of departure for further experiments. We must develop priorities, and that demands a stock-taking. Without an inventory, there is no way to locate the unmade choices that society underwrites by a policy of drift. The rich man's dog drinks the milk the poor child must have to develop normally so long as there is no authority and priority structure to improve the allocation of resources.

Within the social sciences, the quality of the inventory produced will depend on the quality of the concepts used to aggregate populations. A clear distinction is needed between concepts that are useful for locating or *identifying* social problems and the concepts that are required for *dealing with* those problems. In the first case, all that is needed is aggregating concepts which classify people together who share certain specified attributes—"the poor," for example, may be defined to include all those with an income of less than a certain amount each year. Aggregating concepts that are needed for dealing with the problem, however, are different in kind. Here, we need to group together all those persons who will be affected in the same way, in terms of a specified set of dimensions, by a common change in the environment. If the poor as a class is defined in terms of income, for example, members of the class can be treated in the same way by providing additional funds and thus raising individual income. But the normative *impact* of the change in income will depend on a whole range of other factors; the group will not be homogeneous with respect to the normative effect of a change in income level. Income level is only an indicator of other dimensions of life that are considered to have normative significance. For engineering purposes, the population must be aggregated in terms of common changes in the values of these normative variables before reasoned policy decisions can be made. In another context, it seems clear that the number of years of schooling, the salary of teachers and principals, the cost of school buildings, or the teacher-pupil ratio are wholly unrelated to the quality of education provided by a school if quality is construed in terms of the awareness and performance capacity of the students. A common set of normative variables is needed that can be used to compare impacts, and to spell out the effects of altering the values of such intervening variables as social institutions.

In addition to a "population" inventory which can specify the conditions of life of different elements or parts of the population, those *features* of society that have a significant impact on the population will have to be examined. We need to know the actual value standards that society applies in particular situations and their impact on different elements of the population. Which differences are tolerated? Which are considered cause for alarm? What kinds of situations are considered legitimate areas of governmental intervention? Where are collective funds aggregated from and where are they used? Is the society tied to simple incrementalism or does it have some capacity for handling new situations? What of the cognitive quality of discussions of future policy? The flow of information? It is an indication of the utter inadequacy of existing social science, and perhaps of political science in particular, that there has been little effort to collect information of this kind systematically. Even with respect to the impact of particular laws on different elements of the population, political science has rarely gone beyond asking whether or not a given law was constitutional and enforced in the courts, or merely assuming significance on the basis of folklore.

Of course, a social inventory, however detailed, is only a necessary, and not a sufficient condition for reasoned decision. An agreed value system, a priority schedule for allocating resources, is also required, and a social technology would have to be developed that could translate normative standards into meaningful social conditions. The lesson here is that normative and explanatory instruments develop concurrently and not in isolation. At the present time, there is little knowledge of existing social conditions, few signs of an agreed value structure for dealing with those conditions, and little evidence of any genuine capacity to produce desired social changes, even when the need for change is agreed and the full power of government is committed to the undertaking. In many cases, of course, our inability to achieve significant modifications of existing social conditions can be attributed to unwillingness on the part of those who wield social authority, and those who support them, to pay the costs. With respect to the conditions of life of the American Negro, for example, white citizens of a liberal persuasion have been exceptionally willing to accept legal and other changes that could be had at little cost but there has been virtually no serious discussion of the kind of crash program, at very high cost, that would be needed to make really significant changes in the situation in a relatively short period of time. What is more, even if the United States government was seriously committed to the enterprise and *supplied the funds*, there is good reason to suppose that social scientists would be unable to provide a solution to the problem—though they are doubtless willing to accept the funds. How to convince black workers, for example, that they should adopt the Protestant ethic and the behavior that goes with it—punctuality, thrift, hard work, tidiness, and so on? How does one convince the children of the ghetto that they should attend school regularly and work seriously at lessons? The brutal truth of the matter seems to be that we do not know. And despite the desperate need for such information, we are not trying to find out. We need a very large number of inquiries aimed at learning how to get things done effectively and within specified cost limits—presumably studies coupled with suitable experimentation.

The positive implications of a commitment to social criticism and social engineering for systematic social inquiry could be spun out almost indefinitely. Far more attention will have to be given to elementary, primary, and secondary education than is presently the case, not in the sense of puerile descriptions of the socialization process but in terms of identifying the kinds of skills that our children need to be taught, the kinds of performance criteria that can be used for assessing school quality, and the most efficient means of achieving such goals. Education is rapidly becoming the major enterprise envisioned by the Greeks—continuing through life and touching virtually every aspect of life. The sharp separation of universities, public schools, vocational schools, and extension programs cannot be allowed to continue. We can take as our model the two most successful elements in American education: the agricultural school and the physical education program. If social scientists could be trained to perform as effectively as our farmers and football players, the future would indeed be bright. The fact that we cannot produce such training suggests that we inquire very carefully indeed why that is the case. And along these lines, the same considerations suggest that our conception of the proper role of a university in society be modified considerably. By and large, we have tried to mass produce an educational system designed originally for the wealthy and the religious; the result has been colossal expense and dubious benefits. The kind of staff-agency for a particular population function performed by the agricultural schools at their best suggests itself as an admirable alternative to the existing educational apparatus. A school system tied firmly to the occupational structure as well as the inherited culture system, in which work performance and school performance were inextricable intermingled, seems highly desirable. We need to put an end to such curious anomalies as large state universities located in the center of a relatively unpopulated agricultural region, for they make it impossible for the student to combine his education with meaningful employment. Such locations made sense when the transportation system was poor, and the agricultural college wanted to be near its constituents. It also made sense for the Eastern upper classes to isolate their offspring in the relatively safe environment of upper New England during the winter months until reasonable maturity was reached. Today, such considerations are not relevant. The schools should be tied to the cities.

And, of course, to the nation. Here new institutions will have to be created, for if it is fairly easy to transpose present universities into staff agencies for states and localities, staffing facilities for the nation as a whole are less readily converted, unless we are prepared to accept the exaggerated claims of the Ivy League—which I am not. We need national universities that can serve as staff agencies for the nation, training centers for faculty, and models for scholarly inquiry. We need a new model, however, not a reproduction of Harvard and Berkeley on the Potomac.

Pointing new directions, and suggesting reasons for trying them, is one important by-product of the developments that have appeared in methodology in recent years. But the sword cuts both directions, and much could be gained by eliminating current practice as well as adding to it. For much of current social science is a waste of time, and someone needs to say so. Some kinds of inquiry may *eventually* produce useful results (as they may not) but that is not an adequate reason for undertaking them, just as the possibility that a large book may contain some interesting sentences or paragraphs is not a good reason for reading it. The cost of the results may be far too high considering the alternatives available. The quality of social science output cannot be improved without killing off some of the monsters and sports. The live-and-let-live attitude that characterizes relations among guild members is self-destructive. We must be prepared to make discriminations in quality among products, to attack and destroy those of poor quality, and to encourage the others. Otherwise, we shall all be drowned, eventually, in a sea of mediocrity committed to paper. Some of the more prevalent of these intellectual monstrosities are worth enumeration.

Perhaps the most common form of misdirected inquiry in American social science is the aimless institutional description, the purposeless aggregation of data, the pointless repetition of past undertakings. Such activities produce endless books and articles dealing with governmental agencies, obscure people, and obscure laws. They generate history written "for its own sake" and studies undertaken because they "fill lacunae" in knowledge. They produce amateur psychiatric diagnoses of social ills wholly detached from prospective cures, literary criticism based on a particular "tradition," and mindless replications of any studies that have attracted attention and praise in the near past. The characteristic feature of this kind of activity is the absence of any purpose with reference to the environment that might serve to give meaning to the information. There is no testing of expectations, no suggestions of the effect to be expected when people live with particular values or beliefs, no attempt to contribute to our knowledge of the varieties of the human condition and the ways in which they can be modified or maintained. Those involved in such purposeless aggregation author the lengthy biographies of minor figures in history hitherto ignored (and rightly), man the data banks in our computer centers, make exaggerated claims about the "value-free" work they are doing, praise fellow scholars for "maintaining academic standards"... and train others in their own image. It is very depressing.

Every discipline has a place for drones and peasants, of course. The drone is most useful when intelligently directed. But the kind of justifications more commonly offered by intellectual magpies for their collecting lean heavily on two basic fallacies. Some accept the old Baconian belief that the induction problem can be solved mathematically simply by increasing the n of instances and treating the data by sophisticated statistical techniques. Others succumb to the "jigsaw puzzle" fallacy, the belief that every "fact" is valuable because it fits somewhere in the great jigsaw puzzle that man is trying to solve. Unfortunately, we now know that there is no single underlying puzzle, no single machine whose operation we need to untangle. Instead, we have an infinite set of possibilities, depending on human purposes. The fact that a given datum will fit somewhere in some puzzle is quite meaningless unless the particular set can be identified—and that requires a purpose on the observer's part. While such activity is benign rather than vicious, it consumes much time and energy better spent elsewhere, given the present state of social science, hence its rapid demise would be highly beneficial—if unlikely, for the moment at least.

A second type of activity that social science could well do without is the kind of static manipulation of data that makes use of large numbers of variables and generates enormous matrices but is utterly useless because it includes no variation over time. Much of the work done by voting analysts and students of "comparative" international relations falls into this classification. In the classic illustration of the case, an inquirer proposes that all of the nations of the world be divided into three distinct classes: A, B, and C. Having defined the classes and divided the world accordingly, we expect the inquirer to demonstrate by reference to experience that class membership has important implications for the behavior of the nation, in the same sense that an ornithologist's classification of birds tells us a great deal about the kind of behavior to be expected from the different species (robins migrate in autumn, for example). In these cases, however, the result is different. Instead of asking what difference it makes whether a particular country is a member of class A, B, or C, the inquirer turns back and asks what factors seem to be related to membership in those three classes—ignoring the implications of class membership entirely. It is very exasperating.

A third type of study focuses rigorously on a world without people —deals only with such intervening variables as social structure, class and status, political parties, organizations, or "inputs and outputs." The need for abstract and aggregating concepts is obvious, and they can be very useful, but at some point in the development of a study the apparatus must be linked to concrete human beings or remain pointless. If the relations between changes in the value of such intervening variables as party organization, family structure, or legislative procedures and the value of the variables that define the conditions of life of a given population could be established, that would be a different matter. But to study the antecedents to changes in the values of intervening variables without examining their implications for mankind makes inquiry a meaningless ritual, carried out uncritically and pointlessly—with no hope of the results being put to use.

A fourth type of academic undertaking that could be dispensed with is the "heuristic" exploration of particular models or logics without attempting to use or apply them to some empirical situation. Although formal models have an important role in the development of explanations or theories, the accent must be on use or applicability and not on the characteristics of the model without regard to use. For example, though algebra is very useful in social science, we would not ordinarily consider spending time working algebra problems with social science students, yet if a somewhat "sexier" branch of mathematics—matrix algebra dressed up as "mathematical theory of games," for example—is brought to the classroom, that is considered perfectly reasonable, even though we know that the axioms of algebra are in fact often satisfied in social situations whereas the axioms of matrix algebra decidedly are not. In related cases, students are exposed, nay subjected, to games and simulations in which they play roles of various sorts within a defined context. Such activities are widely touted for their teaching value, yet the lessons to be learned from the games and simulations are seldom specified and critiques of the accomplishments of such activities rarely discuss improvements in individual capacity to perform specified operations, relying instead on enthusiastic accounts of the stimulation of participation and reports of enhanced "understanding." The search for parsimonious models whose implications are useful for coping with specified situations ought certainly to continue; it is not furthered, I believe, by mindless manipulation of models for heuristic reasons.

Finally, a few unkind words should be said about those who indulge freely their soaring imaginations. Prophets and poets, Utopians and idealists, ultras of every persuasion, share an utter unwillingness to be bound by the limits of fact and logic. At their worst, the result is mysticism, anti-intellectualism, prophecy, affect manipulation; easily destroyed by argument, though with little observable effect on the speculator. In its milder and more deceptive form, speculation tends to the use of counter-to-fact conditional arguments without benefit of adequate theoretical underpinning, to imaginative instantiation of an argument (which carries absolutely no weight in any dispute), to the substitution of rich detail and plausible narrative for precise concepts, careful observations, and rigorous reasoning, and to the illustration of points rather than the testing of assumptions. The basic fallacy in most such speculations is the belief that examples that are *compatible with* a set of premises though not *enjoined by* them provide support for the premises—a special case of the ignorance fallacy, for non sequiturs are not evidence for or against any proposition. As long as the premise remains unchallenged, speculation can create the impression of saying significant things about the observed world. And given the cultural propensity to admire imagination for its own sake and to overestimate its benefits, and at the same time regard close reasoning as evidence of a lack of human feeling, speculative accounts can go a long way toward convincing a naive audience—I would be prepared to argue that the novelists of this century have done more for Freudian psychiatry, for example, than all of the psychiatrists combined. Speculation, like musical composition, is only interesting when it stays within the limits of recognizable form, hence remains amenable to criticism—and appreciation. What is without limit is meaningless.

.4. "Once You've Made a Revolution, Everything's the Same": Comparative Politics

JORGEN RASMUSSEN

I FIRST heard the words quoted in the title from one of my undergraduate philosophy professors. I do not remember the exact context, but I recall that his course dealt with various main themes of modern philosophy and that in this particular instance he was discussing some of the views of the philosophy of creation and attempting to emphasize the cyclical aspects of this approach. Some of us in his class who were political science majors thought this comment was accurate as well in politics, since despite the destructiveness of revolutions and the intentions of revolutionaries, social processes frequently flow back into the old patterns.

These two, perhaps interrelated, usages of revolution—the cyclical and the destructive—come to mind when I consider the current state of the study of comparative politics. I noted with interest that one of the panels for the 1970 American Political Science Association Annual Meetings, featuring some of the leading names in the field, was titled: "Comparative Political Studies: Did the SSRC-Sponsored Revolution Devour Its Own Children?" As I recalled some of the articles, two of which were written by participants in the 1970 panel, which appeared in the first issue of *Comparative Politics* in the winter of 1968, I felt that the question had been misstated. Instead of appearing in its familiar formulation, it should have been recast to inquire: "Have the children of the revolution devoured their parent?" My first reaction on reading these articles, to return

71

to my philosophy professor's comment, was that one must never lose sight of the understanding that the study of comparative politics must be regarded as a track meet, never as a cross-country run. For were one to make the latter fatal error in perception, he would chase the leaders of the profession over hill, and dale from one new approach and conceptual framework to another, never managing to catch them, always among the also-rans. But once one perceives that the track meet is the more accurate image, he can jog in place with equanimity as the leaders in the race disappear from sight around the first turn, knowing full well that in due time they will come thundering around the turn behind him and, as they lap him, he will be among the vanguard. "Once you've made a revolution, everything's the same."

It seems suitable to recall, in evaluating the study of comparative politics, the conclusions of the most widely known post-World War II diagnosis of the field. Writing in 1955, after the benefit of discussing the subject with various gatherings of political scientists which the Social Science Research Council had sponsored and with a conference organized by the International Political Science Association, Roy Macridis concluded that the trouble with comparative politics was that it was "essentially noncomparative, essentially descriptive, essentially parochial, essentially static, essentially monographic." Noncomparative because even works covering more than one country were no more than "parallel descriptions of the institutions of a number of countries [in which] the interest of the student is concentrated primarily on the analysis of the structure of the state." Descriptive because "there is no effort to evolve an analytical scheme within which an antecedent factor is related in terms other than chronological to a particular event or development [nor] to establish causal relationships that account for the variety in constitutional prescriptions." Parochial because most studies were concerned with Western European countries or related nations such as the British Dominions. Static because studies "ignored the dynamic factors that account for growth and change [to concentrate] on what we have called political anatomy." Monographic because most studies "concentrated on the study of political institutions of one system or on the discussion of a particular institution in one system. [Thus] the relationships established ... hardly attain a systematic formulation that can be used for comparative study, i.e., for identifying variables and attempting to account for them."[1] Summarized perhaps overconcisely Macridis's prescription was "more adequate conceptualization" and "the development of theories at various levels of generalization."[2]

In some ways the accuracy of Macridis's picture of the state of comparative politics in the mid-1950s cannot be contested. In fact he should be congratulated for expressing his views with such restraint. As anyone who has surveyed the literature prior to this time can attest, the percentage of dross or outright junk is astounding and appalling. If these essays, many not even at the level of quality journalism, were the best that reputable journals could find to publish, one shudders to think of what the material they rejected must have been like. Having said this, however, one begins on reflection to have second thoughts about Macridis's diagnosis, especially when, with the benefit of hindsight, one considers the impact of applying his prescription.

Were one of a mind to pray about such things, he well might supplicate: "O Lord, deliver us from further conceptualization and lead us not into new approaches." Regardless of what the situation may have been fifteen years ago, now clearly we are more than abundantly supplied with conceptual frameworks. Yet, as with the Sorcerer's Apprentice, the magical brooms continue to parade to the vat to empty the contents of their buckets. We have reached the point where further conceptualization becomes counterproductive. As Joseph La Palombara has commented, "Concept-refining very quickly degenerates into the scholastic game."[3]

Furthermore, one is forced to conclude either that the great majority of this production fell far short of its producers' claims or that the discipline of political science is unbelievably profligate. For the irritating and disturbing aspect is the lack of acceptance or use of these many proffered concepts. It is almost as though many political scientists fear it would compromise their reputation to be seen in the

[1] Roy Macridis, *The Study of Comparative Government* (Garden City, N.Y.: Doubleday & Co., 1955). The comments quoted appear on pp. 7–12.

[2] Ibid., p. 23.

[3] "Macrotheories and Microapplications in Comparative Politics: A Widening Chasm," *Comparative Politics* 1 (October 1968): 55.

company of someone else's concepts. Perhaps there is something of the maiden-aunt mentality in most people. Even in the swinging 1960s and 1970s the worship of virginity dies hard.

I do not assert, of course, that there are no seminal authors or articles. David Easton's concern with system analysis and Gabriel Almond's various elaborations of structural-functionalism have permeated the field widely. The fact that Almond has been attacked by some for playing with semantics, and is thought by others to be vulnerable to the charge, is instructive, however. For it suggests that while his terminology is utilized widely, many of the users, unlike Almond himself, do not grasp the thinking behind it. Similarly the citation of relevant or similar approaches at the start of most articles and books has an atmosphere of ritual about it; I remain unconvinced that most studies are in any meaningful sense building upon or extending previous work. More mystifying is the failure of many political scientists to employ the conceptual frameworks they themselves have devised or to heed their own injunctions concerning the process of research. Specialization is fine, but I rapidly lose patience with those people who spend their time grinding out advice to others concerning what is to be done and how it is to be done and thus are too busy to get around to doing any of the project themselves.

Consider, for example, *The De Gaulle Republic* by Macridis and Bernard Brown.[4] Were one asked to characterize this book, it would be accurate to say that it is essentially parochial, essentially descriptive, essentially monographic, and essentially noncomparative. As for static, that would not seem to apply to a study dealing with the collapse of one set of political institutions, their replacement with another set, and an assessment of the second set's viability. Yet no integrated theory of political change is presented and tested in the study—France's instability simply is attributed to a lack of consensus in the political culture. The authors seem to have "lost all interest in the formulation of other theories in the light of which change could be comparatively studied."[5] The four concepts—decision making, power, ideology, and political institutions—Macridis discussed in detail in *The Study of Comparative Govern-*

---

[4] Homewood, Ill.: Dorsey Press, 1960.
[5] Macridis, *Study of Comparative Government*, p. 11.

ment as illustrations of how research might proceed more profitably are not the concepts around which *The De Gaulle Republic* is organized, and are not even discussed in any systematic fashion in the book. The concepts do not even appear in the index. I want to emphasize that I am not belittling *The De Gaulle Republic* or its authors. I think it is a useful, worthwhile book and I would welcome others like it. But I must say that I think it requires a fair amount of cheek to write a book like this five years after downgrading most of the rest of the profession for writing books like this.

Perhaps the charge against the study of comparative politics was overstated or the emphasis of the remedies, both implied and explicit, somewhat misdirected. Was the field too parochial? Prior to World War II the politics of Latin America may have been neglected, although I think one could have found some political scientists who had made this their specialty. As for Asia and Africa, how many independent countries were there on these continents prior to the end of World War II? And what meaningful analysis of a country's politics is possible only three or four years after it attains independence? In short, what really pressing tasks had been left undone by the early 1950s in concentrating the bulk of research in comparative politics on European nations? Of course, it would have been a mistake for this balance of emphasis not to have been altered during the 1950s and 1960s as the world political situation changed. But had comparative politics really been derelict in some duty in this regard by the mid-1950s. Would the field really have been substantially further along in understanding political behavior and the political process if a considerably different balance of geographical emphasis had been struck during the first half of this century?

I see no reason why the practitioners of comparative politics need apologize for being parochial, unless their geographical focus implied an assessment of the intrinsic worth of various peoples totally apart from a judgment of where the yield of dividends in new knowledge was likely to be greatest per unit of research time invested. Perhaps some political scientists did feel that any country populated by people with brown, black, or yellow skins could not be worth studying because such people clearly were inferior and had nothing to teach the white man. But this charge would have to be proved, not merely assumed. I would guess that in most cases the heavy emphasis on European studies was simply the product of a researcher's realistic recognition of his limitations. Precisely because European countries were more like ours than were Asian or African nations meant that they were the ones whose politics we were more qualified to analyze. Surely it will be granted that it is difficult enough for an American really to understand French political culture despite many similarities of tradition and ideology between these two nations. And unless he can at least begin to do so he will have little hope of making sense of French politics, to say nothing of being able to analyze them in any meaningful way. How much more difficult is it, then, for an American to empathize with a Burmese. And until and unless he were able to do so, how valuable would his analysis of Burmese politics be likely to be? Such understandings and outlooks are acquired only by a considerable expenditure of time and money. Since the day of the large grant is relatively recent, non-European studies would not have appeared to many political scientists as a live option until after World War II. And then it would take some time for them to "tool up" to do a competent job. Had comparative politics until quite recently been less parochial, the percentage of dross probably would have been even higher than it was. It is increasingly conceded that much of the material published when comparative politics first began to try to save its soul by repenting of parochialism and embracing cosmopolitanism was of a rather low quality and was accepted more for novelty than significance. Other than dealing with another area of the globe it did not come any closer to Macridis's standards of excellence than did much of what had been published on European politics.

   To say that the study of comparative politics was too parochial is to imply that some attention should have been devoted away from European politics because it was receiving more study than was warranted or needed. This implication leads me to inquire how many people you can name who are thoroughly conversant with the politics of, say, Belgium, Norway, or Switzerland. For example, once you have listed Stein Rokkan and Henry Valen, neither of whom is an American, for Norway, and perhaps mentioned Harry Eckstein, of whom else can you think? Belgium, whose language/cultural cleavages are so divisive that one political scientist seriously questions whether it will continue to be a viable nation during the next few years;[6] Norway, which somehow seems to combine some of the worst disabilities of continental political systems with the stability and legitimacy of Anglo-American systems;[7] Switzerland, which is one of the very few cases of a viable federal system despite significant cleavages: all three countries presenting significant, fundamental problems for study. Can it seriously be argued that even now, to say nothing of during the mid-1950s, there is a surfeit of studies on the politics of these countries? Were you advising a foundation on what requests for research support should be granted, could you sustain preferring Burundi, Dahomey, and Niger to Belgium, Norway, and Switzerland, the latter three of which are more populous than any of the former three? (I am quite aware that size alone is not a valid criterion of importance, but I assume that it has some relevance since, so far as I know, no one has yet adopted my idea of writing a book or even teaching a course entitled "The Politics of the Unimportant Countries of Western Europe: Monaco, San Marino, Liechtenstein, and Andorra.")

I am arguing that excessive cosmopolitanism is not to be preferred to excessive parochialism. If enhanced knowledge of non-Western systems has been purchased at the cost of diverting researchers from more penetrating study of the European political process, where, after all, we did have some foundations on which to build, then it is questionable whether the trends of the post-World War II period can properly be labeled "progress." I grant that neither Macridis nor, so far as I know, anyone else has said that political scientists should stop studying European politics. But the reaction to a charge of parochialism is to drive people in this direction. Clearly, in recent years both prestige and money have lain in studying non-European areas. Examine the table of contents of a recent annual report (that for 1968–69) of the Social Science Research Council. You will see listed committees on African studies, Afro-American societies and cultures, Asian studies, Contemporary China, East Asian studies, Economy of China, Japanese studies, Korean studies, Latin American studies, Near and Middle East, and Slavic and East European

[6] George Kelly, "Belgium: New Nationalism in an Old World," *Comparative Politics* 1 (April 1969): 343–65.

[7] Harry Eckstein, *Division and Cohesion in Democracy* (Princeton, N.J.: Princeton University Press, 1966).

studies. For Western Europe? Social Science in Italy. As for the
section of the report on grants, there are headings for grants for
African studies, for Asian studies, for research on Contemporary
and Republican China, for Latin American studies, for research on
the Near and Middle East, and for Slavic and East European
studies. There certainly is some imbalance here, but it is hardly on
the side of parochialism. And as I already have argued, this cannot
be explained simply as a matter of making up for past neglect, since
there certainly are aspects of European politics whose past coverage
has been far from adequate.

Of course, it will be said that many of the ideas, approaches,
orientations, perspectives, and so forth gained in studying non-
Western politics are now making an impact upon the study of European politics. Given the amount of time and money poured into
non-Western studies, one should certainly hope so. For if the various studies of these non-Western areas have no relevance for systems
outside their own area, then they are just as parochial as European
studies are supposed to have been. The essence of parochialism does
not lie in being indigenous rather than exotic. There is no great
advantage in being restricted to one area of the world rather than
another simply because the one has more of an air of mystery—the
inscrutable Orient and darkest Africa—and is a bit farther away.
Had the same amount of resources been devoted to the further study
of European politics, it is hard to believe that we should not have
made equivalent progress—not the same progress necessarily, but at
least an advance of as much significance.

My comments above that many aspects of European politics had
been neglected relate as well to the charge that comparative politics has been monographic; perhaps it was "essentially" so, but this
is not the same thing as saying that it was excessively so. Information (and this touches on the charge of being "essentially descriptive" as well) on some European political institutions, to say nothing
of analyses of their functioning, is extremely difficult to obtain.
There are no thorough, comprehensive studies of either the Italian
or the German constitutional courts, for example.[8] This is so de-

[8]Taylor Cole includes both of them in his "Three Constitutional Courts: A Comparison," *American Political Science Review* 53 (December 1959): 963–84, and examines the German one alone in "The West German Constitutional Court: An
Evaluation after Six Years," *Journal of Politics* 20 (May 1958): 278–307. But neither

spite the fact that eight years were required to make operative the provisions for a constitutional court in the Italian constitution, and that its first president resigned within a year because of the failure of the Government to adhere to one of the court's decisions (shades of "John Marshall has made his decision, now let him enforce it"). This would seem to provide an excellent opportunity to examine the problems involved in any attempt to transplant institutions foreign to a political culture, yet this has not been done.   In Germany the Constitutional Court has made a number of significant decisions, involving such matters as the financing and operation of political parties and the distribution of power between the central and sub-national levels of government.   Yet, after twenty years of operation, no comprehensive monograph has been published.

The answer to why we still lack such studies is in large part that they are not "the thing to do."   If in reply to an inquiry from one of your colleagues concerning your current research interests, you said you were studying the Italian Constitutional Court, what do you suppose his reaction would be?   He probably would regard you as a mossback institutionalist completely out of the mainstream of the discipline.   Studies of this type have been so tarred with the brush of trivial legalisms that no one wants to do them.   Since they lack the aura of being on the expanding frontiers of knowledge, they offer little attraction.   The belief that we can build enduring theories without the benefit of a solid foundation on an extensive collection of monographs is a delusion.   The time has come for a new com-mandment: "Thou shalt not fail to write monographs."

It is difficult to quarrel with the idea that until relatively recently comparative politics has been more the study of foreign governments than the comparison of the political process in various sytems, and that this was not a very desirable state of affairs.   Yet the reaction which this diagnosis has produced seems to be the belief that the quality of a study correlates directly with the number of countries it covers. Very few people, however, have either the time or the abili-ties to be highly knowledgeable about the politics and culture of, at most, three or four countries.   If there is any correlation between

---

of these articles constitutes a full-scale study.   Discussions of particular cases or procedural aspects of these courts have been published from time to time, usually in law journals.

quality and number of countries discussed, it would seem more likely to be that the greater the number the less penetrating is the analysis likely to be. Even a book such as Barrington Moore's *The Social Origins of Dictatorship and Democracy*,[9] which discusses only half a dozen different nations, has been faulted by various country experts for being inaccurate in some respects for the country with which they are most familiar. Admittedly Macridis was not making an argument of this sort in complaining that comparative politics was not comparative; he specifically commented that parallel description of the institutions of several systems was not comparative simply because the study did not confine itself to one nation. But his comments are part of an atmosphere that has grown up that a study dealing with only one country really cannot be of the highest quality—unless, perhaps, that country happens to be a non-European one. One wonders what would have been the fate of such a classic as *The American Voter*[10] had such a criterion been applied in the American politics field.

I don't suppose that anyone has been so bold as to dismiss Robert McKenzie's *British Political Parties*[11] as an insignificant work simply because it does not utilize any "sophisticated" techniques of data gathering or analysis and focuses only on Britain. But at the same time it did not attract the attention and enthusiasm which Gabriel Almond and Sidney Verba's *Civic Culture*[12] did. McKenzie's work, however, is just as significant for anyone concerned with political parties and the democratic process anywhere as is Almond and Verba's. His book is not comparative and yet, precisely because he raises some fundamental issues concerning parties and democracy so clearly and explicates their logical and empirical interrelations, his work has comparative implications.

This really is the essence of Macridis's point, which seems somehow to have been lost sight of. Being comparative has nothing to do with the number of political systems examined, but rather is a matter of making clear one's research framework and basic hypotheses and

[9] Boston: Beacon Press, 1966.

[10] Angus Campbell et al., *The American Voter* (New York: John Wiley & Sons, 1960).

[11] London: Wm. Heinemann, Ltd., 1955.

[12] Princeton, N.J.: Princeton University Press, 1963.

stating one's findings in terms of fairly explicit relations between variables. Then the study becomes relevant to other political systems—becomes comparative—and its conclusions can be tested in other systems to discover the scope—not only geographically, but circumstantially, as well—of the findings.[13] What needs to be stressed loudly, then, is the fact that a study of a single country can be in a comparative context. Thus there is no reason why political scientists in the field of comparative politics should shy away from the idea of being country experts.

Not only would studies which are comparative in this sense help to allieviate the shortcoming Macridis saw in the field being "essentially monographic," but they also would help to cope with the deficiency he labeled "essentially descriptive." The problem here was not that we had too much information, but that it was not gathered or arranged in any meaningful and useful fashion. Unfortunately, here once again the wrong implication seems to have been read into this diagnosis. It seems to have been taken as a warrant for abstraction, as a justification for ignoring details in favor of broad discussions of rather vague influences and tendencies. This error seems to be in the process of correction with the rise of data banks. What distinguishes the best of these from previous similar, although technologically less advanced, efforts—labeled by Eckstein "politically ethnography . . . a matter of content with very little form, a pointless display of interminable exactitudes"[14]—is a greater awareness of the interrelations between a broad range of variables.

What needs to be done to avoid the failure of "essentially descriptive" is not to reduce the amount of information, but to specify more exactly the linkage one sees between the variables he examines, rather than just presenting them and suggesting that the reader should make what he will of them. And there needs to be an effort to discover concomitant variations, not just sequential ones. In this fashion studies can go beyond simply discussing necessary and sufficient causes. In some cases statistical techniques, like factor analy-

---

[13] For an illustration of how this can be done see David Butler and Donald Stokes, *Political Change in Britain* (New York: The Macmillan Co., 1970), expecially pp. 10–12, where they discuss this matter.

[14] Harry Eckstein and David Apter, eds., *Comparative Politics* (New York: Free Press, 1963), p. 12.

sis, may permit attribution of weight of significance to the various factors related to certain circumstances or results. Without entering into a debate between behavioralists and their opponents, I must at least mention, however, the need to guard against allowing the precision of techniques of data manipulation to outrun the precision of the data. At the university where I teach, student grade-point averages are figured to four decimal places, although only letter grades are given and no pluses and minuses are recorded. You can be certain that these averages would contain fewer places were it not for the fact that they are calculated by machine. Apparent precision can mask some indefiniteness and may be more inaccurate than less precise statements. At any rate the point is that it is possible to avoid being descriptive while retaining a considerable concern with the gathering of detailed information and to manage to be analytical without utilizing "sophisticated" techniques of data manipulation.

Just as some of the preceding comments have indicated how some of the various deficiencies in the study of comparative politics are interrelated at points, so also is this true of the shortcoming of being "essentially static." Once study becomes comparative in the way I have discussed, and once it becomes less descriptive in the sense of seeking concomitant variations, it will be very difficult for it not to be concerned with change. It is important to realize that this development will require greater use of historical material and efforts to study noncontemporary events than has been true of comparative politics during most of the post-World War II period. Historical research sites and data have not been "in" in recent years, but they must become so if we are to escape from atemporal research. The same point should be made here, however, as was made in the discussion of how to be comparative. A study can avoid being static even though it focuses on a single time period if it clearly states its findings in terms of testable interrelations between variables. In such a case it is possible for further research to discover how long such relationships have held and to attempt to seek the factors that would explain any change in the relationships. Thus one does not necessarily need to apologize for being static simply because his study deals with a relatively limited time span.

Increased concern with political change also requires recognizing that the balance of research will incline more toward macro- than micro-analysis. The great bulk of historical data available to us deals with structural, rather than behavioral, aspects of the political process. It will be some years in the future before we have built up significant runs of time-series data on many aspects of political behavior through the application of techniques of data collection largely developed since the end of World War II.

The significance that a developmental, historical perspective can have for comparative politics clearly is evident in Butler and Stoke's *Political Change in Britain*, a work which also indicates that some advance can be made even in micro-analysis of past periods, provided that one takes suitable care. By examining the political preferences of several age cohorts, Butler and Stokes recast the question that has attracted the interest of all students of British politics: Why do so many of the working class vote for the Conservative party rather than the Labour party in apparent conflict with their class interests? In their view this has little to do with what has come to be the accepted explanation—working-class deference—and rather is a matter of the relatively late rise of Labour as a major party in Britain and, therefore, the parental politics into which a considerable portion of the British electorate was socialized.[15] Thus by taking an extended time perspective and focusing on change they may have provided a more satisfactory solution to one of the basic puzzles of British voting behavior.

I cannot claim that many of the various points I have been making have not been made by others previously. The same year that Macridis's diagnosis appeared, he and Gabriel Almond and Taylor Cole co-authored a report from a subcommittee of the SSRC Committee on Research in Comparative Politics which specifically noted, among other things, the need for historical and institutional studies of European systems because of the many "areas of ignorance" that still existed. As they observed, "there are legal institutions and processes, about which literally nothing is known."[16] And, as I have emphasized already, I am not really arguing with Macridis, although I do think that he stated the case rather one-sidedly and did not

[15] Butler and Stokes, *Political Change in Britain*, pp. 104–15.
[16] "A Suggested Research Strategy in Western European Government and Politics," *American Political Science Review* 49 (December 1955): 1042–49.

stress sufficiently that the main characteristics by which he described the study of comparative politics were to some extent assets as well as deficiencies. The problem was not so much that they needed to be replaced as it was that they needed to be supplemented. But unfortunately, as I have argued, this was not the way in which this and similar critiques were received. And as seems to be the case with all revolutions, to return to my original imagery, the initial impulse was to go too far and to reject out-of-hand what had gone before, especially because, as is again usual, the followers tended to be more extreme than the leaders.

And thus, to revive the other of my initial images, the race has now passed the far side of the track and is beginning to swing back toward the starting line. Consider some recent comments of Joseph La Palombara, certainly one of the children of the SSRC revolution. The way out of comparative politics' problems, according to him, is to jettison structural-functionalism and systems analysis for—decision making, surely a landmark that the front-runners left behind long ago. He states

. . . in terms of parsimony, I would prefer comparative research on decision-making in legislatures, bureaucracies, political parties—even in elections—to comparative studies of the political socialization of children, patterns of recruitment to governmental roles, or the system of communication found within a society. It isn't that these latter concepts or analytical units are uninteresting or irrelevant; it is that their relationship to the output side of the governmental system remains extremely tenuous since we know very little in fact about what goes on in the "black box" that stands between inputs and outputs.[17]

Similarly Macridis himself has objected to the wide currency of systems analysis.

Scientism constitutes the effort to measure as accurately as possible the weight, scope, and persistence of the input factors, on the purely gratuitous assumption that they are or can be linked causally to political phenomena. The assumption is gratuitous because we have failed as yet to establish any such causal links and because it is doubtful that we ever will.[18]

[17] La Palombara, "Macrotheories and Microapplications in Comparative Politics," pp. 52–78. The quote is from pp. 73–74.

[18] "Comparative Politics and the Study of Government: The Search for Focus," *Comparative Politics* 1 (October 1968): 86.

This certainly is considerably less sanguine than his comments thirteen years earlier when one got the impression that, provided only we conceptualized more adequately, we would be able to establish such links. And although political institutions and decision making had been two of the concepts Macridis had offered in 1955 as a step toward more valuable research designs, yet it still comes as a surprise to read thirteen years later that one of the fundamental deficiencies in the field is "its gross neglect of the study of governmental structures and forms. . . . The central focus of politics, therefore, and of the study of comparative politics is, in my opinion, the governmental institutions and political elites, their role, their levels of performance and nonperformance." [19]

"Once you've made a revolution, everything's the same." In some ways, then, what students of comparative politics need to be told now, are being told now, is that they need to be monographic and to compile more descriptive data than they have been doing. They need to limit their research to a very small number of political systems with whose politics and culture they are fully conversant, even though these may not be exotic lands. They need to worry less about being monographic, descriptive, parochial, noncomparative, and static. They need to be less concerned about devising elegant, original conceptual frameworks and get down to the business of testing the propositions that emerge from previous studies. This means, of course, that the professional journals must cease to prefer abstruse novelty to empirical replication and that research support must not be devoted primarily to elaborate projects of supposedly great theoretical innovation.

Of course, I have overstated the situation—everything isn't really the same. There has been considerable gain. There is a new rigor in the study of comparative politics, and I refer not only or even primarily to statistical precision, which largely was absent prior to World War II. There are greater efforts to state clearly the basic propositions of one's study and to show how these relate to various theoretical arguments. The interrelation between variables tends to be expressed more explicitly. All this may not make political science a "real" science, whatever that may entail, but it is conducive to a

[19] Ibid., pp. 81, 89.

significant advance toward a more accurate and comprehensive understanding of the political process. But we now have gained all that can profitably be derived from the experience of the postwar years in seeking new directions and approaches. The time has come to emphasize the previously slighted strengths in the study of comparative politics.

These comments have been addressed to what might be called the professional or, perhaps, the academic critique of comparative politics, to the concerns and comments of those who desire to strengthen the study of this subject not so much from utilitarian motives as from a commitment to the enterprise of expanding political knowledge for its own sake. This can fairly be termed a professional orientation or commitment. The one thing that can jeopardize the further advance of comparative politics now that the race is swinging around the turn to the starting point, now that we are poised to build upon the strengths of past investigations combined with the greater rigor and clarity derived from post-World War II trends in research would be for this attitude of professionalism to be innundated under a wave of demands for relevance.

I am not extolling the virtues of irrelevancy. Our research as political scientists should not be pointless. The mistake, however, is to assert that it must be socially relevant, when it needs rather to be relevant to the principle concerns of the discipline. I almost am inclined to say, and perhaps a sizable number of people would agree, that the Great Issues are still with us even though the guise in which they appear may change from one generation to the next. The accumulated body of political philosophy and empirical studies provides a wealth of questions meriting further research. Do men and political systems in fact behave as certain classical thinkers reasoned they would in given circumstances, and if not, why not? Do the political relationships discovered to exist in one country at one time apply as well in another system or even in the same one at a different time, and if not, why not? What is the scope and limiting conditions of Tocqueville's belief that revolution is most likely to occur when a period of gradual improvement is followed by a sudden halt or reversal? Why has the federal system of Switzerland endured, while that of Malaysia collapsed, and can the experience of either suggest what can be expected to occur in Belgian politics in the next decade?

Why has the German party system moved toward a two- or, perhaps, three-party system, while that of Italy is even more fragmented than it was twenty years ago? Can this really be attributed simply to the difference in electoral laws? All these and similar questions are not pointless; they are relevant to hypotheses, propositions, theories, findings, philosophies, and so forth that make up the discipline, however indefinite may be its borders, that is generally recognized as political science. Studies rooted in this soil and having as their purpose its further enrichment are the business of political scientists.

Over a third of a century ago Harold Lasswell concisely summarized our basic concerns, *Politics: Who Gets What, When, How.* These are the matters about which political scientists seek to know and understand more. In engaging in this enterprise they need to be aware of the strengths as well as the weaknesses of being parochial, noncomparative, static, monographic, and descriptive; to seek to balance these aspects of their research with their opposites; and not to be concerned unduly if a superficial inspection might suggest that their work could be characterized as an exhibit of the loathsome quintet.

.5. Thoughts on the Purposes of Political Science Education

CHRISTIAN BAY

I

TO SPEAK rationally to this problem requires, I have become convinced, that we first develop a conception of the fundamental purposes of politics.

If we dodge this prior issue, at least one of three things will happen: we implicitly take the value of conventional purposes for granted; we imply without careful inquiries that different purposes should prevail; we speak *around* the issue of what political science education should be for, rather than directly to it.

The fundamental purposes of politics have to do with serving the needs and interests of all men, including those yet to be born. I doubt that anyone would dissent from this general but quite vague notion. But let me propose one further step toward a meaningful point of departure for this inquiry: the most fundamental purpose and justification of politics is to promote a more just society; that is, a society committed to optimal security and freedom for all human beings, on the premise of the equal and infinite worth of every human life.

Some colleagues would no doubt prefer different formulations of their conceptions of political purpose, but I suspect that in substance most of us would agree with this kind of political purpose, *if* or *to the extent that* we admit the legitimacy of asking what the basic purpose of politics should be.

A second premise on which my position will be based is empirical:

all states, and most other large organizations, including political parties, tend to develop purposes and policies at odds with the purpose formulated above, which I shall call *the* humanistically legitimate purpose of politics. While ostensibly many states and political parties proclaim a commitment to "freedom," "a just society," or the like (and thus testify to the widespread belief in the legitimacy of humanistic purposes of politics), it is a well-established law in the sociology of organizations that organizations tend toward hierarchy internally, and externally tend to become the servants of the interests of their leaders and *their* reference groups—groups which are usually overprivileged rather than underprivileged. The larger and more powerful an organization, the greater the stakes of power and privilege, and the less likely that humanistic purposes in actual fact will prevail over expedient purposes. Existentially speaking, in every state we must expect manifest or, more pervasively, enduring latent or hidden conflicts (as a rule rationalized or explained away by eminent scholars and their followers) between ideals of justice and realities of deepening injustice.

My third and final prior premise is only an application of the second one: that schools and universities usually operate like other large organizations, and indeed have close ties with and heavy stakes of power or privilege in their association with state or national governments or with private corporate agencies. Under conditions of academic freedom it is possible for individual educators, and for some university departments, perhaps, to work for, or even to fight for, justice, that is, for the underprivileged against the overprivileged, or at the very least, to keep raising issues of justice in rational, that is, radical, fashion.

Even for a whole profession such as North American political scientists, it is not unthinkable that, with proper education, they could become champions not of the status quo but of a more just society; champions of the humanistic purposes of politics. Political scientists are indeed a privileged group, and the temptations to side with men of power (which they are not) are always great. But with considerable academic freedom and with improved political education it may become possible for increasing numbers of political scientists to find more satisfying lives in the service of justice, or indeed in the service of their own more humanistic, and therefore better, selves.

II

"Politics," as I understand it, should refer to all organized activities aiming at resolving social problems, including the problems of keeping order ("government") and of protecting the weaker, or the less secure and free, against the stronger, or the more powerful and privileged ("justice"). Most generally, the problems of politics are posed by the discrepancies between what is and what ought to be. ("What is" refers also to what will become or what may happen; "what ought to be" in the marginal case could, as in problems of defense, refer merely to increased security for valued aspects of v/hat exits.)

With this conception of politics it is evident that empirical (including behavioral) and normative knowledge are equally essential, if indeed it makes sense to distinguish between the two. For most purposes it is better to say that normative and empirical research[1] are equally essential aspects of political inquiry, or the development of political knowledge: "what is" can be determined by empirical research methods, once the (normative) choices have been made regarding what are the important categories of facts to establish; "what ought to be" can be determined by (normative) choice of fundamental objectives and by (logical and empirical) analysis of necessary, probable, and possible prerequisites, implications, and consequences. "What can be" would in most contexts appear to be a more empirically based, necessary aspect of (or prerequisite of deciding on) what ought to be.

III

Having first spoken briefly to the purposes of politics, and then to the nature of politics, let me now get to the point of formulating, again briefly, some first-order purposes of political science education, along with some reflections, in each case, about their practical implications.

1. As with all education, political science education must aim at liberating the student from the blinders of the conventional wisdom, from political totems and taboos, so that he may make the basic

---

[1] Some purists will prefer to speak of normative analysis and choice, empirical fact-finding and generalization, and logical or mathematical (deductive) analysis.

choices of how to live and of political ideals as an independent person with optimal critical powers. This should keep him, too, from being an easy prey for alternative political dogmatisms.

In practical terms this means that students must be encouraged, not only to catholic reading, but to experimenting actively with governing their conditions of work and, more generally, their lives, preferably at least from high school on, but certainly from the beginning of their college days. And it means that students must have complete freedom of political expression, and access to all available points of view, and that faculties, administrations, and the general community must learn to live with student populations that appear to them unruly (if nonviolent), obnoxious, or unpatriotic. Incidentally, with fewer Spiro Agnew-type adults to provoke them, I doubt that student behavior generally would raise adult blood pressures to the extent that happens now.

2. The top-priority objective of political science education should be to produce graduates who in a double sense are optimally responsible, effective citizens: first, in the sense that they become effective spokesmen for the public interest in promoting justice; and second, in the sense that by their own example and as future teachers (in a formal and informal sense) they influence others, including their elders, to become better citizens. Robert J. Pranger writes that political education, as distinct from socialization, "emphasizes above all the artificiality of political order and the citizen as a creative actor within this order," and aims at developing not merely participants in the ordinary routines of politics but *participators*, or creative contributors to the political processes.[2] I would add that the responsible citizen, committed first of all to the promotion of justice, as a rational person must decide on his own the extent to which, in each situation, he is to work within and outside the legal system.

In practical terms this objective again underscores the importance of learning about politics by behaving politically. With reference to political science curricula, the promotion of responsible, effective citizenship requires empirical skills of comprehension and judgment no less than understanding of more normative issues. Even the

[2] See his *Eclipse of Citizenship* (New York: Holt, Rinehart and Winston, 1968), pp. 44 and 91.

languages of statistics and computer programming, for example, are skills that can make for more effective citizenship; but such skills in the absence of an acquired taste for, and respect for, the importance and complexities of normative issues of politics will produce technicians who in the future ought not to become certified as Ph.D's in political science.

3. I see our universities as charged with a particular responsibility to worry about the future of mankind; no other agencies enjoy the same potential independence from the corporate world, with its many parochial, short-term interests and with its powers to coerce or corrupt or, at any rate, to sidetrack rational concern and inquiry from the disinterested pursuit of the long-term public interest.

Within our universities, departments of political science have a particular responsibility, as I see it, and as I imagine Aristotle would have seen it, had he been around today: political scientists should be more responsible than others for promoting a searching and rational, and therefore radical, dialogue about what must or can or ought to be done, in the interest of justice, or survival, given the state of the nation and of the world.

Perhaps our most immediate task is to promote a free and rational discussion among ourselves and our students, but it seems to me that our peculiar responsibility is to promote and enlighten a continually concerned political discussion within the whole academic community and indeed within our whole society.

The failure to perform this function in the past, by any sizable professional or other community of colleagues or comrades, has had disastrous consequences. In this most powerful country today I believe the possibilities are better than in most others for trying, even at this late date, to make up for our past default as a profession of political scientists.

In practical terms what is badly needed on the campuses are required discussion courses (for all students, not just students of political science or those in the arts or science programs) in public policy and on the Great Issues, courses that will necessitate active participation in discussions and also assignments requiring evidence of careful personal judgments on issues as well as research skills and control of relevant available facts. Beyond that, as soon as it is practical, all political science students heading for the M.A. or the

Ph.D. should be required to spend at least a full year of VISTA or Peace Corps-type work with underprivileged groups, at home or abroad.

4. All scientists must share a concern for truth as an overriding value. Political scientists, too, must value truth, but they must as professionals be equally concerned with justice. Not that truth should ever be sacrificed for justice;[3] but the nature of politics, in my opinion, stipulates a responsibility to do all we can to make truth serve justice.

In practical terms this means that political science education must reflect a concern with establishing the facts as well as the causes or determinants of oppression, of persecution, of need and want, and of denial of elementary human rights; and equally a concern with developing the optimally rational ways by which we can: (a) educate ourselves, the academic community, and the citizenry at large toward a sense of outrage or at least of real concern for the plight of those who suffer; and (b) devise the most promising strategies for inducing governments or other centers of power to repair all needless injustice. The latter concern, the choice of strategies, will of course depend considerably on the former, the levels of political education achieved, both generally and with specific reference to the problems at hand. Strategies chosen may at times involve violations of customs or laws, depending on likely costs and benefits, and notably on the degree of suffering or even loss of life to be forestalled.

There is a lot of loose talk of "relevance" in university education these days, often without specification of "to what." In political science there is indeed a particularly vital need for relevance—relevance to the great problems of justice and indeed of human survival, which confront all of us. Obviously the study of the past and even of what merely *seemed* relevant to past generations of political scientists is not without value toward understanding the present and the dynamics of our own generation's concerns. But in our choices about where to place our emphasis in the education of political scientists it is crucial that we be informed not so much by precedents as by enlightened concern about where the most pressing problems

[3]Let us overlook the obvious fact that in certain types of situations all rational men would agree that some true statements might be so harmful or otherwise inappropriate that they should not be made.

are confronting us today, and what may be their roots. Perhaps, for example, entirely new departmental categories, or new professional combinations, ought to be called for. These, at any rate, are possibilities to which we must be open.

(Parenthetically, may I add that, for many reasons, not least my concern for achieving optimal relevance to pressing problems, I welcome the recent trend toward increasingly active participation by students, especially graduate students, in reshaping our curricula, our institutional arrangements generally, and indeed the structure of our joint concerns in the various departments of political science. I hope we will soon have full parity on most issues—not in evaluation of scholarly competence, however—as a rule rather than the exception. Professors have more experience, by and large, in life and in reading and reflection. Students generally have a keener perception of what is new, and what is in prospect, and also tend, perhaps, to be more honest with themselves and with each other. For a maximally responsible and effective grappling with the awesome problems of politics toward the end of our century, we need a dialogue on the basis of equal dignity and thereby mutual respect between the generations, so that we can all contribute with the best that we have.)

IV

In conclusion a few words on the curricula of political science are appropriate in the light of the above remarks on objectives and styles of learning. I believe that traditionally we have placed too heavy emphasis on (1) fact-learning and not enough on (2) dialectics of judgment, (3) developing more rational, critical use of political language, and (4) establishing political concerns as an essential dimension of reflective living.[4]

I offer these suggestions very tentatively, for reasons that hopefully by now are obvious: the determination of curricula requirements, as much as of styles of teaching and learning, and of general criteria with which to establish the competence of new professionals (as distinct from specific judgments of the competence of individual

---

[4]I leave the issue of training in research skills out of this discussion, because I believe the better departments are doing an adequate job.

candidates), are matters for faculty and students to decide on jointly, and indeed to reconsider and to modify from time to time. As the general dialogues on politics and on the Great Issues change in content or emphasis, so presumably should we discuss from time to time what conclusions to draw for political science curricula.

1. The invention of the bookshelf should have made it unnecessary, in my judgment, to require quite as much factual knowledge of details of political history or institutions or behavior patterns as is now often done. With fast-increasing effective access of students to computer-type knowledge banks, it becomes even more important to make sure that we aim at reducing the numbers of facts to be learned, and instead (a) try to teach our students how to keep improving their judgment with respect to separating essential from nonessential facts (essential to our functioning as citizens, that is, as practitioners of politics, and also to our functioning as theorists of politics, or carriers of general political understanding); and (b) teach our students to do their readings with critical intelligence so that they train themselves to decide on increasingly realistic criteria what to skip over and what to concentrate on and retain.

2. We must shun the supermarket approach in the teaching of either facts or ideas; that is, the teaching that presents wide ranges of materials to the student without judging them normatively. It is not enough that the student be asked to judge for himself, as has often been the logical positivist's or the pluralist's easy way out. It should be the responsibility of the teacher to demonstrate how he formulates his normative judgments, as responsibly as he can, on the basis of optimally explicit criteria.

"Normative judgments" refers, when the materials presented are mainly empirical, to criteria of relevance to normative concerns, as well as to empirical criteria of representativeness, range of ramifications, and the like. When the materials presented are ideas, perhaps mainly normative, the phrase refers to criteria for critical judgment in terms of more basic norms, as well as other, more empirical criteria, such as practicality, psychological implications, and so on.

Ideally, teaching should be dialectic, in the sense that normative premises and inferences are constantly questioned, and weighed in comparison to alternate formulations. Not every teacher can manage to do this well on his own, but team teaching is always a possibility. Moreover, with the right atmosphere of freedom and respect in the classroom, it may more often than not be possible also for the single teacher, among graduates or undergraduates, to elicit good help from his students.

3. What is of enduring value in logical positivism is, I believe, an enhanced awareness of the differences between three categories of statements: those whose (probable) validity depend on evidence; those that depend on logical accuracy or consistency; and those that depend on value commitment, preference, or choice. Not that these distinctions can always be made sharp and clear, but in most statements it makes a lot of difference to clear thinking and communication whether or not the speaker or writer is explicitly concerned to achieve optimal clarity with respect to these distinctions.

Also matters of syntax and grammar are important to clear thinking and communication, and it is often apalling how college teaching, even in political science, has been unconcerned with, or very lax in its concern with, developing competency in mastering the mother tongue as a tool for rational thinking. Qualities of literary grace are mainly for other departments of instruction to worry about, but in the education of political scientists it must be our responsibility to see to it that our students become articulate in writing and speaking to serious issues, as well as thoroughly "language-critical," at least in relation to political discourse. Students should become sensitive to all kinds of irrational, prejudice-promoting, and obfuscating uses of language, to ambiguities and vagueness, to uses of persuasive definitions, to uses of hurrah words and damnation words and other tricks from the demagogue's bag, to conscious or unconscious parading of meaningless or pernicious clichés from the coffers of the conventional wisdom, to needless mystifications by way of academic jargon, and so on. Crisp, direct, simple, yet optimally precise words and statements are not only preferable in political and other prose or discourse; these qualities are essential, I would think, in promoting a more responsible and constructive political dialogue. And that ought to be one special contribution by departments of political science toward a more civilized polity.

4. As teachers of political science we, more than any other group, could and ought to take the lead in attempting to rehabilitate the concept of politics from its present sordid existence as a term of

reference to a semi-commercial bargaining-type game for stakes of power, authority, and other privilege. I have stated my own concept of politics above, as referring to all organized activities aiming at resolving social problems, including the most general problem of establishing order with justice. Not that this concept is mine; it is essentially the ancient Greek conception of politics, going back at least to Socrates, as the art or science most directly concerned with finding ways toward a better human life in a more just society.

As long as authoritarian governments were taken for granted or, as in the Athens of Plato and Aristotle, men of practical power had not yet come to fear the power of political ideas,[5] philosophers could discuss substantive political problems rationally in terms of alternate futures, ideals, and even strategies toward realizing distant ideals. With the advance of more representative types of government, and of democratic aspirations, the salient *problems* of politics tended to become pragmatic rather than substantive; for example, problems of how to engineer coalitions or how to win elections, rather than problems of how to protect or expand human rights.

And the economically privileged classes in modern times gradually, perhaps often without being aware of it, developed a vested interest (especially in the most democratic countries, the English-speaking ones and the North European ones) in *degrading* the activity of politics and the profession of politicians. Under capitalism political life did indeed become commercial in many of its aspects, for example with respect to advertising practices insulting to the more intelligent, competition for voters much as for customers, exchanges of secret deals involving mutual favors, and the like. Since political life was more accessible to public scrutiny, self-serving illegal behaviors that might be commonplace in the hidden chambers of the corporate world would on the political arenas result in recurring scandals, whose immediate practical import each time was to kick out those who were caught and enlist others in the service of the same corrupting interests. And the long-term import was to build into the public consciousness a deepening contempt for politics and politicians—the only agencies and agents that might poten-

---

[5] Socrates was sentenced to death mainly on account of his political style and his temerity to mock the Tribunal that sat in judgment.

tially come to constitute a menace to the interests of the overprivileged; the only potentially rational, disinterested agencies and agents of justice and the common good.

The resulting deepening degradation of the concept of politics became reflected in the teaching of political science as well. Most departments would dutifully continue to offer courses in political philosophy, but these tended to become history-of-ideas courses, with the classical and, one might have thought, perennial ideals of justice and human rights effectively insulated from the practical political arenas of the time.

For a long time the bulk of political science curricula was presented mainly within legal, institutional, and historical frameworks. Then in the 1950s came behavioralism, which again was concerned mainly with understanding established realities, though in a richer sociological perspective. With this "more scientific" approach to the field, "politics" came to refer more explicitly to nothing more than power behavior and consumer behavior relating to government. Concepts such as "justice" and even "the public interest" tended to disappear, as there were no ready measuring instruments available; indeed, these were not considered empirically viable concepts.

But the behavioral approach rendered great services, and cleared the way for a resurrection of politics in the classical sense. While shying away from studies of the principal power elites, behavioralists gradually accumulated mountains of evidence that exposed the pretenses of democracy and bared the realities of oppression and corruption. Orthodox behavioralists tended to remain either "apolitical" students of how the system works or liberal students of how its performance could be improved in various particulars. But their research paved the way for radical "post-behavioralists"[6] (I would prefer to say "radical behavioralists") to challenge the legitimacy of the system, and to go to work to study proximate aims and strategies toward alternative futures—behavioral, educational, institutional—in the service of justice and the public interest.

This brings political science, full circle, back to the basic concerns of Plato and Aristotle, but with immensely improved tools. Though

[6]David Easton's term. See his APSA Presidential Address, "The New Revolution in Political Science," *American Political Science Review* 63 (December 1969): 1051–61.

we now live too close for comfort to several kinds of holocaust, there are grounds for hope as never before, because the nature of the political enterprise has never been as well understood. The power of the individual who can be militant without being irrationally dogmatic has never been greater, paradoxically, than in our complex world, whose normal functioning seems to depend on the vast majority living with one-dimensional semi-consciousness only. Yet a fuller individuality and a fuller humanity seem within reach, for all kinds of people; for example, in situations of nonviolent confrontations, if they are structured and handled in the right ways—and how to achieve that, again, is something we are learning more about, as activists and as social scientists, and particularly if we can combine the two roles.

And that is precisely the point about "establishing political concerns as an essential dimension of reflective living." It is easy to understand the processes by which people becoming de-politicized are essential aspects of oppression in the name of democracy: to become quiescent in an extremely unjust society the so-called citizen must be made to believe that the system is democratic and works in his interest, but yet somehow he must be kept from seeing the realities of oppression and oligarchy. Injustice must be blamed on human nature, and on the human nature of the politicians, above all, while participation in the regular rituals of voting must be seen as the only thing the non-expert but right-minded citizen can do about it. The procedures of so-called democracy become the only fixed realities of the political world, and no one should presume to challenge them.

But "politics" should, I have argued, refer not to procedures but to the substantive aims of justice. As Albert Camus taught us, to become revolted by injustice is a criterion of becoming more fully human, more fully conscious as individuals and as committed members of the human race. "Know Thyself" can then be understood as a call to moral consciousness and to political consciousness. To help each other and our students to heed that call, and to keep relating it more rationally to our expanding political knowledge, surely should be a key responsibility on our part as political scientists.

Part Two: Political
Science and
Action

Introduction

SHOULD POLITICAL scientists mount the barricades or remain stoicly analytic in the ivory-tower comfort of their classrooms, libraries, and computer centers? These options present a rather unreal image of the choices confronting the student of politics because the options seldom are real to anyone who has by choice entered the scholarly realm. Neither is it easy to act without some impact from professional experience, nor to avoid political action. The question more meaningful to political scholars is: How ought political science be related to political action?

This question, of course, has been partially answered in the previous section. It receives more central attention in the following essays because, as the authors view the discipline, the issue is seen as the key to proper standards for research and training. Although the positions of the essayists range from neo-positivist to phenomenologist, the arguments are not so diverse as might be expected. A basic point of departure for the five essays is the recognition that there is an issue to be resolved which ought not be resolved by a retreat to "pure political science"—which does sound a bit stranger than "pure physics"—or to unrestrained activity.

The common point of departure means that the speakers build out to their evaluative standards for action in a fashion that inevitably covers similar grounds and is often in more consequent agreement than their overall perspective might lead one to expect. The narrow scientific rationalism presented by George J. Graham, Jr., can abide

Henry S. Kariel's request for more experimental tests for future possibilities. Avery Leiserson's arguments, which are founded in the tradition of "Chicago realism" that stretches back to Charles E. Merriam, are not completely out of harmony with either Lewis Lipsitz's support for Caucus-oriented reforms or E. W. Kelley's commonsense-plus-science position. Indeed, all five arguments can be characterized as efforts to articulate how political knowledge *can* be used as a proper guide to important political problems. Differences occur both in conception of possible knowledge and the directly related certainty—or better, uncertainty—about possible futures. Perhaps most important is the common agreement, demonstrated throughout the anthology, on the commitment to employ political knowledge to improve human existence as best we can.

The theme of Graham's essay is that human reason can best be employed for human purpose by maximizing political knowledge with the aid of science. He assesses rationality applied to political questions to set forth what political scientists can do distinct from the ordinary citizen. The forms of rationality permit expert study into the necessities and possibilities of society, permitting political science research to contribute to more meaningful social choice. This research, although heavily immersed in norms, can be conducted independently of, and can contribute to assessment of, specific normative choices. These capacities affect the roles political scholars play as political scientists.

The pursuit of social and political possibilities separate from the confines of total commitment to paradigmatic constraints predominant within the discipline provides the key prescription of Kariel's essay. He does not attempt to undercut science so much as to squeeze from it the most expansive perspective possible on the future. The focus of the expansion is the human personality and its development. A more morally sensitive generation of scholars are, in effect, already demanding such an expansion. The expansion requires but a slight shift in perspective—a slight shift with major implications. The shift is to view what is necessary, what is "certain," from the perspective that it is not necessary until proved; that is, experiment to uncover possibilities rather than necessities.

The tradition of realism in political science is brought to bear on this same issue in the comprehensive essay by Leiserson. The searching argument seeks to specify the relationship of commitment and knowledge from a realist's perspective. The complexities of the position, which is founded on both the acceptance of uncertainty and the demand for action, force a fundamental definition of politics and assessment of the effects of the definition on research, analysis, and action. Leiserson makes explicit the realist's refusal to equate politics with everything, thereby avoiding the error that robs the concept of either dependent or independent status in explaining existence. He sets forth value, science, and choice as three interdependent factors whose synthesis leads to action based on knowledge. Further, the proper, albeit complex, relationship between theory and fact is essayed, leading to his standards for appropriate political relevance.

Lipsitz's argument brings forth, in direct language, the disaffection toward the discipline among members of the Caucus for a New Political Science. His charge is not against the means of analysis predominant in political science—his publications demonstrate his mastery of them—but rather against the irrelevance of the research presently pursued to the problems and concepts of contemporary political existence. Indeed, his challenge expands to the point of visualizing American political science as providing ideological support—in the proper sense of Karl Mannheim—for many features of American society. He argues for a new focus toward positive changes in society in terms of satisfying human needs. He sees the proper mode of activity as a social stimulant since the society has a less expansive self-perception than the academy. He discusses the Caucus platform and goes on to additional specific suggestions.

The final essay on political science and action is by E. W. Kelley. His argument, though critical of the present weak state of science in political analysis, moves into arguments in favor of employing political knowledge. The discussion in effect challenges at once both our knowledge and our unwillingness to use it. The application of scientific knowledge, softened (or hardened) by a great deal of information and common sense, is the appropriate stance for the professional. As with Leiserson, classical political problems are seen as remaining important. The task for the political scientist is to muster all the weaponry that can be contributed by political science and then to enter the fray.

.6. Reason and Change in
the Political Order

GEORGE J. GRAHAM, JR.

POLITICAL SCIENTISTS take themselves too seriously, and the subject of their discipline not seriously enough. Or so the recent debates within the discipline might indicate. The intellectual content of the debates is reminiscent of a series of Platonic caves in which each distinct group of dwellers possesses its own particular methodologies and normative perspective, with each group believing its perspective is the only one of any value in interpreting the shadows on the cave's walls.[1] Many political scientists seem more concerned that their own views be accepted than they are about the correctness of their views. Rather than enter into a discussion about which rules ought to be applied in interpreting shadows on cave walls—a topic admittedly pursued in other contexts[2]—it is more fruitful, in light of the theme of this volume, to pursue the question of how political analysis can be related professionally to political evaluation. This seems to me to be the basic problem behind the divisions within the discipline. In other words, how does the subject matter of political science relate to political prescriptions and to action?

[1] The abundance of panels at recent American Political Science Association Meetings grew out of two major groups (Caucus for a New Political Science and Conference for Democratic Politics) and several smaller ones at least feeling a need for independent control for particular orientations and purposes. Independent associations for "specialists" have emerged not only within fields of specific interests, but also for political theory itself (Conference for the Study of Political Thought).

[2] George J. Graham, Jr., *Methodological Foundations for Political Analysis* (Waltham, Mass.: Ginn and Co., 1971).

The first and most important consideration in approaching this problem involves answering a prior question: What specific talents do political scientists possess which enable them to contribute to such an important and critical task as the identification of political exigencies that require prescriptive solutions? In other words, what is it about our subject matter and our means of approaching political questions that defines and justifies our *special* contributions toward improving the political order? One must presume that any special contributions made by political scientists result from something more than the fact that most of us are moral, compassionate, and concerned. Indeed, it is the potential for making special contributions which necessitates identifying and scrutinizing the talents that mold the discipline. This is a difficult task since there presently is disagreement over even the nature of the profession.

Perhaps the critical problem confronting us is explained by the fact that the unifying notion of a discipline of political science has been lost, and subdisciplines based not on subject matter but rather on diverse perceptions of appropriate orientations, methods, and techniques have divided our membership in such a way that each group falls back upon its own standards for interpreting political reality. This dependence upon the group's standards provides the members of the group with an intellectual defense mechanism and raison d'être which justify the seriousness of the group's work.[3] But this is not the same thing as taking political science seriously. Serious assessment of political science requires that political knowledge in its most inclusive form be viewed with the objective of uncovering the capacities and commitments that make knowledge possible.

Political scientists, it is safe to generalize, are committed to the development of a common body of political knowledge. This is the core of the matter. It means that they search for knowledge which can lead to understanding, to explaining, and yes, to improving the political order. The latter objective depends upon the two former objectives because only the capacity to understand and explain political interactions can provide more than an emotional justification

[3]The point concerning "intellectual defense mechanisms" can, of course, cut both ways. Edgar Litt and Philip Melanson, "A Peer Group of Liberals: The Profession and Its Public Discontents," APSA convention paper (September 1969), also use it to criticize standard orthodoxy. Orthodoxy comes in many forms.

for directing or for predicting the consequences of political and social change. Since the former two objectives can be collapsed into the use of reason in political analysis, another objective general enough to claim as consensual becomes clear. The use of reason delimits what can be done in our special role and must be assessed prior to discussion of prescriptions and action. The forms of use of reason, however, vary so widely that each subdiscipline has its own style of analysis.[4]

RATIONALITY IN POLITICAL ANALYSIS

The very diversity of styles employed in analyzing politics provides an appropriate starting point for searching through the uses of reason within the discipline. The basic modes of reason common to all styles, or inclusive of them, can be surveyed. It is of course impossible here to do more than sketch the various modes of reason that have proved important to developing political knowledge, but these modes share common dimensions. *Rationality*, in its most general sense, refers to the capacity for systematic thinking.[5] *To reason*, generally refers to the employment of this capacity for rationality. *Reason*, more difficult to capsulate, refers both to the basis for explanation of conditions and to the intellect. Although these very general notions merely outline a perhaps shaky framework of meaning, by stating them it becomes possible to tack onto them several more specific meanings which will clarify the role of reason in political analysis. It should be remembered that the capacity to apply rationality is not limited to a single style of political analysis.

Perhaps the most specific meaning of rationality as it is used in

[4]Admittedly, different subjects being studied require variation in techniques. But Abraham Kaplan's law of the instrument deserves note: "Give a small boy a hammer, and he will find that everything he encounters needs pounding." *The Conduct of Inquiry: Methodology for Behavioral Science* (San Francisco: Chandler Publishing Co., 1964), p. 28.

[5]The emphasis on "rationality" rather than "reason" permits appropriate limits to the conceptualization which, in turn, permits distinction between rational and *a*-rational thinking (and action). Reason often is viewed so broadly that it fits everything, and therefore identifies nothing. My reference to "reason," thus, presupposes the limits set forth for rationality. The analysis is an outgrowth from Morris Raphael Cohen's *Reason and Nature: The Meaning of Scientific Method* (Glencoe, Ill.: Free Press, 1959).

developing political theory has been borrowed from economics. The assumption of rational behavior under specified conditions has permitted theorists to develop models or abstract analytic theories of democracies, bureaucracies, and even constitutional decisions.[6] This use of rationality, designated as *rationality₁* refers to maximizing behavior pursued by a political *actor* within a set of carefully specified assumptions. Its pure expression is perhaps best typified by Anthony Downs' monk who rationally purges all rationality from his mind in the effort to achieve mystical contemplation of God.[7] The utility an individual assigns a given personal goal is not evaluated in determining his *rationality₁*. Rather, his maximizing behavior, whatever his personal goals are, is the central concern.

This meaning for *rationality₁* is especially interesting from two perspectives. First, the meaning is compatible, or can be made so, with A. J. Ayer's emotive theory of values which permits analysis of rational behavior independent of possibly arational ordering of norms by an individual.[8] It becomes possible for the analyst to study what individuals ought to do to maximize their own values without forcing the analyst to assess those actions in terms of his own cultural or normative standards. Indeed, this possibility improves the theorist's ability to deal objectively with cultures different from his own. Second, but related, there is little reason to presume that an individual would not act according to *rationality₁*, within the limits of his resources. As William H. Riker has pointed out, rational behavior seems to be expected of actors in all political systems, especially in fiduciary relationships.[9] Obviously, as is recognized by the many theorists employing this rational-model ap-

[6]The classics in this field are Anthony Downs, *An Economic Theory of Democracy* (New York: Harper and Brothers, 1957), James M. Buchanan and Gordon Tullock, *The Calculus of Consent: Logical Foundations of Constitutional Democracy* (Ann Arbor: University of Michigan Press, 1962), and Anthony Downs, *Inside Bureaucracy* (Boston: Little, Brown and Co., 1967). The approach has been expanded greatly into the field of coalition theory, represented by William H. Riker's *The Theory of Political Coalitions* (New Haven: Yale University Press, 1962) and Sven Groennings, E. W. Kelley, and Michael Leiserson, eds., *The Study of Coalition Behavior* (New York: Holt, Rinehart, and Winston, 1970).

[7]*Economic Theory of Democracy*, p. 5.

[8]A. J. Ayer, *Language, Truth, and Logic* (New York: Dover Publications, 1946). The use of arational, rather than irrational, is employed to emphasize the nonrelevance of rationality to individual utility ratings.

[9]*Theory of Political Coalitions*, pp. 24–28.

proach, all actors do not—indeed, cannot—always conform to the patterns identified as *rationality*₁ because of imperfect knowledge. But the models nonetheless prove useful in providing general claims about rational behavior which can be compared with real behavior and which often point up empirical discrepancies to be explained, such as why an actor does not pursue a rational course in a given situation. The principles involved permit simulation of settings and predictions about action under the given conditions.[10]

*Rationality*₂ will be used to refer to the logical or mathematical structuring found in models such as those developed to demonstrate *rationality*₁ or empirical deductive theories. Thus, *rationality*₂ is roughly equivalent to the employment of deduction. The activity of deductive reasoning is pursued not only in classical theoretical analysis, but serves as the foundation of formal scientific explanation.[11] It should be noted that the generalizations or assumptions from which one deduces provide the creative dimension of such analysis, with deduction permitting the generation of more particular claims which can be easily studied. If the original generalizations or abstractions are true, then so too must be the consequences generated through deduction. Thomas Hobbes remains the master of such analysis.

The third mode of rationality employed in political analysis is more closely related to empirical theory. Although *rationality*₂ is of obvious significance in this realm of inquiry, most important to empirical analysis are the standards applied for using empirical observations to verify theoretical claims, or *rationality*₃. The major dimension of *rationality*₃ is induction, but it also entails the methodological standards for concept formation, explication, and theory development.[12] The close relationship between these forms of rationality in empirical analysis is clear once it is recognized that the models provide the specific calculus used to relate empirical concepts.

The fourth form of rational analysis can be identified by focusing

[10] See William D. Coplin, ed., *Simulation in the Study of Politics* (Chicago: Markham Publishing, 1968).

[11] Karl R. Popper, *The Logic of Scientific Discovery* (New York: Science Editions, 1961), pp. 59–62, and Carl G. Hempel, *Aspects of Scientific Explanation and Other Essays in the Philosophy of Science* (New York: Free Press, 1965).

[12] Graham, *Methodological Foundations*, pp. 138–66.

on the linkage between the second and third modes. *Rationality*$_4$ refers to the hypothetico-deductive model (H-D) common to most discussions of scientific reasoning, but most clearly explicated by R. B. Braithwaite.[13] The H-D method involves generating verifiable claims which are deducible from theory and then observing whether these claims maintain. Indirect inductive evidence, therefore, supports the general theory from which the testable propositions are deduced. Anomalies among observations indicate that an error exists either in the assumptions or in the definitions of phenomena to which they apply. Seemingly abstract theoretical claims can therefore be grounded in synthetic knowledge.

A fifth mode of analysis is closely related to the hypothetico-deductive model. It is retroduction (R-D), or *rationality*$_5$, which refers to the corrective analysis required whenever an anomaly is discovered. The late Norwood Russell Hanson was instrumental in the revival of inquiry into this method whose tradition stretches back to the dialectic of the Greeks.[14] The appearance of discrepancies among observations forces the theorist to reason upward to the assumptions and the theories for the purpose of discovering errors. The process, the reverse of H-D, should then lead to corrections or replacement of the erroneous elements of the theory and the discovery of explanations for the anomalies.

Further distinctions might be drawn to specify nuances of these five basic modes of rationality. V. O. Key's *The Responsible Electorate*, for example, adumbrates a theory of voter rationality that is fully congruent with *rationality*$_1$, although it is itself an example of *rationality*$_3$.[15] Attempts to deal with rationality of goals have been presented in recent literature as well as in the traditional analysis of politics,[16] but these approaches must be handled through applications of the five modes of rational analysis. They deal with reasons

---

[13] *Scientific Explanation* (London: Cambridge University Press, 1953).

[14] Norwood Russell Hanson, *Patterns of Discovery* (London: Cambridge University Press, 1958), and "Retroductive Inference," in *Philosophy of Science: The Delaware Seminar, Vol. 1, 1961–1962*, ed. Bernard Baumrin (New York: Interscience, 1963), pp. 21–37.

[15] Cambridge, Mass.: Harvard University Press, 1966.

[16] For an example of attempting to "use science" for this purpose, see Fred M. Frohock, *The Nature of Political Inquiry* (Homewood, Ill.: Dorsey Press, 1967), pp. 145–204.

why certain goals should not be part of an actor's utility index, given certain factors in political reality. It should be kept clear that these arguments about goals are not to be belittled. Rather, they are to be treated as completely as is possible within the framework of rationality as applied to political analysis. Rather than attempt to essay all of the nuances possible, an assessment of the commonality of these five modes and their variations will enable us to clarify why classical philosophy attaches so much importance to the uses of reason.

First, logical consistency is a common requirement of the five modes. Inconsistency negates *rationality*$_1$, and makes the remaining modes inoperable. Second, verifiability is central to each mode. The relationship between the theoretical structures developed through rationality and observations of the real world makes such analysis different from mere speculation. Even economic models are considered interesting only when they have empirical applicability. Third, rational thought permits extension of perception beyond mere facts per se to general knowledge which explains them. Thus, man's rationality leads to the development of knowledge—a human creation—which can be used in manipulating and controlling the political environment as well as for explaining it. Most important, it is clear that some form of application of rationality must be employed before sense perceptions can be organized as knowledge.[17] Fourth, each mode of rational analysis employs an explicit and sharable—intersubjectively transmissible—set of criteria for evaluating its employment. Even Platonic meanings, if we follow Leo Strauss in his notion of sociology of philosophy, can be shared once the criteria for understanding are known.[18] This permits us to accept Richard E. Flathman's two criteria or rationality: rational thought requires (a) communication through the employment of language and (b) testability by standards independent of the person applying them.[19]

Uncertainty, of course, plays a critical role in assessing rational

---

[17] Karl W. Deutsch, *The Nerves of Government: Models of Political Communication and Control* (New York: Free Press, 1963), pp. 5–21.

[18] *Persecution and the Art of Writing* (New York: Free Press, 1952), chaps. 1–2.

[19] *The Public Interest: An Essay Concerning the Normative Discourse of Politics* (New York: John Wiley & Sons, 1966), p. 88.

analysis. Each form of rationality is limited by the fact that certain knowledge of real settings will never be achieved. The utility of even abstract, rational economic models depends upon the grounding of the knowledge in political reality: thus all political knowledge is limited by the constraints upon inductive verification.[20] Nevertheless, and this is the beauty of rational analysis, the conclusions from rational analysis are the *least uncertain* available to man. What is more, the standards employed in each mode permit clear specification of the accompanying uncertainty in terms that help minimize the effects of the uncertainty. Rational analysis, therefore, makes clear, within the respective criteria of the various modes, its own limitations, but it also yields the most certain knowledge possible to explain what has been, what is, and what can be.

This commitment to develop such knowledge is what distinguishes political scientist from citizen. He attempts, in a psychological context, to explain and understand the limitations and possibilities that confront political man. He attempts, in a sociological context, to explain and understand the limitations and possibilities that confront a polity. And this is possible within and because of the common and distinct criteria of rationality modes. The outcome is political theory.

RATIONALITY AND ANALYSIS OF NORMS

Political analysis is inherently steeped in values and cannot be pursued without either incorporating or explaining normatively significant phenomena in the theory developed. The categories of analysis that fall within these normative parameters contain diverse elements, both historically and generically. Classical political analysis and the corresponding secondary analyses of the great books only touch on the many types of analysis that must be placed within the category of normatively significant political science. Natural right and natural rights analyses play dual roles both as efforts at political theory development and as variables which are instrumental in explaining normative positions prevalent within societies. Psychological and sociological approaches to creating political theories must deal with political attitudes and social-political belief systems. Political culture, for example, implicitly incorporates the basic nor-

[20]Graham, *Methodological Foundations*, pp. 145–49.

mative assumptions and bases for normative choices within societies.[21] Indeed, political theorists such as Carl J. Friedrich, David Easton, Karl W. Deutsch, and Bertrand de Jouvenel attempt to meet the rigorous standards for meaningful empirical analysis and at the same time to provide within their models explicit or implicit standards for evaluation of societies.

Friedrich's analysis is presented explicitly, providing a set of standards for evaluation derived from applying reason to the experience of mankind.[22] The analyses of Easton and Deutsch incorporate a modernized view of the classical notion of a healthy *polis* in presenting explanations of the conditions requisite for maintaining their respective critical measures or essential requirements for the political system.[23] Jouvenel, in defending political settlement and the art of conjecture based upon the best possible rational political predictions, incorporates both Friedrich's assessment of the importance of reducing conflicts within systems and the systems theory objective of identifying the means necessary for preserving political order.[24] At least when these formulations are treated *as if* they are successful in achieving their own objectives, it is clear that theory can play a critical role in normative analysis. They present models of political reality which can be assessed in explaining and evaluating any normative choice situation.

The important aspect of this relationship between normative choice and verifiable political theory rests in the fact that the theoretical claims can be evaluated by independent standards. A rational model, independent of whether it is based on logically derived consequences from stated assumptions or whether empirical consequences are directly deduced from theoretical claims, provides the means to identify relationships which can be stated as theories in a form susceptible to direct or indirect verification. If observations of reality conform to the model, the assumptions of the model can

[21] Lucian Pye and Sidney Verba, eds., *Political Culture and Political Development* (Princeton, N.J.: Princeton University Press, 1965), and Gabriel A. Almond and G. Bingham Powell, Jr., *Comparative Politics: A Developmental Approach* (Boston: Little, Brown and Co., 1959).

[22] *Man and His Government: An Empirical Theory of Politics* (New York: McGraw-Hill Book Co., 1963).

[23] Cf., David Easton, *A Systems Analysis of Political Life* (New York: John Wiley & Sons, 1965), p. 24, and Deutsch, *Nerves of Government*, pp. 214–56.

[24] *The Pure Theory of Politics* (New Haven: Yale University Press, 1963).

be treated as more or less certain, dependent upon the weight of mustered supportive evidence. This form of political knowledge is based neither simply upon the normative objectives of the theorists who employ them nor upon the objectives of the individuals whose behavior is observed. The knowledge is dependent only on sharable standards for establishing what is verifiable and what is not. Normative choice, if it is to be based on reason, cannot be made without these limitations which are the very requirements for applying reason to the relevant elements of analysis. If verification of theoretical claims in politics can be demonstrated, knowledge so supported provides a foundation for two limitations political theory can impose upon normative choice.

The first limitation is the set of conditions that can be specified for *social sufficiency* in a political system. Social sufficiency can be met by any set of conditions which can be demonstrated as sufficient for maintaining political order. Inductive evidence can be used to demonstrate how varieties of sets of sufficient conditions could (in terms of probability) lead to support for regime forms within specified contextual conditions.[25]   The problems entailed in such specification are complex because more than one set of conditions most certainly would work. Nevertheless, a set of the sets of sufficient conditions could be developed placing limits on which options are possible in a given social context.

The second limitation upon normative discourse, as distinct from normative speculation, is found in the set of conditions that can be categorized as *social necessities*. In this category are included all social conditions and social structures that must be satisfied in every regime form in order that a system survive. Social necessities must be conceptualized broadly because beyond certain limits, implicit in physical human needs, the diversity of means of satisfaction leads to apparently contrary, if not contradictory, sets of sufficient conditions. This is especially clear in dealing with the potential solutions to satisfying emotional human needs with ideological and cultural belief systems.[26]

Although both sets of conditions can be subject to analysis within

[25]Cf. Michael Scriven, *Value Claims in the Social Sciences* (Lafayette, Ind.: Publication #123 of the Social Science Consortium, 1965), pp. 6–8.

[26]Cf. Sebastian DeGrazia, *The Political Community: A Study of Anomie* (Chicago: University of Chicago Press, 1963), and Robert E. Lane, *Political Thinking and*

the limits of scientific epistemology, each set of conditions intro-
duces difficult problems of aggregating individual needs, wants, and
expectations through a societal level theory. Were a readily available theory meeting these needs already constructed, it is highly
doubtful that questions concerning "What should we be doing in
political science?" would seem necessary. Since the requisite theory
is possible, but not available, and since its requirements are specifi-
able, it seems clear that work toward its construction deserves attention since it could resolve major theoretical problems for the
discipline. Both the conditions for social sufficiency and necessity
can be established only through the rigorous application of the many
forms of rationality to political phenomena, and both are dependent
upon, and provide the appropriate bases for, political theory.

Set theoretical models permit the theorist to handle the wide
scope and generality of statements concerning socially necessary and
sufficient conditions while providing sophisticated structures for
dealing with the complex maze of relationships which are so critical
to applying the theory to real-world relationships.[27] Ultimately these
models, whether formal-deductive or partial-inductive, are contingent upon verification of the assumptions through direct inductive
or indirect hypothetico-deductive techniques. Thus, it is but a re-
dundancy to label as "empirical" the political theory so developed.
What is more, even classical and other "essential quality" analysis
present only posited empirical relationships as theory, though the
claims may be very general.[28] Normative political arguments are
dependent on theoretical claims and are usually incomprehensible to
others unless they are demonstrated as consequential to knowledge
of political relationships. The important question is not whether
facts are distinct from values, but *how* empirical knowledge as contained in political theory can be most useful in making normative

Consciousness: The Private Life of the Political Mind (Chicago: Markham, 1969),
especially pp. 334–39.

[27] Partial development of these structures are presented in my "Classical Philosophy and Macroanalysis: Normative Evaluation Standards and Empirical Theory,"
paper presented to the 1971 Midwest Political Science Association Meetings, Chicago.

[28] The generality of a claim as it affects reality does not limit the empirical dimension so long as it does not become tautological; see Giovanni Sartori, "Concept
Misformation in Comparative Politics," *The American Political Science Review* 64,
no. 4 (December 1970): 1040–46.

choices. Every effort to evaluate must recognize that the possibilities for improving the human condition can be pursued only through the use of human reason to discover and to implement political knowledge.

Given that a complete theory of social necessity and sufficiency is not presently available to guide political evaluation, how can the role of reason be maximized? Theory has been and can be developed to provide general knowledge of political relationships. Theory provides the means for understanding, explaining, and even successfully changing the political environment. Even if theory cannot directly prescribe what one ought to do, it can at least settle certain matters relevant to every "ought decision." Political theory, once verified, provides a means for explaining what *is* or *has been* in the world of politics. But more important, it can relate what *can be* in the same world. This is a point of no small importance since theory, once verified, is the best means available for projecting into the future.[29] Prescription deals with the future and what ought to be. Theory deals with what can be. Although knowledge of what *can be* admittedly would include diverse sets of socially sufficient conditions, such knowledge would eliminate conditions that fall short of meeting the requirements of social necessity. And whenever alternatives of goals or policies are advanced as being of normative merit, reason can be employed to evaluate the prescription before normative commitment occurs. Political scientists ought to pursue analysis that will facilitate rational political choices because it is precisely the ability to present the results of this kind of analysis which distinguishes him from the common citizen. How he uses this potential depends upon whether he is committed to using his special talents as a political scientist in political advising or whether he is attempting to promote his personal values under the guise of a specialist.

RATIONALITY AND POLITICAL CHANGE

The significant problems raised by concern over what political scientists should be doing include the assessment of how political science analysis can prove useful in efforts to pursue political action,

[29] Bertrand de Jouvenel, *The Art of Conjecture*, trans. Nikita Lary (New York: Basic Books, 1967).

efforts to make policy choices, and efforts to prescribe specific political objectives. Most political scientists began their careers because they were interested in politics, including proposals for action and prescriptions for change. To ask an individual to ignore this original commitment is at best futile. Rather than pursue such a moot effort, it is more useful to assess the relationship between rationality in analysis and other interests, objectives, and roles which often attract political scientists. The rather familiar trichotomy of roles clearly susceptible to action provides a framework within which this relationship can be discussed. The first of these is the direct involvement of political scientists with government officials and others interested in expert advice. The second is in the area of citizenship education, which is here distinguished from political socialization. The third, and perhaps most controversial, is the area of political activism.

Political advising is perhaps the closest thing to political engineering within the discipline. If political theory capable of accurate prediction of desired consequences of policy choices, domestic or foreign, were available, and if action so based could be correctly assessed as to its probable consequences, both as to expected (or desired) and accompanying (or undesired) consequences, then a major contribution could be made to whomever the advice is given. It is important first to note that any advising that a political scientist pursues merits attention only insofar as it is based on verified theoretical knowledge or it is mere response to requests for specific information. Other forms of advising (moral perspectives, for example) are not really much different from that which could be gleaned from the general public. The point is rather simple. It is in the exercise of the means for rational inquiry in the form of research and analysis fostered by appropriate methodology and techniques that a political scientist is distinguished from others. It is in using these means in searching for answers to politically relevant problems that his role as adviser can be maximized. And it is not his analytic tools which void his efforts to contribute to "relevant" problems, but the decision as to what problems to apply them. In short, his research and theoretical endeavors are what must be pursued if he is to provide special advice in the areas wherein social change will be pursued.

Such capacities raise questions concerning who should receive the advice. The standard form of scientific question-begging—"My job is to report my findings, others decide what to do with them"—is held by many political scientists in common with the physical scientists.[30] The problem deserves brief comment, if only to qualify the general rule of openness. Should political science findings be made available only to those groups who deserve it? Who will not misuse it? The use of political research facilities in election campaigns provides a simple example of situations in which choices of this sort are actually made. Most research reports do not have the same kind of apparent consequences as knowledge necessary for exploding a nuclear weapon, so the question is often dismissed as of little consequence. But research in developing countries has drawn to our attention the fact that certain information collected by political scientists can have immense ramifications. In principle, if we have any faith in the future success of the discipline, the question will become relevant to most research enterprises. It is related not only to the means for potentially manipulating politicization, but to making choices as to what changes ought to be stimulated. The question as to how we, as a discipline, respond to the problem is as significant as our faith in the future success of the discipline in political research.

The question is usually treated in the negative. At a Midwest Political Science Association panel on ethical problems and political research, the prevailing query on this issue was over how to decide when to withhold one's findings from the government.[31] One "call to morality" was the request that, even if governmentally sponsored, the *researcher* should decide whether the information and relationships uncovered should be published or made available. Insofar as the choice is personal, it is of marginal concern. But as a discipline, it is critical that the principle of openness be adopted unless and until some criteria can be set forth justifying preferential treatment in the reporting of research. It is most probable that any individual who does not ascribe to the principle would circumscribe funds for

[30] The fact-value dichotomy frees one more quickly in the seminar room than without. This area is one of searching for most social scientists as is aptly illustrated in Scott Greer's discussion in *The Logic of Social Inquiry* (Chicago: Aldine Publishing Co., 1969), pp. 177–206.

[31] The session was generated by questions over the American Political Science Association's indirect involvement in governmental activities in 1968.

research he may or may not wish to report. The only qualification proposed for the rule, then, is the personal choice not to do research—or at least not to do very expensive research.

The most difficult lesson to learn in social analysis is that the discovery of inequities and social needs is much easier than uncovering a meaningful policy solution to meet those needs within the confines of a social setting. What distinguishes political analysis from other disciplines is the assessment of possible political settlements. This means that solutions must be measured by political possibilities as well as emotive commitment. Poverty, since Aristotle, has been recognized both as a social inequity and as a potential source of grave political conflict in a society. The discovery of poverty in a wealthy society, then, is not so important as the discovery of viable settlements for the condition.[32] And it is this search for settlements of political conflicts which has failed to receive sufficient attention from our discipline—or for that matter, from social scientists in general. Most often, policy projections offered by social scientists have very little to do with the research reported. Data are often used to support the claim that something should be done rather than to lead toward the more difficult, but exceedingly more important, task of developing policies appropriate to the problems.[33] Only within the context of hard research, including both the conditions to be overcome and clear assessment of the limitations posed by the ongoing belief systems and projected consequences of policy changes, can political analysts claim to have met the standards imposed by their academic—or professional—obligations.

Citizenship education suggests that students be trained in applying the rational modes of analysis to politics. It requires that reason and understanding of political life be developed in the individual so that he can perform as a citizen with the advantage of an expanded perspective. Perhaps the bitterest pill is that the student must learn to live in a world without value certainty and to think about problems of normative choice in light of this uncertainty. To be sure, knowledge does not provide a proper foundation for moving from

[32] Recognition of the problem goes beyond Michael Harrington at least to Aristotle.

[33] The problem is richly essayed in Daniel P. Moynihan, *Maximum Feasible Misunderstanding* (New York: Free Press, 1970).

emotive attachment to one set of beliefs to another set which may be no better justified. And equally important, knowledge cannot be used to teach people that problems can be eliminated by a rational attachment to utopian perspectives. The facts of political existence can be sufficiently grasped, however, to realize that the human condition does not change simply through one myth's replacement by another. And equally true is the fact that mere concern over hunger seldom lightens the pains of the condition. Rather, efforts to apply rational solutions to problems such as hunger, and analysis of how to bring about a solution, must provide a more critical element in citizenship education.

Social possibility provides a meaningful entrée to policy analysis.[34] It can, and must, be reckoned with in suggestions for change. The impossible—the empirically impossible—leads into utopian myopics which deserve little attention in citizenship education except in terms of developing maximizing theories (*rationality*₁) for use in affecting political reality. Such theories, however, are not merely utopian because their applicability depends upon contingent conditions. It is more than mere substitution of one myth for another.

Active political participation for members of the discipline adds a difficult dimension to the question: What should political scientists be doing? Activism, however, can consist of those roles pursued as political scientist qua scientist (advising and citizenship training) or the role of political scientist qua citizen. These roles can be traced to the present from classical political philosophy. As a citizen, it is hard to justify any special constraints on the political scientist. But as an individual who is also committed to the employment of reason in political analysis, he must either deny the relevancy of reason or act according to it. Activity according to reason permits him as much freedom as can be achieved within the parameters of social necessity and social sufficiency. If he is so constrained, his action will be different from that of the average citizen.

Much freedom of choice remains, and differences do occur among men so constrained by rationality. But many unfounded options can

---

[34] It is not far off to suggest that the point of twenty years' improvement in political research makes it possible to return seriously, with less ignorance of our own normative involvements, to the proposals and framework of Daniel Lerner and Harold D. Lasswell, eds., *The Policy Sciences: Recent Developments in Scope and Method* (Stanford, Calif.: Stanford University Press, 1951).

be eliminated. More important, grounds for communication concerning the differences is possible. Economics, technology, and contingencies will impose certain constraints on possible social redistributions. The effects of social reform can be assessed without the blinding shades of emotive attachments leading one to delude himself into thinking either that everything is possible or that nothing is possible. Action based upon what has been, what is, and what can be marks the difference between rational and arational normative action. The constraints of reason are often difficult to live with, but they delineate the role and significance of human creativity in political life.

An extension of a significant statement by Sidney Hook is appropriate:

No progress in social learning can be made by driving out one myth by another. If Nazi mathematics and Nazi physics are nonsense, just as much are proletarian mathematics or proletarian physics. [35]

The logic of his statement fits the problems facing the discipline. Challenges leveled against "Establishment" political science do not call science and rationality into question, but rather attack the substantive focus of the discipline. Perhaps the subject matter of our research can be improved; and certainly it is true that concern with techniques, rather than concern with subject matter, leads many of our colleagues into their research projects. These limitations can be overcome without rejecting the foundations for meaningful analysis. Perhaps the present dissatisfaction within the discipline comes from a disillusionment with reason which has led to a return to the attractive comfort of myth, new or old. [36] This unfortunate state reminds one of the fact noted by the late Bertrand Russell: the truth is often missed because it is so seldom sought. Let each seek it from his own perspective, bound together in the search by a common commitment to employing reason in the development of political knowledge.

[35] *Reason, Social Myths and Democracy* (New York: Harper and Brothers, 1940), p. 32.

[36] The disaffection with behavioralism from traditional sources is clearly stated in Leo Strauss, "An Epilogue," in *Essays on the Scientific Study of Politics*, ed. Herbert J. Storing (New York: Holt, Rinehart, and Winston, 1962), pp. 307–27. The arationality of the New Left in politics, which can be carried over to political science, is interestingly assessed in Zbigniew Brzezinski, *Between Two Ages: America's Role in the Technetronic Era* (New York: The Viking Press, 1970), pp. 222–36.

.7. *Possibilities**

HENRY S. KARIEL

> *"Suit yourself."*
> *—American colloquialism*

CURRENTLY FASHIONABLE modes of political analysis deserve acclaim today for at least two reasons: they provide opportunities for participating in a pleasurable if strenuous activity (regardless of the value of the end results) and they effectively come to terms with the surface facts of political reality. Our posterity, too, may find it easy to esteem the contemporary products of the profession of political science should it ever look back and see how an affection for craftsmanship is combined with the ability to please. Moreover, the reward system of the profession should appear as having been nicely designed to promote the present display of talent, ingenuity, variety, and success. There is evidence, in any case, that the prevailing inclination to work hard and to develop ever more powerful analytical tools is welcomed and reinforced within the discipline. All would seem to be well.

Yet doubts continue to be expressed today even by those who govern the profession and engage in what Thomas Kuhn has called "normal science." Partially, there is a petulant resentment among older practitioners, scholars who are made fretful and irritable by the entrepeneurial opportunism of the *nouveau riche*, by the feeling that mindless industriousness rather than scholarly contemplation is

*This essay is a revised version of "Creating Political Reality," *American Political Science Review* 64 (December 1970): 1088–98. Reprinted by permission of the American Political Science Association.

now rewarded by tenure as well as by space in journals, time on panels, positions on editorial boards, cash for projects, and invitations to contribute chapters to books for prospective professionals. It does not pain me, however, to disregard the indictment that comes from this source—not because I suspect its patrician origins but because I believe it is blind to the underlying impulse of empiricism, because it ignores the subversive, liberating thrust of empirical science. I am also prepared to disregard the assorted indictments that come from *within* the dominant paradigm of the profession: intramural critiques, letters to the editor blown up into articles, manuals by technicians more critical of one another's techniques than of their shared assumptions. It is a third kind of indictment— sometimes little more than an angry, incoherent expression of uneasiness—I would like to take more seriously.

What has become annoying to political scientists of diverse methodological persuasions is the profession's inability to frame and illuminate the major events of recent times, events which, because they have run counter to expectations, are perceived as critical. And what makes this failure doubly annoying is that only unaccredited prophets, poets, seers, preachers, and metaphysicians would seem to have foreseen anything like the contemporary crisis in authority. Who within the profession has made our incapacity to govern ourselves—to control the most brutal and the most generous of our impulses at home and abroad—rationally manageable, subject to disciplined statement? One need not go apocalyptic and turn to the major catastrophes of the age to become uneasy about the way our professional activities are disconnected from our concerns, seemingly trivial matters close at hand having proved sufficient to provoke questions. Previously unseen (and presumably irrelevant) parts of reality have suddenly had the nerve to make themselves visible. Pushing their way into camera range, unrecognized and unrepresented men have fought to be perceived, to become relevant if not to professional social scientists, then at least to administrators and legislators worried about the possibility of revolution. Submerged groups (students, women, blacks, cops, prisoners, coal miners, and even army recruits, though not yet patients, teachers, or bureaucrats) have crashed into the mass media and thereby into the arena of politics.

Their emergence (inevitably characterized as an emergency by those within the consensus) has of course been made comprehensible enough on one level: causal analysis has revealed, for example, that the longer and hotter the summer, as at least one article has solemnly concluded, the more likely the outbreak of the lower orders. But while causal analysis allows political scientists to cope with new data, while it allows them to explain the appearance of previously eclipsed men or to demonstrate how to engineer their disappearance, the available scientific explanations nonetheless fail to satisfy. Somehow the prevailing modes of explanation do not enable political scientists to comprehend phenomena as fully as the forms used by some novelists, journalists, poets, or film directors. Political scientists vaguely sense that their approach does not permit them to see their subject matter as comprehensively as they might. They perceive people in motion, but only as reflexes and outputs, as dependent variables, as effects of causes. Privately convinced that men must be respected as agents capable of engaging in goal-oriented action, professionally they nonetheless can see little which exhibits purpose, meaning, dignity, and integrity. As political scientists, they are directed to perceive manipulated and manipulatable data; as men with larger concerns and a greater range of compassion, they aspire to perceive something more, namely, the public significance of others who happen to be outside the prevailing balance of manifest interests. Professionally, they are impelled— whether by memories of scope-and-methods courses or by the innuendos of their colleagues—to confuse science with an edifice of positivist theory and to identify explanations with unambiguous generalizations about neatly assorted variables. As nonprofessionals, however, they are sensitive to the need to challenge what are alleged to be the real attributes of functional systems.

To what extent is it possible to provide professional tools and rewards for such political scientists, for those whose generous moral sensibilities are betrayed by the astringency of their science?

I

I do not believe it likely that we can expand the focus of political science unless we permit our vision and action to be directed by a model of human nature which allows us not only to account for man's private, economic interests but also to recognize his currently less apparent political possibilities. Unless we learn to acknowledge that more may be present than we have yet experienced, the best political scientists—those most torn between the demands of the discipline and their own moral perceptions, those who bear the greatest strains—will drop out of the profession, becoming increasingly unprofessional and undisciplined. They are apt to follow sentiment, ultimately identifying with their subject matter, arrested and absorbed by its sheer presence, surrendering their critical capacities, becoming so thoroughly engaged by aggregated data that they will finally disdain efforts to bestow structure and form on their experience. If they do not go all the way, they will remain as cynics and opportunists who market the products of normal science in order to be least free enough for occasional undisciplined, unprofessional forays into the ghettos of our cities and our minds.

To enable them to move coherently—that is, to make it possible for political science to integrate norms and facts, theory and practice, morality and science, ends and means—I think we will have to ask ourselves whether in our battle against metaphysics, superstition, prejudice, and ideology, we might have won too large a victory. Frankly accepting the idealist overtones of model building, we will have to reconsider the pathetic directive that scientific models are merely to be checked against the common denominator of present experience and inquire how, instead, we might derive a model of political man from barely recorded, ill-articulated, marginal intimations of human possibilities.

Whatever the difficulties today in accepting the discursive styles generally employed for constructing such a model, it certainly has been recurrently envisaged and formulated. I have had previous occasion to identify its outlines by noting what is shared by Rousseau's self-governed individual, Marx's unalienated man, Nietzsche's self-activated hero, Dewey's educated person, Sartre's man of good faith, Fromm's autonomous individual, and Lifton's protean man. We can give further resonance to these available images of human nature by considering the non-authoritarian personality of social psychology, the Hermes-like figures appearing in the various myths of the trickster, the picaresque nonhero of modern fiction, or Gordon Allport's portrait of man as a creature in continuous pro-

cess of becoming. If the result of such an exploration should seem
to resemble an unsorted collection of color slides, there is nothing
to keep us from carefully sorting them, inquiring how they came to
be, and speaking firmly about them with a measure of precision.
This would in any case help make vivid a plausible ideal of the
healthy personality and might encourage us to inquire into ways
for reducing illness.

There is of course a reluctance to permit metaphors borrowed
from medicine to orient political life. Don't citizens, unlike physicians, properly disagree on the ends of action? The application of
the concept of health to political situations is questioned, in other
words, because it would falsely imply agreement on some final ideal,
on some static condition. But I see no need to entertain such a
simplistic notion of "health." A healthy system may well be the *end*
of medical practice; yet there are good empirical grounds for treating biopsychological systems—including the body politic—precisely as physicians or psychiatrists do, namely, as open-ended ones,
as systems which are healthy so long as they remain in process. And
what is characteristic of human beings in process, of men engaged
in political action, is their continuous resolve to display themselves, to remain purposefully in motion, to defy necessity and
assert as much of themselves as they dare. In so doing, men basically strive, as Robert W. White argued in *Ego and Reality in Psy-
choanalytic Theory*,[1] for a sense of mastery. Desiring to master a
progressively richer role repertoire, they welcome and impose order
on their wayward impulses. In order to disclose this self-exhibiting,
self-promoting aspect of political action, studies of attitudes and
of participation, for example, would have to come to terms not
merely with overt behavior but also with unobservable intentions.
Voters would have to be seen as actors in a context which reveals
the expressive aspects of their conduct.

The ground for such a perspective, given its classic definition by
Aristotle, has been characterized as "political space" by Hannah
Arendt. In terms echoing George Herbert Mead no less than
Aristotle, she has tellingly identified it as

... the space of appearance in the widest sense of the word, namely, the
space where I appear to others as others appear to me, where men exist not

[1]New York: International Universities Press, 1963.

merely like other living or inanimate things but make their appearance explicitly.... To be deprived of it means to be deprived of reality, which, humanly and politically speaking, is the same as appearance. To me the reality of the world is guaranteed by the presence of others, by its appearing to all; "for what appears to all, this we call Being," and whatever lacks this appearance comes and passes away like a dream, intimately and exclusively our own but without reality.[2]

Man's natural need, in this view, is the opportunity to *be*, to gain public recognition by making witnessed and comprehended appearances, thereby becoming significant to others.

That precisely this—no less *and no more*—is man's universal need is still hard to acknowledge. It has found implicit support in statements such as the epilogue of Amitai Etzioni's *Active Society*,[3] a thoroughly lucid discussion of human inauthenticity, a term given meaning by his review of authentic basic needs. Yet whatever the appeal of such essays, they still respond to the essentialist question of what human needs "really" are. Needs continue to be specified as if some ontological heaven had to be decked out with an assortment of reifications.

To accept the spirit of Etzioni's discussion but avoid its residual Platonism, it should be useful to recall the tradition of empiricism and see it expressed in part of Herbert Marcuse's work. His approach is at once far less idiosyncratic than his critics claim and far less complicated than his prose allows. Derived from Hegel, it gives rise to that "unhappy consciousness" generated by the tension between the reality we know all too well and the reality which remains unconfirmed and unrealized—those unacknowledged intimations of life that the prevailing organization of society continues to repress, those unspeakable dimensions of ourselves from which we are kept alienated. Our needs will make themselves known to us when surplus repression—repression in excess of what men need—is eliminated.

To be sure, we feel that Marcuse's argument begs the question: Just how much repression *do* men need? But the kind of conclusive answer we tend to look for simply cannot be had within the empirical tradition. We crave abstract, unconditional answers whereas

---

[2]Hannah Arendt, *The Human Condition* (Chicago: University of Chicago Press, 1958), pp. 198–99; the quotation is from Aristotle's *Nicomachean Ethics*.
[3]New York: Free Press, 1960.

Marcuse will rightly provide us only with hypothetical, conditional ones: *if* you reduce repression, his hypothesis states conditionally, *then* the ability of men to harmonize their conflicting drives is likely to be enhanced. Put differently: if reality were changed, men would be more apt to bring a greater variety of experiences into meaningful relationships.

But, we might persist in asking, how valid is this proposition? For those empiricists not aligned with the established present, there is only one way to find out. We must proceed by acting as if it were valid: we must be prepared to invest in it, to try. The procedure is of course the familiar pragmatic one. Taking risks, we must attempt to *violate* whatever is alleged to be reality, whatever equilibrium positivists certify to be real. We will then either lose our wager or else compel reality to yield, learning (by doing) that, to the extent that we succeeded in pushing back the coercive forces of the wilderness, we will have gained in manageable experience, in political space. If we win, we will have learned that we did not *need* the prevailing degree of postponed gratification, that we did not need to hate as much in life and in ourselves as we believed. We will know that there was, in Marcuse's phrase, "surplus repression." We had felt we needed to live more amply—and we found out (if we survived) that, yes, we *could*. Clearly, to accept this experimentalism for discovering one's needs is to see how diversionary it is to draw up an abstract inventory of human needs, how such academic exercises function ideologically and keep us in line.

What we need—not what we want—we will only discover in practice, only by treating present systems of domination and necessity as if they used greater violence and more discipline than necessary. Because the surplus benefits elites, only non-elites or unattached outsiders are likely to be motivated to engage in testing—that is, probing in ways not yet legitimated, acting violently.

It cannot quite go without saying that a commitment to testing, to political life as an ongoing, self-consciously conducted experiment, poses troublesome practical questions that no abstract theory can presume to answer. Experiments—like revolutions—may be so intoxicating or exhausting that they make us frantic or listless, diminishing us in the very process of conducting them. Of course, we can advise (and compel) men to make only such choices which are likely to make their *continuous* action possible; we can direct them *not* to violate others whom they yet need as irritants to promote their own personal growth. The difficulty, we know, is that every course of action forecloses some future options. In short, it is not very helpful merely to instruct men to avoid self-destruction and seek self-enhancement. Forced to make specific choices while unable to see far ahead and yet responsible for the *totality* of ourselves (including a future self which includes our present enemies), we are confronted by the most practical problems of priorities and tactics. To reduce the risks of self-destruction while promoting self-enhancement in practice, we surely need all the positive knowledge we can accumulate—whether by drawing on the conditional conclusions of cost-benefit analysis or comparative research. We must seek to know with a measure of certainty what will keep us from violating both our potential self—our present enemies—and those institutions required to realize it.

This pragmatic approach is implicit in Etzioni and radicalized by Marcuse (who follows Dewey as much as Marx). It makes human needs the test of existing regimes and leads us to define alienation in naturalistic terms, forcing us to move beyond institutions and roles that prescribe *needless* destructions of the self. It sustains the drive to provide an empirical basis for a conception of man as an open-ended, multifaceted being, as an actor resisting every certified truth, naturally given to posturing, simulating, performing, playing, equivocating, innovating, testing, improvising—in sum, acting.

Were we to welcome such a view of political man and permit it to work on us at least as an analytical construct, our attention would be drawn toward those presently unknown elements of experience which the newly formulated model would integrate but not assimilate, which it would esteem for being what they are. No doubt, we might hesitate to confront those elements in their fullness, not wishing to see and discuss them publicly. After all, they are still private and taboo, only to be felt and fondled (as Norman O. Brown has insinuated), or at most to be related, like Portnoy's elaborate complaint, to one's analyst in private sessions as privileged communications. Yet if we should find the economic and psychological resources to learn to speak up, we would expose repressed dimensions, expand our political consciousness, and gradually establish those eclipsed aspects of life which still fail to live up to our model, which remain in repose, waiting to be exhibited, stimulated, and activated.

Our model, in other words, would serve to alert us to the gap between what we might be and what we are, between political possibilities and the present reality. When this gap makes us sufficiently uneasy, we will unavoidably feel impelled to close it. Our model would, therefore, do more than create awareness and direct attention: it would induce us to act, to test environments in order to make them yield. To use it would enable us to implement the Kantian view that society is not something "out there" to be studied, but rather, as Etzioni has said, "a human grouping we collectively organize and are free to restructure, within certain limits we seek to understand and untighten."[4]

When we compel reality to accommodate our model of political man—when we are successful both in pretending to *be* such men in sheltered laboratory settings and in extending our laboratories—at least some of the practices and institutions commonly alleged to be real will emerge as changeable. As our environments then turn out to be less intractable than we thought (or have been instructed to think) our action will defy and jeopardize the prevailing order of commitments: a functional division of labor, the distinction between private and public sectors, the system of fixed social and biological roles within hierarchical organizations, government by a plurality of elites, the market economy, the identification of security with military power, the separation of means from ends, and finally the organized repression—whether in the family, private associations, or public institutions—of action and pleasure, of politics and play.

Basically, such an approach follows Melvin Tumin by challenging existing captor-captive, superior-subordinate relationships. It questions the structures of power established in schools, prisons, hospitals, political parties, industrial plants, academic departments, professional associations, and nation-states. Postulating political realities dialectically opposed to manifest ones, it negates empirically confirmed experience. The imposing social structures which have

[4] Ibid.

been discovered by a nonexperimental, nonpragmatic, positivistic social science are thus treated as targets for a political science determined to test their value—their value always in the relation to the structure of human needs. Political science thereby comes to terms with whatever the powerful insist is given—given by providence or merely by the process of history, the wisdom of the founding fathers, the necessities of industrialism, the iron law of oligarchy, the immutable nature of man, or the discoveries of a halfhearted empiricism more intent on finding answers "out there" than on honoring its own critical, negativistic, reality-defying spirit.

II

If some form of political science is to restructure our sense of reality—to give new meanings to life by engaging in what Dewey called "social reconstruction"—what are the relevant procedures? How is "reality" best tested to make it satisfy basic human needs?

Before urging the obvious—namely, the extension of programs for experimentation, simulation, prototyping, and participation—I should note that *non*participation has assumed at least two forms, and that we have been warned, I think to excess and for the wrong reasons, only about the one which involves the construction of empirically empty frameworks, mathematical systems, and formalistic analytical models. Anti-behavioralists might well acknowledge that there are worse activities than efforts to provide abstract designs whose exhaustive meaning is their public existence, that the kind of abstractions welcomed in the arts—John Cage's resounding silences or white scrupulously painted on white—need not be rejected in the social sciences. The more insidious form of nonparticipation is that of irony. Having previously written on the uses of irony (and having left matters less than clear), I would merely like to remark—not argue—that the ironic mode should be regarded as appropriate only when nature is as intractable as Sisyphus found it or else when it is infinitely pliable, only when nothing whatever can be done about our fate or, alternatively, when all is so well that we can actually disarm, play freely, and reverse roles at will.

Attracted by the ironic posture, we tend to overlook that it demands an inhuman suspension of judgment—the refusal to discriminate, the determination to accept nothing as finally serious. Unintimidated by their humane sentiments, the practitioners of irony have of course given us some stunning accounts: Alexis de Tocqueville's account of equality, Max Weber's of bureaucracy, Joseph Schumpeter's of capitalism, David Riesman's of the lonely crowd, Thorstein Veblen's of the higher learning, John Kenneth Galbraith's of the techno-structure, Harold Lasswell's of the garrison state, Samuel Huntington's of the military virtues. And from the perspective of our survey research centers, individuals have suddenly emerged as if they were characters of modern fiction. In Harold Kaplan's words—which refer to Theodore Dreiser, John Dos Passos, and John Farrell, and not to Angus Campbell, Philip Converse, Warren Miller, and Donald Stokes—

... we are impressed by the fumbling irrelevance in the subjective consciousness of their characters. They are portrayed in terms of rather simplistic laws of psychological and social behavior, while their own consciousness is groping, penetrated by only brief glimpses of light. The field of vision is at the extreme of externality, so preoccupied by the super-personal design of social and biological process that the agents within it seem mindless.[5]

Torn out of context—removed from their authors' unexpressed moral impulses—these accounts of fated institutions and put-upon individuals exhibit a capacity for fastidious detachment, for objectivity and disinterestedness. The posture is serenely nonpartison. There is no interaction with the phenomena, no experimental intervention—only rigorous clinical passivity, observations made in cold blood. Because their authors are manifestly uninvolved, their work enables us to see more of life than we normally permit to fall within our range of vision. The ironist magnifies and thus makes visible what we are otherwise reluctant to recognize—our fixations, compulsions, addictions, and limitations, our behavior. He removes us from ourselves—at least our active selves—and shows with barely concealed pleasure how little we amount to and how well we behave. At the same time, he unwittingly shows *himself* to be someone who condescends to scrutinize his data. His very prose reveals his self-restraint: *controlling* his sympathy and his rage, he displays his superior power—the power of aloof ob-

[5] Harold Kaplan, *The Passive Voice* (Athens, O.: Ohio University Press, 1966), p. 9.

servation. To understand him, to sympathize with him, we need merely recall Truman Capote standing by in cold blood (as we still do) when the State of Kansas proceeded to execute the objects of his study.

Yet an exclusive commitment to such a posture—ever tempting for social scientists who aspire to gain status by separating emotion from fact—is not justifiable, as I have said, unless intervention is futile and absolutely nothing can be done to satisfy our diverse human needs. During such desperate times, we may rightly prevent despair and assign ourselves some activity, exercising what freedom remains, diverting ourselves and escaping necessity. We may then observe and leave a record. When nature (or the state) is implacable and the end is near, that may be the only way to leave one's mark.

To be sure, *no* case, as we fear late at night, is other than terminal. But to go on, to save what we can, we may nevertheless pretend to the contrary and mock reality. Careful probing of reality may suggest that we still have options, that some of our needs—most basically our need to live, to amplify our existence, to communicate—may still be satisfied. When this becomes evident, we have no warrant for irony. We are then called on (not by some abstraction but by our needs) to *integrate* the role of observer and actor, of scientist and citizen, to join ethics to policy, norms to facts, and theory to practice.

It should be apparent at this point that action to bridge the gap between man as a value-creating being and man as a value-neutral analyst of the predicaments of others will necessarily be symbolic (as all action is) and, more specifically, that for social scientists it is likely to be literary, that is, ideographic and discursive, capable of elaborating new contexts to reveal the limits of the old. The accounts of the political scientist—his markings, his symbols—will be derived from what he believes to exist beyond accredited reality—beliefs he comes to express and hold by virtue of his experience, his sympathetic involvement.

But if his literary act can scarcely be said to "explain," if his claims are not verifiable because they do not refer to experiences others have had, on what ground can we possibly accept his testimony? What will testify to his veracity?

I would urge an effort to recover the oldest of tests, the one

Aristotle applied to drama: our performances are successful insofar as they enable us to comprehend the polarities of our existence, leading us to take fuller cognizance of them, inducing us to identify visions and interests which, when unidentified and merely experienced, terrify and paralyze.

We will *know* that an author's work is successful only in practice, only as he demonstrates his ability to establish more parts of ourselves and our environment than we had dared to admit into our presence. The critical and wholly empirical question is to what extent his symbols have moved us to confront and accept progressively more complex realities. To the charge that he might simply lie, there is but one response, namely, that he assuredly does, that at least so far the truth has not been told. What is at issue is not the fact that he makes things up—depriving "reality" of its success—but, as Nietzsche noted, the effect of his fabrications. To what extent do they make a greater variety of experience manageable? Do they embody a maximum range of bearable interests?

Still exploiting Nietzsche, I would have us assent to ventures which serve to multiply meanings and create new possibilities, which appropriate new space and new time. The newly created realities must demonstrate that the established ones do not have an exclusive claim to the political arena. The new ones must supplement or negate the prevailing ones. They will have to compete with the great hit plays (plays experienced as real enough, however, by anyone involuntarily involved in them) put on by corporate boards, university administrations, welfare bureaucracies, National Guard units, peace research centers, or other institutions for crisis management. Successful writing teams, as Donald Fread has noted in defending his own play, *Inquest*, have staged performances such as

"The Gulf of Tonkin" and "The Black Panther Will Get You if You Don't Watch Out." And there's the play called "Why Don't They Take a Bath?" "The Body Count" is a wonderful comedy of the absurd. . . . There is also that wild satire by Sidney Hook and other liberal humanists who have told us to use the democratic process. . . . There is the story of "The Outside Agitator," the great continuing adventure series which began with the Palmer raids. . . . [6]

[6]Quoted in the *New York Times*, May 3, 1970, p. D-6.

At issue for a political science determined to offer counter-realities is not the morality of whatever skits and plays happen to be staged but the likelihood of their expanding the political life of those affected by them. A reality-creating venture is of value to the extent that, *without destroying self-awareness,* it leads men toward increasingly complex realms of being, freeing them to be progressively more playful and political, more active and alive. But the final test, one social scientists might tentatively wish to apply first to doctoral dissertations, must be its impact on the author himself: Does the very process of ordering experience give his life a greater measure of meaning? Does it enable him to gain access to additional dimensions of himself?

Although I have been referring to literary acts, there is no reason for political scientists to confine their activities to them. Physical spaces are no less stages for action. Ever since Machiavelli pointed the way, we have in principle been prepared to treat societies, too, as artificial creations, quite deliberately designing them so that they might maximize opportunities for developing our capacities, so that man-made institutions might generate as much variety and conflict as we can bear without being overwhelmed.

If the political scientist's familiar environment fails to move him—if it strikes him as inert, dull, fatuous, or torpid—he might, therefore, seek to become the author of more complex social enterprises, rearranging society, doing violence to it by probes, tests, irritating questionnaires, and disconcerting research designs until it provides him with more stimulating material. Accordingly, he will be violating and restructuring social settings, creating synthetic spaces for experimental purposes, encouraging new things to happen in what had been stable, well-managed enclaves—whether these are welfare bureaucracies, university departments, or professional associations. His purpose is not, however, to bring about some supposedly desirable state of affairs from which men will eventually benefit. It is to increase public knowledge of public possibilities in the very process of public action. Engaged in what Robert Rubinstein and Harold Lasswell have called "prototyping," he will seek to make a conspicuous record of his interactions, leaving as coherent an account as he can of the meanings of each of his successful probes.

The experimental probing I am urging might well begin modestly at the very places political scientists find themselves at work—their classrooms, departments, institutes, or colleges. Were each of these arenas to be treated lightly—as if they did not quite amount to what is proclaimed by course descriptions or catalogue prose, as if they held unfulfilled promises for participation—they would be saved from easy success and dramatize the possibility of social reconstruction. And were action to be accompanied by efforts to publicize the experimental process, we would be offered practical demonstrations of theoretical possibilities.

In this view of the activities of political science, the practitioner attempts to *express* what he is doing, interweaving theory and practice. Aware of his own operations, seeing them as others might so as to communicate his experience, he uses words to circumscribe the world for himself and others, to come to terms with the mindless forces of nature and society. He thus makes new experience accessible to himself and to others. In a word, he politicalizes it.

This procedure is but analogous to the experiments of those contemporary artists whose work, in the words of Thomas Messer, who was speaking as director of the Guggenheim Museum, "is impossible for collectors to collect, for museums to show, for dealers to handle, for critics to appraise. . . ." *The new constructs aim at including the spectator, at bringing in the outsider.* They are at once more embracive and more fragile than the constructs of contemporary political scientists.

Should political scientists proceed to transform hierarchical, goal-oriented administrative systems into equalitarian, process-oriented political ones, they would be engaged in the kind of artistic enterprises that impel us to become aware of ourselves, that enable us to fill spaces, invent alternatives, impose perspectives, and establish connections. Should political scientists subject themselves to the discipline required to complicate and break up stable social environments, they would create vulnerable structures which remain embarrassingly open and which, like pregnant pauses, demand participation. They would then embrace empiricism fully and invite distrust of even their own conclusions—indeed, all completed work. Their very tone would then be that of the novelist as narrator who has given up the omniscient voice. They would decline to speak as authorities—in effect following *Finnegans Wake* which, as Charles Newman has noted, is "the first great book without a single sentence we can *trust*."

Those who have invested in the prevailing social order are understandably anxious about the ambiguous and therefore untrustworthy features of every new structure. They expect reliable findings. Screening project proposals or research applications, they are reluctant to support scholarly activities which merely promise a wider sharing of the satisfactions of participating in social experimentation. For them, this is hardly enough. They expect unambiguous payoffs in the form of conclusions reached. Yet when pledged to an interactionist, anti-positivist paradigm of political science, we must necessarily view such a demand for specifications as misguided. Unable to advance knowledge of our findings, we can at best merely pretend, seeking support for our enterprises by operating on the principle, as David Bakan has said, of being "one ahead":

To be "one ahead" means to apply for a grant for a piece of research that one has already conducted, and to use the money thus obtained to conduct further research. When one thus works "one ahead" it is possible to write rather splendid applications. Cynical as this approach may appear, it is actually sounder from a scientific point of view than good design. For the fact of the matter is that good research into the unknown cannot be well designed. . . .[7]

To be sure, since we do have empirical knowledge of the pre-conditions for "good research into the unknown"—the requisites of innovative activities—we can request support for promising approaches. But just as Marx declined to discuss the classless society, we should not go further and identify the functions of prospective social arrangements. We should have been warned by that obsessive preoccupation with detail and affection for logistics characteristic of utopian thinkers from Henri de Saint-Simon to G. D. H. Cole, realizing that our problem is to live up to the epistemological demands of a transactional paradigm by making both knowledge claims and future experiences conditional on action. There is no alternative but to resist all requests from foundation officers to blueprint and illustrate and specify what it would mean finally to create

[7] David Bakan, *On Method* (San Francisco: Jossey-Bass, 1967), p. xiv.

new political realities, what it would mean to expand the political present and bestow political qualities on nonpolitical time and space. We simply cannot *know* what it would mean until the moment our resources are exhausted, until our research grant has been spent—when, presumably, our application for the next grant is already being processed.

Given this persuasion, the political scientist's concern cannot be with learning something from what he and his colleagues have done but with accentuating and intensifying the very process of acting. The rewards for him and others come not at the end of the game—in the form of answers, results, conclusions, findings, predictions, explanations, or hypotheses confirmed—but in action itself, in the curiously gratifying knowledge that one's ability to maintain one's balance under stress is being continuously tested—and that one has not, at least not yet, succumbed.

To gain in sympathy for such balancing acts, perhaps it is sufficient to remind ourselves that openness is a long-standing convention of empirical science—in fact, characteristic of all institutions that reject finalities by compelling men to review their conclusions, interrogate one another, and add to their burdens. Perhaps it is necessary (if not sufficient) to *welcome* what Sheldon Wolin has seen fit to reject: the skepticism of behavioralists which has "abolished all privileged beginnings," their "animus against tradition," ultimately their faith in a "self which has been purged of inherited notions."[8]

The professional demands made by such a radicalized empiricism—one which constitutes what Herbert Simon has called the "sciences of the artificial"—are obvious enough. Committed to the openness entailed by valuing man as self-governed agent and repelled by procedures and organizations which frustrate us *needlessly,* we are forced to identify practices which fail to serve our natural needs—specifically our need to take turns in playing diverse, mutually incompatible roles. And as we become sensitive to whatever forces arrest our development, we may learn to appreciate educational institutions which move men, in Marx's phrase, "to do one thing today and another tomorrow" without ever compelling any-

[8]"Political Theory as a Vocation," *American Political Science Review* 63 (December 1969): 1068.

one, if all goes well, ever finally to embody merely one of his various functions.

III

I have been asserting, in sum, that a model of political man as value-creating being would serve to direct attention to current non-decisions (or at least to incomplete ones) and that it would induce us to transform oppressively present organizational structures and attitudes. Moreover, I have maintained that in order to create new meanings and to construct new realities, we should avoid detached ironic postures and instead seek to interact with our environment, whether (1) by offering the kind of accounts of phenomena which induce both reader and writer to take cognizance of more of life than is immediately present or (2) by experimenting in practice, in either case demonstrating the satisfaction of achieving not some end-result but of being engaged in expressive activities. The final test of both of these frankly provocative, intrusive strategies lies in their power to bend what is alleged to be unbending, to expand political experience.

Becoming aware of the desirability of engaging in either vicarious or actual experiments may be all that is feasible today. As we proceed to employ obtrusive measures, we may recurrently find ourselves thwarted (even if consoled by textbooks that teach the uses of unobtrusive research techniques). Unable to be effective even while stationed near the levers of power, we may learn that action is futile and agree with Raymond Williams "that if we move at all we put at risk every value we know, since all the actual movements, all the actually liberating forces, are caught up in a world of reciprocal lying and violence, with no point of entry for any sustained action...."[9] But even though recurrent defeats may teach us that this is true, it still remains possible to define our political situation and make its pathos explicit. If these are not happy times, they may nevertheless be partially redeemed by our being generous with words and calling them what, in the end, we found them to be.

To accept this strategy requires welcoming scientific modes that do more than dignify the vulgar successes manifest at the center of

[9] "Parting of the Ways," *Commentary* 47 (February 1969): 73–75.

our public life. It requires extending ourselves, surrendering some of our hard-won methodological principles, and seeking to incorporate the flotsam and refuse now at the periphery of consciousness. The proper procedure—my reiterating the point in a new context may now help make it more plausible—is necessarily experimental and discursive, for we reach unknown, unnamed territory only by discoursing, advancing ideas as scouts, sending our words out to appropriate new worlds, using our language to relate inchoate experience to what is established, well-formulated, and familiar. Were we to value this use of the imagination as a distinctive discipline, we would move lightly and playfully through new territory, receptive to its promise, proceeding (as in life) in ever widening circles. We would at the same time remain prepared to retrace our steps so as to avoid more trouble than we can tolerate. Retreating when necessary, gaining confidence by being as redundant as I have been, willing to publish variations of our essays again and again, we would ultimately demonstrate that the new territory can be managed, that it has been secured, and that we can risk moving ahead.

There is no point in documenting the obvious and showing how effectively the conventional diction and present organization of political science discriminate against such reality-creating, expressive action. A pragmatic activism finds few legitimate outlets within the normal curriculum. Defying paradigmatic expectations, such activism is perceived as undisciplined and irresponsible. It is seen to reduce the discipline of political science (like physics at its best) to the level of the humanities. Even worse, it leaves us exposed to what remains the gravest of all charges—that we are unrealistic. Our problem, I think, is somehow to accept the charge and not plead guilty. This will entail not only affiirming that it is all right to outwit reality but also demonstrating every step of the way that the escape from necessity, however agonizing, gives pleasure. It will require treating one's own work—indeed, the whole of political life—quite seriously as a form of play.

Were we to reconceptualize politics itself as play, I believe we would be led to recognize the prevailing modes of analyzing and diagnosing political behavior as ideological, serving those who reserve the pleasures of play for themselves. We would be led to suspend our heavy rhetoric and attempt a lighter tone, risking ambiguities and puns, arrogantly speaking of political reality as if it did not exist, enclosing our most precious possessions in quotation marks— "the individual," "private property," "deterrent credibility," "the free world," "the democratic process," "the curriculum," "political science," and—why not?—"reality." We could thus indicate that these marvels are only *so called*, that we have made them all up and that—given wit and passion, courage and luck—we might yet remake them to suit ourselves.

.8. Realism and Commitment in Political Theory

AVERY LEISERSON

THE REALISTIC ORIENTATION

THE REALISTIC tradition in political thought is generated and maintained by preoccupation with conflict, tension, opposition, contradiction, paradox—the antinomies of human experience. All of us differentiate and classify, contrast and reconcile, analyze and combine, take apart and reconstruct. But the believer in the absolute, whether idealist or authoritarian, relativist or pragmatist, for different reasons refuses to accept "unbridgeable gulfs" between the formal and the real, the one and the many, the ideal and the material, the true and the useful, the theoretical and the practical. Whether or not he goes through the terrible agonizing of Augustine, or of Dostoevski's Grand Inquisitor, or of William James, he ends up merging one term into the other for purposes of action, affirming one and denying the other in this imperfect world, and rationalizing the necessity of doing what one wills or must (*"ich kann nicht anders"*).

Contrariwise, the first mark of the realist is his acceptance of conflict and opposition as a "given of human existence": (1) conflict between powers (gods, values), (2) opposition between authorities (rulers, elites, experts), (3) the tensions and hostilities of differences among equals, (4) the paradoxes of similarities between opposites. The realist lives with, is known by, the contradictions of experience he maintains in his own life. Even here there is contradiction. The realist is very insistent that the conflicts he maintains are genuine, as opposed to nominal or frivolous word play, the cynical denial of consequences. Nothing infuriates him more than the assertion that reality is nothing but sheer personal selfishness or will to power. For the realist, conflicts and contradictions are part of an objective order of events that exists independently of his approval or disapproval. Genuine conflicts are not psychological entities to be eliminated by an act of will, mental phenomena to be assumed or explained away by definition.

Second, realistic acceptance of conflict does not entail mere passive contemplation or verbal manipulation of symbols, although these are surely forms of adjustment response not limited to realists. The true realist finds commitment and satisfaction in discovering conceptualized terms, operative ideas, which emphasize "how things are" and help to explain how the conflicting parameters and variables of existence can be transformed into modified patterns of living (belief, concept, and act). The realist insists upon considering operative conditions, as well as specifying appropriate value criteria, for action; he wants to calculate consequences and effects as well as to elaborate statements of belief and indulge in ritualistic obeisance to preferred symbols and goals. In emphasizing "the methodology of achievement," he tends to overestimate the importance of conditional and process factors, just as the believer in values and motivation overemphasizes purpose, end, ideal. And then, to confuse things further, the practical, effective realist publicly dissembles his concern for conditions and means, and clothes his acts in the rhetoric of beliefs and ends.

Third, the realist tends to look for conceptual and behavioral innovation as an aspect of, or contained in, the past and present, rather than requiring a complete break or quantum jump. In this respect, however, he does well to take a more relativist view (or perhaps this attribute is also a nominal or rhetorical one), for history is continual witness to the lesson that changed conditions may turn impossible goals into the most practical means.

This paradox is peculiarly apt in politics, which is so often defined, incompletely and partially, as "the art of the possible." Another example is the conception of politics as power, "the capacity to produce intended effects," which neglects or overlooks that politics is the distinctive area of life where leaders and public officials are held responsible for unintended events and unanticipated consequences, as well as rational or reasonable failures. Again, we find emphasis upon the distributive aspect of politics ("Politics is who gets what, when, and how"), forgetting that politics is also the building and maintenance of the city, the state, the system of public or world order. And still another: "In politics there are no solutions, only settlements."

The point is not that these definitions are witticisms, or convenient, shortcut simplifications. Politics is both effective advocacy, leadership of partial, limited group interests, *and* action on behalf of what is believed to be the common, inclusive, *public* interest. Politicians are constantly expected to reconcile the irreconcilable, to devise modes of adjusting attitudes and behavior between persons and groups who sincerely entertain opposed views of what the public interest requires, to find ways of persuading people to do and to assent to (accept and adapt, if not like and agree) actions that are necessary for the good of the commonwealth, which they would not do if left to their economic interests, class or group preferences, or personal volition. Politics and political theory undoubtedly include more than collective conflict and problem solving,[1] but we may start with the assumption that the two attributes of the realistic orientation, conflict and the conditions controlling conflict in the public sphere of life, may be stated analytically in terms of concept, belief, and act or choice (see Figure 1).

Politics is the arena of public conflict and adjustment of conflicts among powers (persons, groups, nations, worlds), *of changes in the truth parameters controlling their behavior*, and *of changes in the values attached to the constants and variables of end-means conditions controlling the achievement of collective goods*. Politics includes, but

---

[1]As problem solving, there is a remarkable analogy between political settlements, innovation in natural science, biological evolution, and philosophical dialectic, at least on the macro-level of changing conceptual outlooks, if not the micro-level of laboriously verifying the formal or material truth of theories and laws. The analogy should alert us to the dangers, in one direction, of over-facile, self-interested, or self-deceiving *semantic freedom* to define words and meanings as one wills (the mathematician Carroll's Queen of Hearts; "radical phenomenological subjectivism"), and *methodological positivism* (materialism, empiricism) and *logical determinism* (idealism, solipsism) in another.

Figure 1. Categories of Knowledge, Differentiated by Two Dimensions of Experience: Judgment and Interpretation

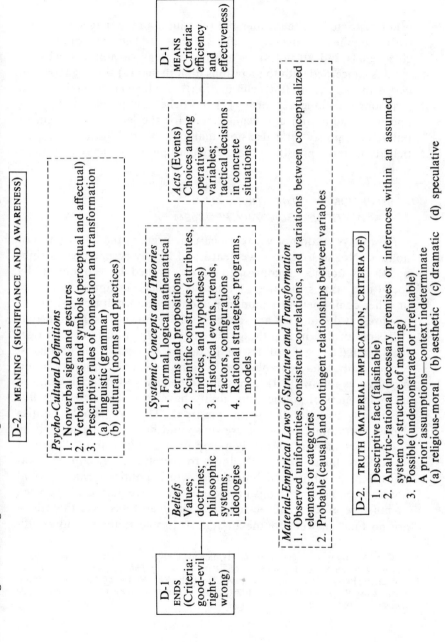

is not restricted to, the leadership (conduct) and management (control) of public controversy (conflicts within and between popular and elite beliefs and attitudes). The methodology of political achievement is concerned with the relations underlying: (1) the organization *and* disorganization (not elimination) of violence, coercion, and sanctions of public authority, (2) the belief conditions of support-rejection, alternation and replacement for the legitimate system of public law, policy, and decision making, (3) mobilization of participation and opposition, to particular public policies and decisions.[2]

ASSUMPTION OF "THE POLITICAL": THE ANALYTICAL BOUNDARY PROBLEM

Nowadays we do not waste much time arguing the importance of politics. Not so long ago, we heard and largely accepted such shibboleths as politics is controlled or determined by economics, by social and class structure, by interests, beliefs, instincts, by sexual or other components of human personality and culture. Many of our present discontents are related to the contrary assumption that "all is political," or, that things have to be politicized in order to get them changed, as if politics could decide or resolve all problems. Semantically, an acceptable formulation of the contemporary mood might go as follows: "If things are to be changed through politics, the parameters of political possibility have to be politicized." But this simply assumes the main question: Does or should politics decide everything, or, what are or should be the limits to politics and political action? Much contemporary verbiage about "the end or death of liberalism" boils down to regretful or gleeful observations that the limits and boundaries which politics formerly could not transcend (some things are beyond or above politics) have been or must be eroded and destroyed. The realist suspects that there are no final answers to the boundary problem; times and condi-

---

[2]C. E. Merriam, *Prologue to Politics* (Chicago: University of Chicago Press, 1939), especially pp. 16–84; B. de Jouvenel, *The Pure Theory of Politics* (New York: Oxford University Press, 1963), chaps. 1–3; K. Deutsch, *The Nerves of Government* (New York: Free Press, 1964), chaps. 1–2; R. A. Dahl, *Polyarchy* (New Haven: Yale University Press, 1971).

tions change, and successive generations transform the boundary meanings.[3]

Let us concede the centrality and importance of politics, in at least four empirical respects:

1. the distributive struggle to influence or control through government and law the production and allocation of natural and human resources;
2. to maintain, or to displace and overthrow the underlying legitimacy-consensus that supports the coercive machinery of tax payment, military service, law enforcement, and dispute settlement;
3. the authoritative articulation, settlements, and regulations in varying areas of collective life, of priority conflicts between: (a) individual-group, (b) group-public, and (c) individual-public values and interests;
4. the institutionalization of conflicts in leadership selection and replacement, and in policy formulation and decision making (rule), between the few (elites and activists) and the many (the factionalized, divided, apathetic, uninformed and alienated people, citizens, or members of the political community).

Appreciation and reflection upon the ubiquity of these processes in human affairs makes it easy to assume the universality and all-inclusiveness of politics, until it is remembered that the same claim has been made for theology (thirteenth century), celestial and physical mechanics (seventeenth to eighteenth century), social-structural and biological evolution (nineteenth century), and in the twentieth century psycho-cultural determinism, biosocial (general) systems theory, and cybernetics (communications and decision theory). Confronted with these pretensions, the realist, political or otherwise, wonders whether the advocate of each "science," or area of human knowledge, has not sought to identify the *analytical part* (politics, theology, physics, biology, sociology or psychology, or combinations thereof) with the *total context* of human meaning and experi-

[3]F. Newmann, "Approaches to Political Power," in *The Democratic and Authoritorian State* (Glencoe, Ill.: Free Press, 1957), chap. 1, on the politics-society boundary; C. E. Black, *The Dynamics of Modernization* (New York: Harper Torchbooks, 1967), chaps. 3-4, on the politics-economy boundary.

ence. Logically, of course, politics cannot be both identical with reality and at the same time an independently controlling or dependently determined factor, without involving a tautology or contradiction. Rejecting as presumptuous the claim that politics is everything, the realist opts for the more modest assumption that it is an aspect of the human personality and human society's survival effort, partly to adapt itself to, partly to control, its internal and external environment (human and physical). As an aspect of human knowledge and experience, politics may at times be an assumption (a given or a constant); it may at others be an independently controlling or causal factor; and under other conditions it may be a dependent variable influenced or controlled by other variables. Abstractly, formally, mathematically, we may assume anything: this does not make it true in the world of human experience, nor does it mean that our assumptions make no difference—herein lies the importance of human values and beliefs, which are ultimately implicated and involved in our cognitive truth or reality concepts.

It is truly staggering to contemplate the requirements of demonstrating the validity of the proposition that politics, along with the other sciences of human knowledge, is an aspect of reality, hence related to the other areas and aspects of human experience. One implication would be that each science, each aspect of reality, contains within itself similar conceptual elements. It would be a hardy individual indeed who would impute analogous base elements and laws controlling their structure and transformation to physicochemical atoms or mesons, biological cells or genes, human personalities, racial or economic groups, and political societies. Another implication would be that each science or area of human knowledge and behavior go through parallel processes of change and development in their basic, elemental, conceptual structure. The correctness of these assumptions cannot be proved directly, but we have the testimony and heritage of philosophy, logic, and mathematics to support the scientific belief that: (1) we may investigate and clarify the logic of the relations that hold between assumptions and inferences, regardless of the truth or falsity of either; and (2) we may compare and evaluate the correspondence (degree of fit) between hypotheses derived from our conceptual categories (differentiations and the relations assumed to exist between them) and observable events, acts, behavior. If, in our modern era of specialization, the older absolute line between matter (chemistry) and energy (physics) can be broken down with the aid of mathematics, logic, and technology, and if parallel processes can be detected among lower organic levels of molecular biology and psychogenetic processes of human learning and adaptation, surely political scientists are well advised to cultivate their own elemental structural concepts with a view to discovering their interactive relations at least with those of their sister sciences, not excluding philosophy, formal logic, mathematical statistics, and technology. In abstract, formal language, the political aspect of human experience "should be" investigated as a variable that influences, and is influenced by, other pertinent variables of human experience.

But we need substantive meaning and content along with definitions, formal rules of reasoning, and procedures of confirming empirical propositions. One basic dimension in experience is the ends-means dichotomy, one term of which in politics, as in the other human and social sciences, is provided by the element of belief (value, purpose, goal). A belief as to what we assume the reality context to be is distinguishable from, but related to, the analytical concept (structural element, attribute, category, construct, or cognitive idea) whereby knowledge of reality is to be investigated, tested, or falsified by reasoning and data. This distinction establishes the relation between the philosophy and the scientific theory of politics when we differentiate between assuming and discovering principles of general political knowledge. A third element is the *act* of choice or decision between alternatives set by perceived, operative variables and criteria of value in particular conflict situations in which individuals and political collectivities are impelled or galvanized into action. Belief, or criteria of purpose and value, differentiated symbolic classes or categories of objects or events out of which belief and value statements (hypotheses) are constructed, and choices among varyingly efficient or effective means (technologies, resources, procedures) for achieving the value-object state of affairs desired, thus provide the terms for articulating the relations between the philosophy, the science, and the practice of politics.[4] Formally,

---

[4]G. E. G. Catlin, *Systematic Politics*, (Toronto: University of Toronto Press, 1962).

linguistically, assumptionally, each term could be defined so as to include the others, that is, we might define all of politics in terms of belief, of analytical concept, or of choice; but we might also define each in terms of its relationships to the others, and this I submit is what the realist has in mind when he posits the importance and inquires into the relations between ends and means.

What works in practice is not the sole test of truth, whether considered in a philosophical, scientific, or practical context, although it comes closest to describing the criterion of efficient and effective action. Even the most practical politician admits the most efficient and effective political means is not necessarily right, which is to say that he recognizes there is a larger or different universe of meaning than political effectiveness. Suppose we place the three categories of belief, concept, and act on a meaning-truth dimension, differentiating them on the basis of the operations by which we manipulate: (1) symbols of psychocultural, affective, or linguistic significance; (2) rules of logical, formal reasoning; and (3) procedures of investigating and verifying material-empirical laws, uniformities, relations between specified variables under observed and observable conditions. As in the case of the means-end dimension, each truth operation may be analyzed and judged to be inclusive of, superior to, or mutually exclusive of the others, but again the realist assumes that they should be analyzed not as things or entities in themselves but in terms of their relationships to each other. Innovativeness and creativity are problematic and contingent; they may or may not grow out of man's efforts to adapt to necessities imposed by his beliefs, material circumstances, and knowledge, including technology; they may or may not emerge from his freedom to choose among alternative means of acquiring and expending his resources for discovering and changing the value and truth dimensions of human experience.[5]

To sum up the foregoing discussion, politics is visualized as that aspect of human behavior which involves the effects and consequences of the most inclusive system of legitimate authority within a given political unit upon the units of power and influence within it (belief); the parameters and variables which control and influence

[5]C. J. Friedrich, *Man and His Government* (New York: McGraw-Hill Book Co., 1963), pp. 1–18.

the exercise of public, official authority (concept), and the choices (acts) made by individuals and groups inside and outside the system to change the values and weights attached to the controlling parameters, the beliefs, concepts and practices of persons and groups composing the system. In conventional language, the philosophy and science of politics study leadership-followership relations within and between persons, groups, and politically organized societies, and the institutionalization-transformation of those relationships in contexts of public controversy (opposition) and potential application of sanctions of physical coercion, settlement, and consent.

THE "CONCEPTUAL SYNTHESIS" PROBLEM

The paradox of the realist outlook is illustrated by the charge that he is not "really" maintaining his conflicts and contradictions: that, as he uses them, belief, concept, and act are actually all concepts; and that concept, or the base term of logico-empirical thought, includes both belief and act. It is easy to deny, but difficult to refute this accusation.

The charge goes thusly. First, at this speculative level of abstraction, there is little or no chance of finally demonstrating what is ultimately real or true. "The ground of all existence is humanly incomprehensible." Second, we may readily admit that human life, if not organic existence, seems to consist in symbolic interaction and transformation, meaningful communication, between "selves" seeking to adopt, understand or control their human and physical environment.[6] Third, meaning and truth may be judged by at least three conceptual criteria: psychosomatic-cultural definitions, the formal laws of logico-rational implication, and the material-physical scientific uniformities or laws governing the relations, operations, or transformations between diverse phenomena. So we may admit the abstract possibility that human symbolic interaction and transformation may be interpreted as belief, as act, or as concept.

In reply, the realist can only say to the "believer" that in the world of human beings neither belief and value systems nor definitions and premises can establish the material truth of empirical propositions.

[6]G. H. Mead, *Mind, Self and Society*, ed. C. W. Morris (Chicago: University of Chicago Press, 1934); E. Cassirer, *An Essay on Man* (New Haven: Yale University Press, 1944).

He points out to the pragmatist and existentialist that action is grounded upon implied or explicit beliefs and concepts that may be too broad, narrow, relevant-irrelevant, or blindly efficient-inefficient in dealing with what is assumed to be the problem. To the idealist, phenomenologist, or nominalist, he asserts that too easy identification of belief and attitude with cognitive truth concept blinds us to the distinction between refutable and irrefutable hypotheses. In sum, the realist denies that he is a conceptualist in the sense of postulating that concepts are things in themselves; he approaches and envisages reality with concepts that enable him to discriminate and describe how significant conflicts and contradictions between concepts (partial aspects of reality) can be related and explained, not assumed or solved by definition. Insofar as we consciously differentiate reality from unreality, we do so by means of "propositions (belief-statements) expressed in linguistic (conceptual, symbolic) forms with meanings referring to relations between such terms and specified states of facts" (acts, events).[7]

It does not help very much in politics to show that, on the metaphysical level, we are all realists to an extent, or are at liberty to adopt an idealist or existential position. In the world of human experience, politics begins with the disjunction between the truth that men require a system of coercive authority in order to govern themselves, and the truth that this coercive system involves conflict between desirable goals or principles, each of which possesses valid grounds for human belief in its truth.[8] What shall be done when men assert that one principle shall control in the sphere of the other? (Example: freedom of the press and the public right to know vs. the government's right to classify and act on information that in the public or national interest is restricted to a few.) Political truth becomes that which is publicly believed and accepted; rational and factual truth, that which individuals and minorities know to be true although the nation perish, the world mock, and the community kill the dissentient who challenges its gods. Rational truth is also relatively powerless, hence contemptible and ignominious in the face of

---

[7]M. R. Cohen, *A Preface to Logic* (New York: Henry Holt & Co., 1944), chaps. 2–5.

[8]A. L. Lowell, *Conflicts of Principle* (Cambridge, Mass.: Harvard University Press, 1932); H. Arendt, "Truth and Politics," in *Political Theory and Social Change,* ed. D. Spitz, (New York: Atherton Press, 1967), pp. 3–37.

popular belief and political authority, but both opinion-beliefs and factual truth contain a quality of coercive power that men of power recognize as dangerous to their positions. Paradoxically, free nations cannot survive without active citizens willing to face imperious consequences and act on the presumption that what they believe to be fact can be realized as true. To paraphrase Hannah Arendt: "Persuasion and violence can destroy truth, but they cannot replace it [hence] constitutionally governed countries recognize that they have a stake in the existence of [truth-seeking] men and institutions which the political realm does not, subject to certain conditions, control." But what are the limiting conditions and costs that both truth seekers and public authorities must accept, and how are they to be authoritatively defined and maintained?

Realistic political theory assumes the following:

1. Man believes, but sets himself goals and purposes which are not necessarily consistent with his belief and value systems; moreover, he tries to achieve his goals by means which are not necessarily the most efficient or effective, particularly when he insists upon maintaining a plurality of goals.[9]

2. Man seeks truth, but the processes of discovering the necessary conditions under which general laws and uniformities of natural and human relationships hold true include his own and his fellow-men's ignorance and self-deception: refusal to admit the possibility of truths in which he cannot believe, and persistence in maintaining against the facts doctrines and concepts in which he wants to believe.[10]

3. Man's actions occur in a natural, material setting in which some factors can be manipulated, controlled, or varied while others may not, that is, they must be assumed, held constant, or taken as beyond his control. Subject to these limitations, he may increase or decrease his ability to control or influence his destiny by investigation, planning, and developing a policy-making and decision-making

---

[9]Machiavelli, *The Prince*; Hobbes, *Leviathan*; S. Wolin, *Politics and Vision* (Boston: Little, Brown and Co., 1960); G. Kateb, *Political Theory: Its Nature and Uses* (New York: St. Martin's Press, 1968); W. Letwin, "Social Science and Practical Problems," in *The Great Ideas Today: 1970* (London: Encyclopedia Britannica, 1970), pp. 93–137.

[10]J. S. Mill, *Logic*, Part VI; J. Bronowski, *Science and Human Values* (New York: Harper Torchbooks, 1956); A. Kaplan, *The Conduct of Inquiry* (San Francisco: Chandler Publishing Co., 1964).

process that allow him to: (a) clarify the choices available to him, (b) calculate the alternative costs of changing one or more of the conditional variables affecting his and his fellow-men's behavior, (c) make acceptable choices among alternative available means, and (d) reconstruct the belief preferences of the proximate and distal policy makers upon whom application of means depends.[11] But action in the sense of explicit articulation of preferences and action in the sense of achievement of intended consequences, even for the most absolute dictator, are further apart than the opposition between action and thought, or concept and belief.

The urge to simplify, the "wish to believe," the propensity to *fuse* belief, thought, and action (philosophy, theory, and ideology; religion, science, and behavior; purpose, necessity, and choice; instinct, constraint, and will) has produced magnificent systems of rational thought. Not one, however, from Plato's *Republic* to Stalin's *Foundations of Leninism*, from deTocqueville's *Democracy in America* to Weber's *Economy and Society* or Freud's *Civilization and Its Discontents* succeeded in describing political, cultural, or economic systems then prevailing. This suggests that, beyond rational system building, scientific positivism, and ideological simplification, political theory (along with post-positivist discoveries in mathematics and logic, physics, biology, psycho-cultural and systems theory in anthropology, sociology and psychology) requires a "dynamic structuralist" conception of man and political society, envisaging the possibility of successive (over time) structural states of homeostatic equilibrium governed by logico-empirically discoverable, conceptualized relations among conditions set by belief, resources (including knowledge and technology), and choice.[12] Analogously, "systems of self-regu-

[11] Bentham, *Principles of Morals and Legislation*; N. Bukharin, *Historical Materialism* (1923); C. E. Merriam, *The Role of Politics in Social Change* (New York: New York University Press, 1936); K. Mannheim, *Man and Society in an Age of Reconstruction* (London: K. Paul, Trench, Truber, and Co., 1940); H. D. Lasswell and D. Lerner, *The Policy Sciences* (Stanford: Stanford University Press, 1951); J. G. March and H. Simon, *Organizations* (New York: Wiley, 1958); C. E. Lindblom, *The Policy-Making Process* (New York: McGraw-Hill Book Co., 1968); K. W. Deutsch, "Political Theory and Political Action," *American Political Science Review* 66 (March 1971): 11–27.

[12] E. Voegelin, *Order and History* (Baton Rouge: Louisiana State University Press, 1957); G. Almond, "Political Theory and Political Science," in *Contemporary Political Science*, ed. I. Pool (New York: McGraw-Hill Book Co., 1967); S. Huntington, *Political Order in Changing Societies* (New Haven: Yale University Press, 1968);

lating, symbolic transformation" seem to describe behavior of sub-human organic, individual, and social collectivities; selfhood seems to develop out of a nonrational process consisting of interactions between "internal" necessities and a variety of possible modes of response to environmental requirements for survival as a relatively stable, "system state" of logico-empirical connection at any given moment or period of eternity. Societal reflexes (habits, institutions), reason (symbol-concept formation and transformation), and choice therefore each appear to be part of a natural (partly given, partly acquired) process whereby the organic, individual, or societal unit equilibrates the conflicting-converging elements of existence into more or less ephemeral structural units, and, in a limited sense, guides the inevitable selection from internal-external pressures, modes and rates of response, of change from one system state to the next. Change, history, or process becomes the story of selecting among the possibilities of adjustment and adaptation in the temporal flux; science, the investigation and elaboration of the necessary conditions and relations between elements composing the living system "stabilized, interactive adjustment" at given "moments" of time.

Belief gives the self its criteria of value (worth) and significance; logic and science, the conceptual tools for understanding the truth of things; choice, the elemental realization that man must act whether he chooses to live or die. The three exist together in constant tension, struggling for priority in the formation of selfhood or personality, which no sooner "develops" than realizes the necessities of survival and adaptation to change, internal and external, until further adjustment becomes intolerable or impossible. Exclusive commitment to one is illusion. The worship of reason neglects practical consequence and produces fantastic dreams beyond the wildest irrationalities of superstition and magic. To postulate "the priority of the act," without reference to standards of value and conceptual reality-discriminations, is to blind oneself to the ambiguity of human motivation (least effort as well as self-interest,

---

Claude Levi-Strauss, *The Savage Mind* (Chicago: University of Chicago Press, 1966); W. E. Moore, "Social Change," *International Encyclopedia of the Social Sciences,* vol. 14, pp. 365–75; A. Rapoport, "Some System Approaches to Political Theory," in *Varieties of Political Theory,* ed. D. Easton (Englewood Cliffs, N.J.: Prentice-Hall, Inc., 1966), pp. 129–41; J. Piaget, *Structuralism* (New York: Basic Books, 1970).

frivolity as well as moral indignation, idol worship as well as rational curiosity, personal aggrandizement as well as human welfare). Total rejection of values apart from individual experience leads ultimately to the denial of differences between life and death, good and evil, the important and the trivial, truth and error. Exclusive reliance upon belief is no less ambiguous: it may introduce order and clarity, but it may jumble everything together into meaningless chaos. It may challenge men to face realities or summon them to mindless deeds and sacrifices in the name of evocative and justifying symbols.

Against the absolutism of idealism, conceptualism or affective action, the realistic synthesis offers *not* the contemplative passivity of moderation, but *action* subject to knowledge of asymmetrical, limiting principles and costs; *commitment* to the standards required for "mapping" a comprehensible structure of relationships between belief, thought and action; and finally, awareness that the choices and decisions of action may have destructive and suicidal as well as constructive and liberating effects.

THE BELIEF-CONCEPT DISJUNCTION AND
THE PROBLEM OF POLITICAL DATA

Because facts cannot be data until ordered into some kind of meaningful context or system, it is too often presumed that the data concerns of the classical and normative philosopher are completely opposed to those of the empirical and scientific theorist. Few would deny that they differ, particularly in respect of their training and attitudes toward: (1) preferred techniques of data collection and analysis; (2) observer responsibility toward his human data sources of information, understanding, and involvement; and (3) the important problems and points of departure for research. But suppose we were to take as the interesting question, notwithstanding their mutual preferences for isolation, how normative and empirical theorists' work is related, *assuming that their foci of interest are different*. The belief-concept disjunction is not to be "solved" in the sense of eliminating it, anyway, and certainly not through professional symposia, conferences, or negotiations in the expectation of quick and easy verbal agreement on definitions. Perhaps the most to be hoped for by such means is the reduction of mutual ignorance as to motivations and assumptions, plus possibly increased appreciation of personal qualities and areas of skill.

With respect to the first difference, techniques of data collection and analysis, the important point is that well-ordered, systematized procedures of inquiry are not the primary bone of contention. Refer, for example, to Deutsch's nine politically relevant "data categories."[13] Even if value-oriented theorists are primarily interested in only three of the nine (elite data, historical and documentary materials) they are not necessarily *against* sample population surveys, electoral and legislative voting data, case studies, or other types of mathematical, economic, and social aggregative statistics. True, they may be indifferent, or inclined to ask whether this or that piece of data-oriented research is worth doing, but their primary interest is to determine (find or apply) an appropriate criterion or standard by which to interpret the significance of the research data. This interest, purpose, or function includes "the right" to emphasize and elaborate political aspects of the data that do not emerge explicitly from the conceptual categories employed by political statisticians or scientists, of which indeed the latter may not even be aware. Of course, evaluative criteria and data categories (variables) may be totally disconnected, that is, refer to wholly different levels or universes of meaning, in which case there is no overlap. Insofar as it may be assumed that there are possible or potential alternative "structures of significant meaning" within which the scientific hypothesis of conceptualized relationship makes only partial or limited sense, explains only part of "the problem," there is still the need to assess and evaluate the "program" for which the data was collected and analyzed. This is another way of saying that as long as there is no disagreement about what the data reveal, scientific categories are not being called into question; but as soon as there is dispute as to what the data mean, whether they are fully explanatory of the problem, there is a legitimate question as to whether the scientist-technician's concepts and analysis are adequately determinative or controlling. Whether we say this evaluative function belongs to the philosopher, the politician, the "responsible" public official or citizen, the point is that interpretation of the discrepancy between explicit standards of evaluation and technical data analyses cannot be left to the scientist or data expert alone.

---

[13]K. W. Deutsch, "Recent Trends in Research Methods in Political Science," and discussion thereof, in *A Design for Political Science: Scope, Objectives, Methods*, ed. J. C. Charlesworth (Monograph #6 of American Academy of Political and Social Science, 1966), pp. 149–237.

Value (program) criticism and specification has another function in connection with data collection and analysis. One result of the mid-century revolution in amounts, kinds, and methods of data processing has been, not unnaturally, widespread experimentation with coordination, "confrontation," between different kinds of data in order to produce better conceptual "understanding" of political processes or systems. Examples are the Elmira study of 1948 presidential voting (voter perceptions and group-process behavior); the Survey Research Center's study of representation in the 1958 congressional election (voter perceptions and legislative voting); the rash of studies investigating the correlations between indexes of economic development, political structures, and policy outcomes. Useful as these enterprises in data processing and hypothesis testing are, it is not nearly so clear as to whether they have improved our theories and models of political structure and dynamics.

Again, it is easy for the data-oriented investigator to brush aside such criticism as overly cosmic or global, irrelevant to his "limited" hypothetical purposes. The question remains, to what extent do the categories and methods of data analysis advance our understanding of politics if they are not connected to a more satisfactory theoretical model than the assumption that votes are a function of personal beliefs and group identification, or a finding that structural arrangements and resource distributions are 75 percent or 84 percent explainable in terms of the intercorrelations between four to seven variables, for example, cultural norms, social stratification, institutional organization, and personality. Such a question is not answered by saying we will know more when we learn how to combine content and aggregate data analysis with interview sampling, or when we can measure more precisely the degree of variation and margin of error in the correlations between personal perceptions, mass beliefs, elite decisions, and resource distributions. It goes to the realization that any science, including that of politics, has three distinct operations which have ultimately to be integrated: (1) "information-processing," (2) "hypothesis, model or theory-construction," and (3) "definitional clarification, categorization, and systematization." [14]   The value theorist may not be much help in

---

[14] J. B. Conant, *Modern Science and Modern Man* (New York: Columbia University Press, 1952), especially chap. 3; T. S. Kuhn, *The Structure of Scientific Revolutions* (Chicago: University of Chicago Press, 1962).

solving technical problems of data processing and hypothesis testing, especially if he insists that only systematic, synthetic, grand theory is worth doing. Insofar as scientific progress consists of paradigmatic and conceptual transformation, model building and hypothesis reformulation, and continual reassessment of the logical implications and interconnections of propositions (which no scientist would reject as being "too metaphysical"), theoretical training in speculative political thought and formal, abstract reasoning is no less a requisite of competence than that of the mathematical statistician and computer programmer.

The second point of overlap between value observational standpoint of the analyst to his data is often referred to as the "value problem" in the philosophy of science and "sociology of knowledge" when the objectivity of social research is called into question. In the light of the belief-value disjunction, this problem is not one of describing the psychological motivation or sociological conditioning of research, or the logico-philosophical tenability of such distinctions as that between factual and valuational truth or between definitional and empirical propositions.[15] The belief-concept disjunction requires us to emphasize not only the differences but the relationships of normative and cognitive theory, the connective linkages between reality perspectives (beliefs) and logico-scientific concepts in dealing with the available data with respect to what we take to be a problem. In these terms, the question is *not whether* judgmental values enter into the scientist's work (clearly they do in the selection of problems, relevance of data, legitimacy of inferences, interpretation of results), but *how* the scientist applies in his work the values of truth, reason and freedom in collecting, analyzing, and interpreting data (intelligence) about individual and group behavior inside, outside and through the formal political system.[16] The real-

[15]The question of a "value-free or neutral science" may not be dead, but it is now pretty clearly recognized as a non-question. No one seriously denies the Weberian differentiation between analyzing a problem in terms of one's personal value-position and analyzing it in terms of a standard of reference, meaning or explanation. The basic question is whether intersubjectively definable political beliefs, theories, hypotheses, are amenable to discussion in terms of evidence (arbitrary and irrefutable vs. non-arbitrary and falsifiable propositions). Cf. W. G. Runciman, "Sociological Evidence and Political Theory," in *Philosophy, Politics and Society*, ed. P. C. Laslett (London: B. T. Blackwell, 1962), pp. 34–47.

[16]H. D. Lasswell, *The Analysis of Political Behavior* (London: Routledge and Kegan Paul, 1947); D. Lerner, ed., *The Human Meaning of the Social Sciences*

istic perspective is not one from which values are totally excluded from data collection and analysis, but one in which the *openness* of the research process is maintained, partly to the interpenetration of data with both alternative cognitive dimensions and standards of valuation. The truth-value of this perspective lies less in what the philosopher-scientist believes truth, reason, and freedom to consist of than the *competence* with which he applies his observational, analytical, and judgmental skills to the data of his chosen problem.[17]

Finally, with respect to the supposed divergence of normative and empirical theorists with respect to "the important issues" or problems of political science, there are so many different referents involved that a clearing operation is necessary to enable us to visualize the interdependence as well as the opposition of the two groups. In the first place, the discipline's stage of development is an extremely salient factor. Without going back to the differing time perspectives of Plato and Aristotle toward the problem of revolution, for example, it is worth remembering the three major periods of development in American political science: (1) the parturition-infant growth period symbolized by J. W. Burgess and Columbia in the 1880s and 1890s; (2) the interdisciplinary, functionalist led by C. E. Merriam's "Chicago school" in the 1920s and 1930s; and (3) the thrust toward "scientific behavioralism" in the 1950s and 1960s.[18]   Both internal-disciplinary and external-environmental variables operated at each period to alter the then-current conception of "important problems" to work on and the contemporary styles and strategies of research. Concern with the perennial problems of power, justice, freedom, equality, and the balance between private, group, and public interest or common welfare, in different accents permeate the literature of all three periods.   Even the most mathematically and statistically oriented research of the 1960s can

---

(Cleveland: World Publishing Co., 1959), chap. 1; C. W. Mills, *The Sociological Imagination* (New York: Oxford University Press, 1959), chap. 10; H. L. Wilensky, *Organizational Intelligence* (New York: Basic Books, 1967).

[17]G. C. Lewis, *An Essay on the Influence of Authority* (London: J. W. Parker, 1849); K. Polanyi, *Faith, Reason and Society* (Chicago: University of Chicago Press, 1946), chap. 2; J. Bronowski, *Science and Human Values* (New York: Harper Torchbooks, 1959); A. Leiserson, "Science and the Public Life," *Journal of Politics* 29 (May 1967): 250–51.

[18]A. Somit and J. Tanenhaus, *The Development of American Political Science* (Boston: Allyn & Bacon, 1967).

be interpreted as an extension of the eighteenth-century mercantilist effort to place political knowledge on a surer foundation of *reliable intelligence* in the service of the nation—a theme that has emerged quite explicitly in the fields of international politics and comparative political development. In historical perspective, the scientific study of politics has never wholly divorced conceptual from normative analysis, however wide the variation in methodological emphases and preferences for particular observational standpoints.

A second source of confusion with respect to the lack of agreement on the important problems of political science lies in the failure to discriminate between "theoretical" and "observational" (or "empirical") concepts,[19] that is, to assume that meaningful theory consists of *either* one or the other instead of discovering the appropriate role of each and showing in technical terms the rules for transforming theoretical and observational concepts into a minimum number of formal, abstract concepts and propositions (assumptions) from which empirically testable hypotheses are logically derivable. The difficulty is not that empirical theorists and normative theorists cannot exhibit a considerable consensus upon a descriptive list of topics or problems with which political science is concerned.[20] The problem arises when such terms as authority, representation, responsibility, power, organization, justice, obligation, freedom, are assumed to have only that meaning arising out of their function in an a priori structure of logical explanation (which is then, so to speak, imposed on the data); or when, from the other side, it is assumed that only concepts abstracted from empirical observations can be combined and aggregated into an acceptable scientific theory. Neither procedure, alone, is sufficient: the former because of its indifference to descriptive application and falsification problems, the latter because it generates so many descriptive variables and categories of ambiguous reference as to defy reduction or assimilation into a parsimonious, consistent set of logically powerful, explanatory universals. Formal and empirical concepts have somehow to be

[19] G. Sartori, "Concept Misformation in Comparative Politics," *American Political Science Review* 64 (December 1970); 1040–46; S. M. Lipset, *Politics and the Social Sciences* (New York: Oxford University Press, 1969), pp. ix–xxii, 65–70.
[20] APSA, *Goals for Political Science* (New York: Sloane, 1951); L. Lipson, *The Great Issues of Politics* (Englewood Cliffs, N.J.: Prentice-Hall, Inc., 1960); H. Eulau and J. March, *Political Science* (Englewood Cliffs, N.J.: Prentice-Hall, Inc., 1969).

combined, for, without the aid of the former, the widely hailed "middle-level" process of hypothesis construction and testing cannot bridge the gulf from descriptive generalization to abstract, systematic theory on the level of atomic theory in physics or the genetic apparatus in molecular biology.[21]

Lastly, the lack of intersubjective agreement in political theory does not arise so much from inability or failure to recognize important problems or from preferences for particular types of data or techniques of data analysis (this highly desirable personal differentiation occurs within all fields of knowledge and science). It comes from disagreements and uncertainties over such questions as: (1) whether political-system factors are independent (causal), dependent (to be explained), constant or given in relation to such variables as cultural norms, social (demographic) class, economic (productive skill and income), and psychological (perceptual, affective, and identification) variables; (2) the merits of causal theory vs. multiple factor analysis in model building; (3) the plethora of interdisciplinary "approaches" and terminological points of departure; (4) the ambivalence in the discipline over the issue of whether political science is a basic social science at all or whether it is really an applied science of politico-administrative-engineering research, seeking to link the efforts of the social and behavioral sciences with the efforts of intellectual and political elites, groups and nations to mobilize the convergent-conflicting mass aspirations and goals of mankind.[22] Small wonder that political and social science theory is not sure of its conceptual points of departure for attacking problems of war and peace, scientific intelligence in public policy making, controlling and directing technology, achieving stability and change in industrially developed and emerging nations, offsetting group alienation and personal incentive in bureaucratized, segmented societies, institutionalizing consensus and cleavage in pluralist and hegemonic democracies. The most recent methodological exercise in political science self-analysis finds our theoretical commitments not

[21]See the remarkable volume edited by Philip Handler, *Biology and the Future of Human Life* (New York: Oxford University Press, 1970), especially chaps. 1 and 14.
[22]S. Wolin, *Politics and Vision* (Boston: Little, Brown and Co., 1960), chap. 10; A. W. Weinberg, "Criteria for Scientific Choice," in *Reflections on Big Science* (Cambridge, Mass.: MIT Press, 1967), pp. 65–84; V. C. Ferkiss, *Technological Man* (New York: New American Library–Mentor Books, 1970), chaps. 7–9.

toward integration but separatism in three directions: (1) contextual-linguistic analysis, (2) construction of formal theories, (3) codification of empirical generalizations about political behavior.[23] On the positive side, it is worth noting that while these trends represent centrifugal forces, viewed methodologically, they also constitute the intellectual operations necessary for the construction of a unified analytical model for all political systems. Unfortunately, belief in the desirability of such an instrument does not provide the conceptual and technical linkages that make the integrative enterprise a directly feasible goal.

POLITICAL RELEVANCE AND THE
"LEVEL-OF-ANALYSIS" PROBLEM

Just as modern scientific theory finds it necessary to discriminate and integrate the descriptive, analytical, and systematic levels of truth, the classical "ends-means" dimension of human goal achievement faces the problem of integrating the levels of goal expectation, strategic assessment of means, and specific policy choice in particular situations. The rationality assumption of classical ethical theory, notwithstanding recognition of its limitations as a rule for directing behavior by individuals, social groups, organizations, or nation-states, retains its preeminent position as the theoretical criterion of "correct" judgment, at the price of handing over to the judge, manager, executive, administrator, or man of wisdom the task of practical decision. The "theory-practice" distinction accentuates the pejorative difference between "higher and lower" levels of decision, so that the label of "realistic" if often applied as an epithet to means-rationality, which perhaps accounts for the general feeling that the distinction is not really sound on either moral, scientific or practical grounds. When will we reach the state of being able to admit frankly that the contextual meaning of rationality shifts when one is concerned with uncertainty over desirable goals in the abstract, the analysis of efficient means when agreement upon a goal can be assumed, and the complexities of specific controversial situations whether or not full information is lacking? We might then be better able to examine the question of whether the problem of inte-

[23]Eulau and March, *Political Science*, pp. 51–56.

grating general-ethical, economic-rational, and sociopolitical action theory in terms of adopting *what participants believe to be right* as an integrative criterion of social judgment instead of oscillating between an extrinsic, ideal standard of "in theory" and a "practical" standard of efficient means for evaluating practical decisions in the observable world of human political choice.

This is not a simplistic suggestion to assume a single, dominant, psychocultural world view (Consciousness III for Consciousness II) as an independent variable controlling socioeconomic and technological factors. Such a procedure merely transforms into another variation of the chicken-egg proposition of whether personality and culture controls economics and biophysical conditions, or vice versa. Neither does it imply complete ethical relativity in which cultural and moral standards are to be viewed simply as a numerical consensus, majority, or multimodal distribution of personal opinions on any given issue. The starting assumption of realistic action theory is not an effort to find a foolproof, logico-empirical model which establishes the priority of any one level of ethical, rational, or psychophysical causality over the others, but to find appropriate conceptual tools for relating ethical generalizations (criteria), cognitive instruments of policy and program analysis, and practical modes of relating applicable criteria to particular contexts of application.[24] The value problem is to recognize the legitimacy (proper role) and utility of each level of judgment; the conceptual problem is to reduce the empirical uncertainty and ambiguity with which the elements constituting the problem of choice can be stated, *once the analytical level has been decided*;[25] the practical problem is to maximize the utility satisfactions achievable in terms of the divergent belief-values maintained by participant decision makers.[26]

Just as the level-of-analysis problem on the meaning-truth dimension requires discrimination in terms of the advantages and limita-

[24]A. Edel, *Ethical Judgment* (Glencoe, Ill.: Free Press, 1955), pp. 296–97; C. L. Schulze, *The Politics and Economics of Public Spending* (Washington, D.C.: The Brookings Institution, 1968); G. M. Lyons, *The Uneasy Partnership: Social Science and the Federal Government in the 20th Century* (New York: Russell Sage Foundation, 1969).

[25]J. D. Singer, "The Level-of-Analysis Problem in International Relations," in *The International System*, ed. K. Knorr and S. Verba (Princeton, N.J.: Princeton University Press, 1961), p. 90.

[26]J. S. Mill, *Utilitarianism* (1863).

tions of each level of abstraction, so the belief-action dimension, consisting of end clarification, means strategy, and tactical-choice determination has to be differentiated, not jumbled together by the wishful assumption that a single, correct process of authoritative belief can be imposed, by an act of will or thought, upon the conflict of ethical imperatives, the limitations of abstract thought, and the difficulties of applying strategic principles in concrete historical situations.[27]

Systems theory, the contemporary replacement for the postulate of a global human rationality or a godlike transcendent will, has undeniable heuristic advantages. It provides a framework of analogy and communication between scientific workers on the biological, psychological, and societal levels; it focuses attention on problems of conceptual and category construction; it points to the subsystem and environmental components of system-action.[28] Unfortunately, it has not yet been shown to be helpful in clarifying the connections between value theory, operational research, and policy formation; and it fails to provide a satisfactory account of system-transformation and change.[29] *Policy science*, after twenty years, remains essentially in a programmatic stage, not having untangled the linkages between a general theory of policy formation and the variety of applied areas of policy knowledge, or again, between national-normative and "optimal" models of the policy process.[30] Nevertheless, even if policy science retains a primarily "applied" connotation, it deserves encouragement because it focuses attention on the limited

[27]R. Aron, *Main Currents in Sociological Theory*, Vol. II (New York: Basic Books, 1967), especially chapters on Pareto and Weber.

[28]T. Parsons, *The Structure of Social Action* (New York: McGraw-Hill Book Co., 1937), and *The Social System* (Glencoe, Ill.: Free Press, 1951); A. Kuhn, *The Study of Society* (Homewood, Ill.: Dorsey Press, 1963); D. Easton, *A Systems Analysis of Political Life* (New York: John Wiley & Sons, 1965); J. G. Miller, "Living Systems: Basic Concepts," *Behavioral Science* 10 (July 1965): 193-237.

[29]*Functionalism in the Social Sciences* (Philadelphia: American Academy of Political and Social Science, 1965); F. Riggs, "Comparative Politics and the Study of Political Parties," in *Approaches to the Study of Party Organization*, ed. W. J. Crotty (Boston: Allyn & Bacon, 1968); A. W. Gouldner, *The Coming Crisis in Western Sociology* (New York: Basic Books, 1970).

[30]Y. Dror, *Public Policymaking Re-examined* (San Francisco: Chandler Publishing Co., 1968), chaps. 1, 12–15; R. Bauer and K. Gergen, eds., *The Study of Policy Formation* (New York: Free Press, 1968); A Ranney, ed., *Political Science and Public Policy* (Chicago: Markham, 1968).

role of scientific knowledge as an input element in the policy process, and it emphasizes what scientific theory builders tend to reject or forget—the conditioning influence of structure upon inputs and outcomes of the process.[31]

From our truth-action paradigm, we might expect the most promising fields of theoretical innovation to develop at the intermediate level, where the analytical operations of concept and hypothesis formation intersect with the strategic assessment of value-oriented action programs. This standard points to no particular institutional or conventional field of knowledge, and if history is any guide, suggests that the ripest areas are likely to occur in interstitial zones of common concern to several of the empirical social sciences. These are not far to seek. The study of comparative political systems, frankly seeking a dynamic theory of development and change, has been extraordinarily productive in the past fifteen years, and provoked an amazing amount of theoretical crossing of lines between the disciplines. The field of political behavior, attitudes, and beliefs, at one time almost wholly embedded in the psychology and sociology of voting, is showing signs of turning once more to its earlier fount of inspiration, public opinion management, ideology, and *communications theory*, for a more satisfying theoretical focus. And the students of interest group, political party, and administrative behavior, for twenty years deeply divided between advocates of "scientific" survey research methods and devotees of applied-policy involvement, have begun to look toward *organization theory*, in both informal models and in statistical-comparative, cross-national ones, for theoretical simplification and systematization.

Space does not permit substantive elaboration of these trends. From the standpoint of the level-of-analysis problem, which has confounded and still continues to confuse functional theorists, it is significant that communications theory (including the political culture school) concentrates on the level of individual attitudes toward the system, discriminating belief-images, expected or preferred

[31] Lyons, *Uneasy Partnership*; National Academy of Science, *The Behavioral Sciences and the Federal Government* (Washington, D.C.: 1968); National Science Foundation, *Knowledge Into Action: Improving the Nation's Use of the Social Sciences* (Washington, D.C.: 1969); National Academy of Sciences, *Behavioral and Social Science Research in the Department of Defense* (Washington, D.C.: 1971).

values, and personal factors affecting percepts (messages) of sensible experience.[32] Organizational theory focuses upon the conditioning influences that formal organizations exert upon the achievement of limited human values, modifying individual beliefs, perceptions, and expectations of ultimate system performance.[33] Political systems analysis, accepting as controlling data for authoritative policy choice the beliefs, expectations, and perceptions of individuals involved and participating in organizational and interorganizational decisions, focuses on: (1) the production of types of data relevant to system-level predictions concerning the consequences of alternate ways of modifying the environment of interpersonal and organizational behavior, (2) taking account of changes in popular expressions of value demands and expectations (symbolized policy), and (3) keeping in mind the requirements of legitimacy-support for the system of public order.[34] The integrative political idea is the concept of *leadership as coordination:* the institutionalization of personal and symbolic capacity to inspire mass popular belief to structure and restructure an effective decentralization of public authority and opposition, and to convince the several, often conflicting, autonomous centers of authoritative (elite) decision making that they

[32] R. M. Williams, *The Reduction of Intergroup Tensions* (New York: Social Science Research Council, 1947); O. Klineberg, *Tensions Affecting International Understanding* (New York: Social Science Research Council, 1950); E. Goffman, *The Presentation of Self in Everyday Life* (Edinburgh: University of Edinburgh, Social Science Research Centre, 1956); R. E. Lane, *Political Life* (Glencoe, Ill.: Free Press, 1959); A. Rapoport, *Fights, Games, Debates* (Ann Arbor: University of Michigan, 1960); K. Boulding, *Conflict and Defense* (New York: Harper & Row, Publishers, 1962); J. D. Singer, *Human Behavior and International Politics* (Chicago: Rand McNally & Co., 1965); T. R. Gurr, *Why Men Rebel* (Princeton, N.J.: Princeton University Press, 1970).

[33] H. Metcalf and L. Urwick, eds., *Dynamic Administration* (New York: Harper and Brothers, 1941); C. I. Barnard, *The Functions of the Executive* (Cambridge, Mass.: Harvard University Press, 1938); H. Simon, "Recent Advances in Organizational Theory," in *Research Frontiers in Politics and Government* (Washington, D.C.: The Brookings Institution, 1955), pp. 23–44: M. Olson, *The Logic of Collective Action* (Cambridge, Mass.: Harvard University Press, 1965); C. E. Lindblom, *The Intelligence of Democracy* (New York: Free Press, 1965); A. Downs, *Inside Bureaucracy* (Boston: Little, Brown and Co., 1967); J. D. Thompson, *Organizations in Action* (New York: McGraw-Hill Book Co., 1967).

[34] Cf. note 10 supra; L. W. Pye and S. Verba, *Political Culture and Political Development* (Princeton, N.J.: Princeton University Press, 1965): I. deSola Pool, *Contemporary Political Science* (New York: McGraw-Hill Book Co., 1967).

should operate constructively and adaptively with respect to their component elements and environment claimants, rather than destructively, ruthlessly, suicidally.[35]

A final word on the role of political valuation (program analysis) as the intellectual operation most likely to integrate the truth dimension of science and the choice dimension of action. The first bridge consists in the assumption that science is concerned with the construction of ideal (conceptual) systems applicable to the human as well as the inorganic world, and that the formulation of connections (relationships) between conceptualized elements that hold good with a fair degree of approximation under specified conditions is an intellectual operation common to the empirical sciences both of nature and of man. The second bridge consists not in the assumption that human desires and aspirations are final causes or directly knowable objects in the human sciences, but accepting them as organizing principles for ordering and for judging what is worth doing, what is illuminating and valuable, whether in the physical, organic, or human worlds. Whether considered as data or as guiding principles of judgment, values cannot be excluded from scientific analytical operations. Finally, the integration of belief-values, the concepts of understanding, and the choice-judgments of action, comes about not through immediate, emotional reaction, but as a result of an arduous, detailed process of clarifying and refining our hypotheses as to what is necessary (programs of scientific or administration action) in order to achieve specified ends. Notwithstanding the attractiveness and compulsiveness of our human propensity to assume the necessity, completeness and definiteness of a single ideological "system" or set of value criteria to be brought into being, political and social science should view politico-ethical valuation as a continuing process of reducing uncertainty and indeterminacy on the part of individuals, politicians, and administrators, as to the moral consequences of factual dilemmas in balancing (harmonizing) the conflict considerations involved in practical-choice situations.

[35] D. Marvick, ed., *Political Decisionmakers* (New York: Free Press, 1961); D. Apter, ed., *Ideology and Discontent* (New York: Free Press, 1964); D. Rustow, *Philosophers and Kings* (New York: George Braziller, 1970), especially pp. 4–29.

.9. Vulture, Mantis, and Seal: Proposals for Political Scientists*

LEWIS LIPSITZ

ON THE front of the September 21, 1969, *New York Times Sunday Magazine*, Claes Oldenburg stands in his sneakers, brown pants, red shirt open at the neck, and dark glasses, leaning "negligently" against his latest creation: a 24-foot lipstick mounted on a tractor. This creation, entitled surprisingly "Lipstick (Ascending) on a Caterpillar Track," has been purchased for $6,000 by Yale University alumni, students, and artists to present to that august university as a new sort of monument: 3,500 pounds of consumer culture. According to the *Times* story, if Yale, in its traditionalism, decides not to accept this monumental gift, the "Lipstick" may move on to Harvard.

But what has this to do with out society, and with political science? If one turns to page 29 of that same issue of the *Times*, to the article about Oldenburg, one finds that article prefaced by a quote from Herbert Marcuse. Marcuse here is talking about previous Oldenburg creations, such as the giant hamburger. He says:

> If you could really envision a situation where at the end of Park Avenue there would be a huge Good Humor ice-cream bar and in the middle of Times Square a huge banana I would say—and I think safely say—that society has come to an end. Because then people cannot take anything seriously: neither their President, nor their Cabinet, or the corporation executives. There is a way in which this kind of satire, or humor, can indeed kill. I think it would be one of the most bloodless means to achieve a radical change.

*An earlier version of this essay appeared in *Polity* 3, no. 1 (Fall 1970): 3–21. Reprinted by permission of the Northeastern Political Science Association.

The task of radicals then seems clear. Gather the necessary resources to buy up land both in Times Square and at the end of Park Avenue, commission supersculptures from Oldenburg and on the appropriate day proclaim the end of society. There seem, however, to be some serious problems with this approach, since as a student of mine pointed out to me: "We've already had bananas in the White House." Yet somehow society as we know it has not come to an end, I think I can safely say.

Clearly, Marcuse's hypothesis needs further research. One can imagine brilliant applications for research funds to the National Institute for Mental Health or the National Science Foundation designed to explore the relationship between pop art and the foundations of the social order: studies no doubt requiring a comparative perspective to make theoretical sense. But perhaps this is enough of a joke, if it is a joke. Marcuse's remarks about the potency of pop art remind me of the work of precisely those people that Marcuse himself has long opposed: those conventional social scientists who imagined they were telling us about life "like it is" when they were filling the air with assumptions as comforting and tenaciously held as Linus' old blanket.

In a time of revolutionary destruction and technological anarchy we heard about "incrementalism." In a time of the manipulation of mass publics we heard about "democratic stability." In a time of great wealth and great poverty we heard about "deterrence." Many of us who became professionals in the 1960s discovered in graduate school that our interests in politics became somehow diverted as we became more professional. And we found that what most professionals were doing seemed at best irrelevant to the major social and political problems of our time. Kenneth Rexroth describes in this short poem the way many of us came to feel about our discipline and its descriptions of political life:

Vulture

St. Thomas Acquinas thought
That vultures were lesbians
And fertilized by the wind.
If you seek the facts of life,
Papist intellectuals
Can be very misleading.[1]

My own respect for the profession I am engaged in reached some sort of low point at the American Political Science Convention in Washington, September 1965. The bombing of North Vietnam had begun in February of that year. The Dominican invasion took place in April. "Teach-ins" followed, culminating in the May 15 debate. Then came the first really long, hot summer. Some weeks before the convention, all members of the Association received a special invitation to attend an exclusive State Department briefing. Clearly, Washington officialdom was worried about what political scientists were thinking. The briefing was well attended, and frustrating. Some of us tried to question the official version of things, but found it difficult to make ourselves entirely clear. Most significant, there were very few questioners. And it seemed clear that most of the hundreds attending were, at the least, not openly critical of what their government was doing. Then the convention itself—its main components were dreariness and irrelevance. Hardly a word about the significant issues of our time, or any time.

This was not a tolerable or defensible situation in itself. But what made it outrageous was that political science was actually anything but irrelevant. Despite the impression the convention or the main professional journals might give, social scientists were involved in the making of significant political decisions—pacifying Vietnam; designing the bombing; creating the Diem regime; thinking about a "war" on poverty. Moreover, the political science profession as a whole gave evidence in the main thrust of its work of a shamefully thoughtless endorsement of the American status quo; an endorsement built into the assumptions and often explicit in the conclusions of much research. Political scientists consciously or unconsciously served a society they then understandably were incapable of confronting critically. Rexroth has another poem called "Mantis":

> In South Africa, among
> The Bushmen, the mantis is
> A god. A predatory
> And cannibalistic bug,
> But one of the nicer gods.

[1]This and the two other Rexroth poems in this article are to be found in his *Collected Shorter Poems* (Norfolk, Conn.: New Directions, 1968). All three are part of a sequence called "A Bestiary."

Likewise, we too had our gods, but I think I say now—and safely say—they were not among the nicer gods.

So it seemed in September 1965. Since that time it has become increasingly difficult for social scientists to give uncritical or unconscious endorsement to America. We have seen some changes since then. It is no longer possible to say that the conventions are totally irrelevant, though they continue to have a very long way to go in order to become genuinely useful. We have seen sharp critiques published, some in the leading professional journals, that revealed the comfortable underlying assumptions current in the profession.

I assume, then, that there already exists a growing awareness of several things: first, that on the whole, political science has recently functioned as an ideological support—though perhaps a feeble one —for many features of contemporary America; second, that many of the "conservative" assumptions implicit in political science research —the cult of stability, the acceptance of Cold War formulas—have also been employed in shaping government policies; third, that political science research ought now to reflect some new priorities and orientations; fourth, that these new priorities and orientations ought to be reflected in our teaching and in the sort of policy-making judgments we make (whether we're asked to judge or not). Implicit here is a desire to create a different sort of society, or, at any rate, to change many aspects of the present society. But there is also a desire to understand reality more fully, in terms of its potentialities as well as its momentary crystallizations. Much of what social scientists wrote ten years ago now looks hopelessly myopic; and what is perhaps worse is what was not even being thought about. The war, racial struggles, new conflicts, have awakened some of us to the need to define our tasks in different ways.

But what are the new priorities of a new political science? Let us look briefly at some of the most significant critiques of the old political science and see what they tell about what a new political science would involve. I propose here to look only at a handful of the many critiques that have recently been made. But I think an examination of this handful will make clear the implications of the main lines of criticism.

POLITICAL SCIENCE AND HUMAN NEEDS

First and probably most significant is the work of Christian Bay. In his many recent articles, and implicitly also in his earlier book, *The Structure of Freedom*, Bay has criticized the "systems" orientation of political scientists.[2] He has argued that despite their proclaimed empiricism and relativism they implicitly assume that Western or especially American democratic forms make for the best of all possible worlds. He pointed to Robert Dahl, S. M. Lipset, Gabriel Almond and Sidney Verba, among others, as men whose work is deeply committed to the survival of the existing order, and ignores the suffering that is perpetuated within that order. He has distinguished between politics and what he calls "pseudo-politics," and has argued for a focus on human "needs" as opposed to "wants." Many of us, and rightly, have trouble sometimes knowing the difference between a need and a want, or between politics and pseudo-politics. And many also sense an aristocratic or elitist preference behind such distinctions. Bay himself is aware of these problems and has attempted to operationalize his ideas more precisely.

Bay's fundamental position is based upon a belief that political systems ought to be built to fit the nondestructive potentialities of human nature as closely as possible. Democracy, such as it is, or even as it might be if improved, can only be justified by references to satisfaction of human needs, such as the need to survive. In this, Bay is following in the tradition of "liberal" theory. And he has himself cited Hobbes as a theorist, who despite his pessimism, retained this fundamental insight—that political institutions could only be judged in terms of the basic needs they were to serve. Yet Bay rejects Hobbes' ferocious gloom and calls on political scientists to play the role of physicians who seek to heal the ills of the body politic. He expects that all political systems will need serious criticism and radical improvement when viewed from the standpoint of

[2]Among the Bay pieces I refer to are *The Structure of Freedom* (Stanford, Calif.: Stanford University Press, 1958); "Politics and Pseudo-politics . . . ," *American Political Science Review* 59 (March 1965): 39–51; "The Cheerful Science of Dismal Politics," in *The Dissenting Academy*, ed. T. Roszak (New York: Pantheon, 1967); "Behavioral Research and the Theory of Democracy," unpublished manuscript; "Political and Apolitical Students: Facts in Search of Theory," *Journal of Social Issues* 23 (July 1967): 76–91; and his article on Civil Disobedience in the *International Encyclopedia of the Social Sciences*.

the satisfaction of basic human needs. The political scientist then is the doctor who must seek out his patient, who must recognize the patient's unwillingness to change, and seek to make clear not only the cure but first of all, the illness and the possibility that cure can be had. This of course is the ancient task of the intellectual: to force the recognition of ignorance and travail, and to suggest that it needn't be so. Perhaps I should say that this is the ancient task of the isolated intellectual, the man about whom Marx said that he "interpreted" the world while the task was to "change" it. Marx here is raising the issue of the means through which change can be achieved, and the role of intellectuals as part of those means. Bay has not dealt with this question fully, though it is clear that he believes that a critical social science might have a substantial impact on public policy, and also that universities could serve as model communities for the rest of society, teaching lessons by experimental example.

Bay himself has several suggestions about research concerning human "needs." He indicates first that needs can be understood in relation to the occurrence of pathologies, such as suicide, mental illness, homicide, alcoholism, drug addiction. This is similar to the argument Erich Fromm made long ago in *The Sane Society*. Fromm attempted to raise questions about the "sanity" of affluent Western societies by pointing out that many of these countries had relatively high rates of such pathologies. Fromm's argument, like Bay's, has many problems. But they both have the significant merit of directing our attention in the proper directions. For both of them it is not enough for political scientists to confine their work to a study of politics in the narrow sense, and to confine their standards of evaluation in the same fashion. Rather, the social analyst is required both to see politics as an architectonic science in the manner of Aristotle, a science that can encompass all of life's variety; and the analyst is also required to concern himself with the individual soul on its journey. One bridge between these two interests that Bay has suggested is Abraham Maslow's concept of a hierarchy of human needs. Bay argues for the tentative, critical acceptance of Maslow's hierarchy as a working beginning which will allow us to judge and make recommendations concerning various political systems. Given such a hierarchy, Bay seems to be telling us, we can see which human needs are being met and which are not and for whom in a given society.

Bay himself has yet to undertake such work but his arguments have had their impact. Professor Timothy Hennessey,[3] for example, in concluding a survey of recent work in the area of political development, including work concerning the American states, argues that future work in this area must orient itself more clearly toward the discussion of ways in which political systems meet human needs, and specifically calls for concern with Bay's concept of "objective security." Hennessey sees this concept as involving in part freedom from threats to the individual's life, health, and ability to provide support for his family. He plans to study the state of "objective security" in various nation-states over a period of time and to attempt to relate the variations to political and other factors such as socioeconomic characteristics. Hennessey's attempt is to tie a concern with political change to the meeting of what he considers to be basic human needs. Probably implicit in these ideas is Bay's argument that a society is as free as its underdogs, and the related argument that the underdog, like all of us, is only capable of freedom if his most basic needs are being, or have been met. Bay himself has never developed the policy implications of these agruments in terms of social priorities except to say that capital punishment should be abolished. Beyond this, I think, we can only imagine the broad outlines of the social policy perspective that flows from such a position. Yet this is similar to many other arguments Bay has put forward, particularly in *The Structure of Freedom*—for example, his arguments concerning psychological and potential freedom. The policy implications of these positions have yet to be spelled out by anyone. This is a matter partly of normative imagination and courage, but it is also partly a matter of difficult and patient research.

There is one other concern of Christian Bay's that matters to us here and that is his interest in rebellion. Bay has maintained that Camus' "rebel," the man who disobeys, who rebels in the name of human solidarity, but also the man who acknowledges the need for rules and for decency, that such a man is the appropriate model for democratic life. In connection with this, he has sought to establish a strong and clear-cut place for civil disobedience within democratic theory and has criticized those who have assimilated democratic

[3]T. M. Hennessey, "Consideration of Theory and Concept Formation in Comparative Political Analysis," paper delivered at the Midwest Political Science Convention, April 1969.

theory to pseudo-democratic reality. He juxtaposes his model of the "rebel" to Almond and Verba's model of the deferential participant, or Berelson's idolization of mass apathy. The "rebel," Bay claims, is the man free enough of deep-rooted personal anxieties to challenge the prevailing norms of his society and to develop a humanistic perspective of his own. Bay has related these concerns for freedom from inner anxiety and freedom to act upon humanistic concerns to the process of personal development. Rebels are made, not born. The rebel is a man who is extending the range of potential freedom because his own inner development has freed him to grasp the existence of this potential. In Bay's mind, then, if we understand the humanistic rebel we can understand more fully what is lacking in our society.

Clearly, Bay's concern with disobedience leads to a concern with obedience and to the socialization process. And this is the second area I want briefly to examine. Perhaps the word socialization itself ought to clue us into the underlying conceptualization, and its assumptions. Socialization is not a term we would usually associate with independence of mind and a critical perspective. Rather, it is associated with questions of support or opposition, with affiliations based on barely conscious associations and fears. If we talked of political education instead of socialization, perhaps this distinction would remain clearer.

The area of education and of upbringing generally is a crucial one for a new political science. A new political science would have to go beyond the work of Easton, Hess, and Greenstein. It would have to take account of the obedience experiments Milgram[4] has reported on. It would have to carry further back into childhood the concerns of certain of the researchers on student activism. For example, it would need to understand how the ground is established in childhood for independence and humanistic rebellion in adolescence and adulthood. In doing so, it will have to concern itself with child-rearing practices, the role of educational institutions, and other institutions that influence these capacities. What is essential, however, is that future socialization research have before it a model of that "democratic" man whom we are seeking both in our world and, however hopelessly, in ourselves. This means that regime legitimacy becomes one concern among others, and not the exclusive focus of

[4]S. Milgram, "Some Conditions of Obedience and Disobedience to Authority," *Human Relations* 18 (February 1965): 57–76.

concern. Further, as Richard Flacks has suggested, there is a growing conflict between what he calls "two of the great shaping institutions of the contemporary period—mass higher education and bureaucratic authority—a contradiction which has to do with opposed definitions of competence embodied in each of these institutions."[5] Perhaps Flacks tends to overdraw this contradiction in the light of current student unrest, but it is clear that increasing numbers of young people are dissatisfied with both educational bureaucracy and other forms of bureaucracy. This is a development that Paul Goodman articulated long ago in that oldie-but-goodie, *Growing up Absurd*. Without attempting here to analyze and evaluate the roots and qualities of this dissatisfaction, it probably makes sense to say that the mere existence of this discontent creates possibilities for fruitful change, and that such change can only be dealt with reasonably by political scientists if they have some idea where they want to go.

The third area I want to touch on is democratic theory itself. Clearly, assumptions about "democracy" serve as a basic backdrop to much of the work in American politics, political development, and comparative politics, not to mention political theory. We have recently seen some important changes in the nature of the arguments about democracy. I have already indicated some of the criticisms Christian Bay has offered in this area. But others have reasoned in different directions. Returning to some of the root ideas of liberal theory, various critics have called for a revival of interest in participation as an essential element of democracy, and have contrasted this emphasis on participation with the more common identification of democracy with competitive political parties. Jack Walker,[6] criticizing Dahl and others, has argued for a new interest in mass movements and protest as essential parts of the democratic process. Peter Bachrach[7] has called for the democratization of day-to-day life, particularly at the workplace. Others have emphasized decentralization as a way of allowing for greater participation and the anticipated good consequences of greater participation. There are several dif-

[5]Richard Flacks, "Protest or Conform: Some Social Psychological Perspectives on Legitimacy," *Journal of Applied Behavioral Science* 5 (April-May-June 1969): 127–50.

[6]Jack Walker, "A Critique of the Elitist Theory of Democracy," *American Political Science Review* 55 (June 1966): 285–95.

[7]Peter Bachrach, *The Theory of Democratic Elitism, A Critique* (Boston: Little, Brown and Co., 1967).

ferent arguments about these consequences of increased participation. Some have talked of the value of participation for personal development—much as Aristotle argued that a man could not realize his full human potential except by joining in the work of the polis. A related argument sees political participation as something of an antidote, providing people with alternative means of expressing discontent and rage. Another way of thinking about participation is in relation to the accurate representation of people's interests and views. Without involvement people will not see what their interests are and will not be able to make them vividly known.

Another element in the critique of democratic theory is the concern with non-decision making, developed especially by Bachrach and Baratz.[8] This concern has, at the very least, awakened democratic theorists to the significance of those issues that are not raised, those questions not asked, those powers not challenged, those energies not mobilized, those analyses not developed. Perhaps ten years ago such concerns may have seemed quixotic, but they don't any more. This interest in non-decision making is important not only because it tends to lead to a deeper exploration of power relationships, but also because it reveals to the political scientist the potentialities of his own role. It is far more comforting to believe that men are inherently nonpolitical, as Dahl proclaimed in *Who Governs?*, and to look only at those issues that are already in the public arena, than to believe that men are potentially political, depending upon the issues at stake and the possibilities of fruitful action. The second perspective implicitly puts to the analyst the question of what role he is to play in the process of revelation and conflict.

Little, however, has been done in the area of democratic theory beyond the critique of the old and the suggestion of guidelines for new work. The research currently going on concerned with anti-poverty programs and the participation of the poor may provide us with more help in understanding the meanings and potentialities of participation. Yet this is to conceive the issue too narrowly. What about Bachrach's emphasis on participation at the workplace? Here we come up against one of the major taboos of contemporary politi-

[8] Peter Bachrach and Morton Baratz, "Decisions and Non-decisions: An Analytical Framework," *American Political Science Review* 57 (September 1963): 632–42.

cal science—the structure of the socioeconomic system. Though many of us may hope for some equalitarian reforms of the existing order, how many of us are willing to indicate in our work our sense that the existing distribution of wealth, of privileges, and deprivations in our society is radically wrong? Yet, if we are to think through the issue of participation, it is necessary to question exactly these matters. Only when we do so can we begin the utopian work of imagining alternatives.

Let me conclude this brief survey on developing tendencies of criticism in political science by looking briefly at international politics. Just a short time ago, Marshall Windmiller published an attack on dominant trends in the field of international politics. His paper was titled "The New American Mandarins,"[9] and this title referred to the many students of foreign policy and international affairs who were so closely identified with U.S. foreign policy that one could expect no serious criticism of it from them. Of course, at the present moment there is no lack of critics of U.S. foreign policy, including many of its old supporters. The lesson to be learned is probably not that men profit from past mistakes, though undoubtedly there is some learning going on; rather, the soberest lesson is that nothing fails like failure. Had American policies in Vietnam succeeded, or involved only small cost, as for example in the Dominican Republic, one wonders how many people now would be bothering to serve as critics of those "successful" policies. Nonetheless, in the short time since Windmiller's critique was published, some changes have occurred. It is not that one cannot still imagine a Project Camelot finding willing social scientists; it is that counterprojects have also developed. The Concerned East Asian Scholars are offering critiques of the accepted assumptions of their discipline. Others are becoming more sensitive to the costs of the international system, and in particular, to America's ways of doing business in it.[10] These

---

[9]In *The Dissenting Academy*.

[10]See, for example, Bruce M. Russett, "Who Pays for Defense?" *American Political Science Review* 63 (June 1969): 412–26; Marshall Windmiller, "Toward A Value Maximizing Foreign Policy," paper delivered at the APSA convention, September 1969; J. David Singer and Paul Winston, "Individual Values, National Interests and Political Development in the International System," paper delivered at the APSA convention, September 1969.

developments do not constitute a reorientation of the field, but they do indicate a growing sensitivity to the underlying issues of the international division of wealth, the dangers of the arms race, and the domestic consequences of militarism. Perhaps if the Vietnam experience does nothing else, it will free students of international affairs from a myopic perspective that looks out on the world from American boundaries. Fundamentally, the central tasks of students of international politics are also concerned with the meeting of human needs. In the terms of their fields this should express itself in a concern for demilitarization, international redistribution of wealth, and opposition to empire building regardless of the disguises in which it may express itself.

What I have been describing here, sketchily and hopefully, is perhaps more of a mood than an achievement; more a growing perspective than a movement; more a troubled conscience than a new life. Nonetheless, when I read Kenneth Rexroth's poem, "Seal," I think it describes what many of us are feeling:

> The seal when in the water
> Is a slippery customer
> To catch. But when he makes love
> He goes on dry land and men
> Kill him with clubs.
> To have a happy love life,
> Control your environment.

Our task then is to protect the seal, except that what Rexroth is referring to here is something within men themselves. The seal is a symbol of what loves and what is vulnerable. And the club symbolizes why it is that deterrence is only successful when we achieve it within ourselves. The task of the social sciences is, at the minimum, to help us control our environment in the name of pleasure and vitality. But this is not merely to rephrase the slogan "Make Love Not War," since what is required is the more intricate task of making lovers not warriors. We all know perfectly well that, unfortunately, making love can help destroy and conflict can help to liberate. Our problem then is to defend men's needs against their most formidable enemies, the complacency and destructiveness of the human species.

THE PROFESSION: "A PEER GROUP OF LIBERALS"

I began this paper with a joke Marcuse played on himself. Let us turn back to Marcuse now and look at what David Braybrooke had to say about him in a recent review of two of his books.

Marcuse's global criticism—his anti-rationale of the American system—however erroneous in detail, has been a better guide to the overall output of the system during the past dozen years than the rationales provided by non-Marxist social scientists, however instructive these rationales have been (in ways Marcuse completely ignores) with respect to the relative uses of bargaining polyarchy, hierarchy and the price system or with respect to the real advantages of incremental decision-making. Marcuse would have expected evils of the magnitude that have emerged, not merely something like Vietnam, violence in our cities, masses of Negro youths festering without jobs or expectations, starvation in South Carolina, but evils like these, prolonged, inflated, beyond the capacity so far of the system to cope with them. To the other thinkers (I speak for myself among them) these events have come as unpleasant surprises. It was not perhaps beyond the capacity of respectable social science to predict them one by one, but the rationales did not anticipate all those things going wrong together, and to such a degree.[11]

But this "success" of radical criticism (and there were others besides Marcuse who made such criticisms) does not resolve for radical social scientists what their appropriate work ought to be. As a result, radical professionals are at present going through a period of self-questioning, bafflement, and creativity in attempts to work out for themselves a reasonable style of work in a profession and in a society that they find they cannot often tolerate.

Before I attempt to chart out some of the sorts of work I believe political scientists, including radicals, should be doing more of, I want to turn to the profession itself, since some of the changes I am going to suggest call for new directions in the profession rather than in the individual researcher. Edgar Litt and Philip Melanson use the term "a peer group of liberals" to describe political scientists.[12] They elaborate their argument about the narrowness and contradic-

[11] David Braybrooke, "Marcuse's Merits," *Trans-Action* 6 (October 1969): 51–54.

[12] Edgar Litt and Philip Melanson, "A Peer Group of Liberals: The Profession and Its Public Discontents," paper delivered at the APSA convention, September 1969.

tions within the profession in a recent article that is unusually insightful.

I am not going to summarize the Litt-Melanson argument, but I do want to select those portions of it that are relevant here. They argue basically that the threefold development of professionalism, behavioralism, and scientism has had drastic effects on the work and role conceptions of political scientists. They maintain that these developments "have had unanticipated consequences so as to prevent us from acting collectively on behalf of political inquiry and intellectual freedom. A narrowly conceived professionalism is inimical to liberal programs lest they result in cognitive dissonance for the individual scholar, disruptions in interpersonal relations within the discipline, and disturbances in the political environment that might curtail our social benefits from governmental, corporate, and foundation interests."

Litt and Melanson see professional norms acting as "defense mechanisms" that shield political scientists from unpleasant realities. What they describe as the "profound public discontent of political scientists" is caused by the gap between our professed liberalism and the actual norms of our professional and associational life. They see a narrow concept of professionalism, allied with a narrow concept of scientific work, being used to weed critical activists out of the profession. They see political science having its impact on public policy mainly by supplying the legitimacy of "disinterested expertise." They imagine a different situation and state that:

If the vast majority of political scientists conceived of themselves primarily as critical intellectuals rather than as scientists; as clinicians concerned about the public allocation of esteem, power, and participation rather than as methodologists, then realization of these self-concepts would greatly alter the cognitive and behavioral dimensions of the profession.

They cite as evidence of the problems of the discipline the fact that only one article about Vietnam has appeared in the *American Political Science Review*, and that of 924 articles published in the *APSR*, the *Journal of Politics*, and the *Political Science Quarterly*, between 1959 and 1969, only 6 percent dealt with policy analysis "in the broadest terms." Austin Ranney, recent editor of the *APSR*, has pointed out in reply to criticisms of the journal, that he simply did not receive very many articles about Vietnam. If political scientists were writing them, they were sending them elsewhere. This confirms the point Litt and Melanson want to make: it is not conscious manipulation that inhibits professionals from broadening the meaning of their profession, but a deeply rooted notion about what sorts of work deserve to be called professional or scientific. Litt and Melanson believe that appropriate reforms can be instituted which will revive the liberalism of the profession, but this brings me to the final section of this paper where I want to set out my own recommendations for change.

CONCLUSIONS: SUGGESTIONS FOR CHANGE

It is clear that the Caucus for a New Political Science proposes to alter the tone and dominant tendencies of the profession. And it is also clear that the Caucus calls for a more open and explicit professional concern with changing our society for the better, not merely serving it as it is. The Caucus does not propose to turn the profession into a political action group, but rather to recall it to a deeper concern with its own values and to the troubling problems of our time. Much of what I have to say from this point on is summarized in the Caucus's election platform; a document that reeks a bit of rhetoric, but, like an antipasto, has some salty surprises.

A. Research

I. Taking "human needs" seriously

(a) We need a different set of standards for judging regimes. We need to take into account attempts to deal with mental and physical illness; infant mortality rates; life expectancy; full employment; and job security. In doing so, we need to take account of the "equality" of treatment available—and particularly, the security and freedom of the least secure and least free.

(b) Dealing with "potential" freedom: Here we have to be concerned with developing a capacity for freedom for independent thought, freedom from manipulability. The current socialization literature, for example, thinks about education in terms of a fit with a particular regime. Instead, we need to think about education as mobilizing a man's potential freedom. To this end, we need distinctions between different sorts of education and their contributions to intellectual liberation. The structure and content of the mass media also should be studied with these goals in mind.

(c) Comparative welfare state politics: Given the parochialism of most American students and of many social scientists, we need the remedy that would be supplied in part by detailed, normatively meaningful studies of alternative methods of organizing social life—Swedish methods of town and country planning; Danish health care; Yugoslav workers' control; Cuban education. We do not need another text describing the British parliament.

II. Altering priorities

(a) The inequities and oppressiveness generated by many existing structures and processes need to be explored:

1. The structure of military hierarchies and military justice

2. The structure of penal institutions and practices

3. Bureaucracies which develop "custodial" attitudes toward their clients.

In all of these cases, and others like them, it will not be enough to prepare an indictment. We have to explore how patterns of vested interest develop and how the "problems" look as conceived by the people who make significant decisions within these institutions.

(b) Oligarchies:

1. The inner structure and external influence of associations such as AMA, ABA, AFL-CIO

2. The strategies of industries such as drugs, tobacco, and automobiles in attempting to block legislation or in coopting federal bureaucratic processes

3. More particularly, the lobbying function within the Defense Department remains to be explored—the detailed documenting of the "military-industrial complex" awaits this work

4. The influences of private power (oil, mining, etc.) on foreign policy making

5. The effects of the American military on foreign policy—for example, the role of the military in the Dominican uprising of 1965, or in Greece

6. How dissident views are kept in hand within bureaucracies, such as the State Department

7. The structure of the internal security establishment—ranging from the FBI to state HUACS.

(c) Creations:

1. We need "scenarios" of ourselves—not in the manner of extending existing trends, but with an eye toward altering some of them. For example, how to restructure the allegiance of poor whites in the South; assessing the possibilities for a new party of the Left in America; evaluating various strategies for radical movements; how to encourage greater participation by the apathetic under different circumstances; how and whether to decentralize various political structures.

2. Peace research: We need, not only the sorts of critiques of strategic thinking that we have been getting, and not only recommendations for disarmament and arms control strategies and the peaceful settlement of disputes—we need also political assessment of how such strategies can be put into practice.

III. *Normative clarity*

(a) It is time for a new burst of utopian thinking—but one attentive to the attempts to create new forms of community and sensitive to the problems and limits of these attempts. We need to imagine and sketch out alternative social structure, family structures, alternative development routes for the poorer countries, alternative sets of priorities for the richer countries. We have to take into account different sorts of incentives and rewards and their possible uses. In connection with this we ought to look again at the thinking of guild socialists and others who suggested alternative ways of organizing portions of social life.

(b) Ethics and radicalism: We need to develop further the work that Camus began on the ethics of violence and the moral issues involved in radical change. We will have to reflect here on the ideology, organization and tactics of radical movements, and the decisions of such groups if they gain power. There has been a dearth of empirical work on the subject of nonviolence. Martin Luther King's campaigns, for example, were far less carefully studied than the riots that followed them. It seems in order to concentrate more of our efforts on the study of more or less peaceful methods of change.

(c) New forms of survey research: Contemporary survey research is often insensitive to the grievances and moral problems of individuals. We don't need another survey telling us that voting behavior is related to opinions about candidates and parties. A more exploratory sort of survey research would attempt to probe beneath the usual surface and achieve a deeper picture of the latent tendencies in political life.

I hope it is clear from the argument to this point that given our problems as a profession, we should act *as a profession* to remedy them. Therefore I want to go beyond recommendations for new areas of research to indicate the kind of tasks the profession can take on in the attempt to create a new political science:

B. Professional Action

I. Recognition of the teacher's role: As suggested by Litt and Melanson, as well as the Caucus, the APSA should consider the creation of rewards for good teaching, and opportunities for post-doctoral teaching fellowships. Litt and Melanson argue that such rewards will, first, help to legitimize attention given to that large but neglected constituency, our students; and second, help to to create intellectual independence from professional norms.

II. University reform: As a profession concerned, at the minimum, with liberal values and democratic norms, we should be concerned with the power structure of universities themselves. The APSA should stimulate research into university reform.

III. Academic freedom: The Association should implement the potentially significant Academic Freedom resolution passed at the 1969 Convention. This resolution calls for APSA sanctions against departments that discriminate on political grounds in hiring and firing. The resolution has many other important things to say, including a recognition that we need to rethink the problems of academic freedom. We ought to get started on this as soon as possible.

IV. Relevance

(a) There have been varied suggestions about how the profession could make itself more "relevant" to the problems of the society in which it enjoys a relatively privileged position. Litt and Melanson suggest a Committee on Political Science in Human Welfare whose function it would be to "provide for the general public and scholarly community the facts and estimates of the effects of critical alternative policies...." David Easton, in his presidential address, suggested an action group with membership from all the social sciences. Again, some have called for regional clinics where political scientists could bring their expertise to bear on the social problems of a particular area.

All of these considerations deserve some attention, but let me suggest two others that I feel have higher priority: first, I believe the APSA should select a few neglected but significant problem areas and attempt to stimulate research in these areas. One obvious area that suggests itself right now is the structure of the military and the problems of military justice. This is an area with acknowledged widespread abuses of fundamental rights and decencies, and an area that any serious person ought to be deeply concerned about. I am not arguing that this must be the area selected, only that the profession ought to stick its neck out by making such a choice, in an area of controversy. Second, I believe our regional conventions could be better organized to reflect the concerns of the regions in which they are located. For example, in the South, the problems of the region are rarely reflected adequately in the convention proceedings; yet we are aware that this is the most backward and authoritarian area of this society, also the poorest.

The question of "politicization" of the APSA by the Caucus has been an issue in the two election campaigns of recent years. It is notable that in the 1970 campaign, some of the best-known members of the profession alleged that Hans Morgenthau, the Caucus's presidential candidate, sought to take over the Association and to use it for political purposes. There is no need here to explore the exact language employed by the Caucus, its candidates, and the critics. The general concern is quite clear: "politicization." But in the context of the APSA, what does such a charge mean?

It might imply, first, that APSA funds would be used for flagrantly political purposes. Yet, the Caucus has never advocated such allocations; moreover, it would require a majority of the APSA Executive Committee to approve them. Second, it might mean that the APSA would go on record as opposed to this or that, passing resolutions like a pizza maker twirls pizzas. Yet, such resolution passing requires approval of the membership. The fear of politicization of the Association, I believe, is more a vague anxiety than a pin-downable allegation. The Caucus has, if anything, urged the Association to break its political ties, for example, the Congressional Awards. On the other hand, it is true that a Caucus candidate once elected president of the APSA would be far more likely to speak out on current issues and to take initiatives that might or might not have wide support among the members. In other words, a Caucus president would be a more active leader, hopefully for the better. It is just this activism many fear since certain people and groups no doubt might be offended by presidential actions, or statements. I would argue that such activism—hopefully of an intelligent and measured sort—would stimulate debate and discussion within the Association and perhaps within the larger society. It would not mean that the Association would abandon its professional duties and commitments, nor that members would be driven out of the Association because of their political views. "Politicization" would amount, in practice, to slightly more controversial leadership.

In his recent book *Earth Household*, Gary Snyder—a poet and student of Eastern religions—argues that:

There is nothing in human nature or the requirements of human social organization which intrinsically requires that a culture be contradictory, repressive and productive of violent and frustrated personalities.[13]

[13]Gary Snyder, *Earth Household* (Norfolk, Conn.: New Directions, 1969), p. 91.

Snyder articulates the great hope that the species can transcend its self-destructive tendencies and can return to its own nature and the larger nature of this world with a certain harmony, peacefulness, and grace. Perhaps. We don't know. I'm not sure Snyder knows, except perhaps for himself, and perhaps though he has found his way, it is not a way suitable for others. Still, we ought to recognize the troubles of our time and do what we can, whether or not we have a vision of the future or of the inner world that satisfies us. It is hard to build without a utopian vision, yet we have already seen the horrors utopian visions can bring with them.

A student came to see me after a recent class and told me how frustrating the discussion had been. First one point of view had been criticized, then the other, then the critics had been criticized, and then a criticism of the critical critics. Too much. What did it all have to do with living a reasonable life, for oneself, or assisting others in doing so? Not clear. The student said: "You know, I'd better spend my time giving out contraceptives or fitting diaphragms. At least that would be something *useful*."

And indeed it would be useful. But then, who was to decide how these birth-control devices were to be distributed, and who to furnish the resources? These were political decisions. And so we were back again with our concern with politics. But maybe this student's frustration should be a guideline for all of us—that if the "Seal" does not prosper, our work is in vain.

.10. *Political Science as Science and Common Sense*

E. W. KELLEY

GENERALLY, THE world would be no worse off without political scientists, or at least I would be sorely taxed to show the contrary. Insofar as there are particular exceptions to this claim, I suspect individual abilities and energies are responsible, rather than the fact that the exceptions belong to the American Political Science Association.

In this context, to speculate on the directions the study of political phenomena will take in the near or distant future is both unrewarding and hazardous. The hazard comes in trying to predict norms or values for a profession that is internally drawn and predominantly internally responsive. No large body of lawful knowledge exists to guide its work; most political scientists do not know what laws would look like anyway. No extensive externally derived demands are placed on the profession in such a manner that its work can eventually be judged by others as worthwhile or not, relevant or not.[1] Just how am I to make a sensible guess as to what techniques, toys, and terms will be employed, say, twenty years from now? To attempt this would be like guessing which potential poets under twenty-five will be popular among their peers twenty years from now. I am not good at guessing such things, particularly when I am not neutral with respect to what one might come up with. Hence, I take a different tack: the question I intend to deal with is what

[1] There is much internal criticism concerning this last point, however.

political scientists might *sensibly* be doing twenty years from now. The response falls into three categories: political scientists might try to do science; they might study systems of valuation and the classical political questions concerning man and the relation between man and the state; they might apply common-sense knowledge and what scientific knowledge they glean to the implementation of particular, valued goals.

We will consider each of these categories in turn, but so that our initial assertion will not be considered irrelevant to matters pursued here, we will also evaluate current professional activity as it claims to fall under any or all of these three categories.

POLITICAL SCIENCE AS A SCIENCE

Knowledge of the political and social world around us, like knowledge of the physical and biological world, is not rare. We "know" that most men of wealth or control over economic resources prefer private to public charity, do not favor highly progressive taxation and other redistributive measures, tend to vote Republican, and so on. We may even speculate about the thought and psychological processes that account for our claims. Possibly on the whole what we know is true, but exceptions abound. If we distinguish further among the vocations and avocations, the generation in which wealth is gained, the education, professional or otherwise, and ages of the individuals we "know" about, what we know is not true of those in each possible category. If for some reason we need this more detailed information, we obtain it. In doing so we are probably not yet doing science, but we are exhibiting one feature of that task: we are trying to express our factual knowledge about modalities so that fewer or no exceptions are involved. This knowledge does not follow analytically from the definitions of the modal categories. At the end of this analysis we hope to have descriptions of each modal category that are unexceptionally true. If we then pay attention to the particular features of our environment that give rise to the distribution of individuals in our categories, we might call these features boundary conditions, which if present will assure the validity of our descriptions. Then we pose hypotheses, guesses about laws, statements we believe to be true when the boundary conditions are realized.

Let us now restate what is going on in the simple terminology used to describe scientific knowledge. Our knowledge becomes more assessible to others and hence more public as we come to greater agreement concerning the referent of our words. Presumedly when we refine the use of a word, referent is more exact, but not necessarily more confining, than was previously the case. Consider "conservatism." The word obviously has multiple and in some men's minds contradictory referents; so much so in fact that we often feel obliged to preface the word conservative with "economic," "racial," and the like to communicate in casual conversation with informed others. If we are concerned with this state of affairs we may, like McClosky,[2] attempt to find some shorthand into which we can condense at least part of most men's meanings for the term (hence his reliance on what he calls the validity of his scale). Literally taken, McClosky's scale gives exact referent for how he is going to use the term "conservative." The scope, range of application, or alternatively, the extent to which the property so defined is exemplified is fairly general. In this instance, then, "exactness of referent" is not synonymous with "restricted in scope or application."

The uses of "conservative" are so varied, however, that the possibility of offering many hypotheses true of all who are conservatives in almost any meaning given that term is slight. Hence we may wish to make further distinctions; to define concepts which name some properties that may not appear so ubiquitously, but that may be found to be uniformly related to others. In doing science we are at least as concerned with theoretical significance, the appearance of concepts in laws, as we are in the extent to which the properties named are exemplified.

Hypotheses are guesses about laws. Laws always have an "if..., then..." form, however this may be disguised or augmented in a particular instance. Usually associated with the laws are boundary conditions, those other properties that must be exemplified if the law is to obtain. Laws state the contingent and usually universal association of properties; laws are not about facts. Facts exemplify properties. There are no laws about France or about voters now or in the past alive in the United States. These facts and others may exemplify the properties named by the concepts in laws. In this

[2]Herbert McClosky, "Conservatism and Personality," *American Political Science Review* 52 (March 1958): 27–45.

context, surveys are almost always surveys of fact, or better, of some of the properties that a large number of facts (usually people) exemplify. As such surveys may (but by no means always) be used to gather evidence relevant to a particular hypothesis(es), but no hypotheses are "generated" automatically by analysis of survey data. Usually at best, any survey only provides one rather inexact instance of evidence relevant to some particular hypotheses.

One must be careful not to equate "hypothesis" with "associated with" or "related to." The latter terms are often used to describe the results of data analysis, but as such they only describe a widely found state of affairs for any particular set of facts—namely, that two properties as exemplified by *these* facts are not randomly associated, where random association has a clear and defined meaning (incidently, an unexciting one—more on this later).

When one has a number of hypotheses or laws, one is sometimes said to have a theory. The laws may be axiomatically structured (we have none of these in political science) or may simply involve overlapping sets of concepts. "Theory" has some other uses in political science, some intentional, some not. One meaning is that of a picture or kind of heuristic outline of the way political systems are. Let us not be unkind and point out that in science a heuristic is such for something else *in* the science; instead let us give a simple way in which the word "system" is used in science and see how a "theory" of the political system stacks up.

A system can be thought of as a set of facts, properties, and laws containing the concepts naming these properties. The facts presumedly exemplify the properties named. The solar system is the classic example of a system. The facts are the sun, nine planets, moons, etc.; the properties are position (three values for each fact), momentum (three values for each fact), and masses (one value for each fact). The laws are, say, Newton's. These forenamed things, and nothing more, are part of the system: the color of the moon is not part, even though the moon (fact or in other words—thing) is. Further, the solar system is a closed, almost complete system. By this we mean that the laws contain only those properties named (the color of the moon is not lawfully related to its relative momentum) and that the set of bodies, sun, planets, moons, etc. are the only ones that need be considered to obtain future and past knowledge of the state of the system with respect to the position, momentum, and mass of facts in it. To know, say, the position of the moon at some point in the future, we need know only the present positions, momenta, and masses of the bodies in the solar system and the laws. In principle these features of more distant stars are relevant, but their affect is slight; hence we call the system almost complete.

A political system could be composed of facts, properties, and laws, also. These must be specified, however. Only some properties, not all those we could observe would be part of the system. Possibly only some facts, some things, people, behavior, institutions in a political system exemplify these properties. Presumedly, all the properties referenced would appear in laws, or at least guesses about laws, which are posed. This description, of course, does not characterize "systems" as political scientists use the term. In fact, to decide how political scientists use the term is difficult. Sometimes it appears to refer to everything that is political and might be lawfully related to anything else.[3] All things then are divided into categories: inputs, supports, interest aggregation, articulation, etc. None of the concepts naming categories appear in guesses about laws. Further, in a scientific context the breakdown of the political world into these categories cannot be judged to be useful. If the breakdown is meant to be heuristic, one must pose the question: What laws or guesses about laws have resulted? Publicly posed heuristics can be favorably judged only when public knowledge has resulted. Further, since the referents for the categories are not exact, we can dispute what falls under some particular categories on the margin. The categories, then, probably do not have sufficiently exact, shared meaning even to be possible terms in laws or guesses about same. Often this is the result of a not uncommon confusion between the scope or range of application of a term or theory and the precision with which it is used or applied respectively. The latter is essential in science.

In fact, the injunction to use words that have exact, shared meaning is one of only three characteristics that seem general to the scientific enterprise. We must know what we seek knowledge about and this knowledge is presumedly to be public knowledge. A second

[3]David Easton, "An Approach to the Analysis of Political Systems," *World Politics* 9 (April 1957): 383–400; Gabriel Almond and James S. Coleman, eds. *The Politics of the Developing Areas* (Princeton: Princeton University Press, 1960), Introduction.

characteristic of scientific endeavor is that it seeks general knowledge, knowledge expressed in unexceptional laws. The third is that when reports of particular observations of properties are combined with statements giving laws or guesses about laws and together a logical contradiction is formed, something must give. Guesses about laws must be changed, terms redefined, boundary conditions altered, or the guesses must be discarded.

TWO METHODS OF POLITICAL SCIENCE AS SCIENTIFIC METHODS

In the early part of this century, in attempting to replicate and extend some of Mendel's work, biologists became interested in the association of genetically independent traits in populations. If the traits were indeed independent, a very particular pattern of joint exemplification should appear. This pattern is termed random association: it is a rare event and is *expected* to occur only in a theoretical context like that just described. Since the randomness expected is not necessarily perfectly exemplified in finite populations, biological statisticians developed an array of knowledge of the sampling distributions of various measures of deviation from random association. This work extended to properties measured on all levels and continues today.

Social scientists, however, seem more interested in all the other cases, those which exemplify the nonrandom association of properties in populations. For some reason it is presumed that descriptive random vs. nonrandom association is of some general scientific importance. This is almost never the case; the way in which two properties are statistically associated in a population almost never has any bearing on whether that data is consistent or inconsistent with a guess about a law. Consider a hypothesis involving the following contingent association of length of residency and opposition to state eminent domain proceedings. In towns under ten thousand in population, more than half the residents of more than ten years' duration will go to court. While overly particular, this formulation will serve our purpose: in a particular town it matters not whether the exact figure is 55 or 95 percent. The behavior of residents of less than ten years' duration is irrelevant to the hypothesis. Unfortunately, all these factors influence the calculation of a measure of nonrandom association (say, phi or Yule's Q). Hence, data from all relevant towns can be consistent with the hypothesis, but the measure of association between length of residency (dichotomous variable) and taking eminent domain to the courts can vary from town to town. In some rare case, random association between the two properties may obtain; the same percentage of long-term or other residents may go to the courts. This is irrelevant to the hypothesis as long as that percentage is greater than 50.

Sometimes particular percentages are placed within guesses about laws. Say that in the above example our guess was that between 75 and 80 percent of the long-term residents went to court.[4] In each town the data would be either consistent or inconsistent with this guess. This could be directly ascertained in each town by examination of the relevant cases: the behavior of the long-term residents. In its summary form, this behavior is represented in only one row of a contingency table. Again the behavior of the short-term residents is irrelevant.

Alternatively, the hypothesis may assert that more long-term residents go to court than do short-term residents. A direct comparison of the relevant percentages in the contingency table for each town is then appropriate. Notice that if the hypothesis is correct, nonrandom association between length of residency and going to court will obtain in each town. The manner in which it is nonrandom association between length of residency and going to court will obtain in each town. The manner in which it is nonrandom, though, is largely irrelevant. One gets all needed information by comparing percentages.

We could continue with more examples, but instead we shall indicate how similar observations hold for measures of association used for properties measured ordinally and intervally. All this material is dealt with at much greater length elsewhere.[5]

Hypotheses involving ordinal properties are most simply of a more than–more than form. In particular, *defined* sorts of populations, if one individual has more of Property X than another individual has, then the former has more of Property Y. Obviously to test this hypothesis one must select those populations that meet the

---

[4]The reader is again asked to forgive the author the silly simplicity of the example. Given no body of lawful knowledge to draw examples from, the point is best made simply.

[5]E. W. Kelley, *The Methodology of Hypothesis Testing*, in press.

stated antecedent conditions and *make paired comparisons* between individuals in each such population on comparative properties X and Y. Sometimes the hypothesis may state that the majority or some percentage of paired comparisons are in the same or opposite order on the two properties. Many variants are possible. Regardless, ordinal measures of association seem to have no bearing on testing these hypotheses. The principle reason for this is the manner in which such statistics treat tied cases.

Two individuals may always be tied on a comparative property. Our hypothesis may be that in the type populations we are considering, of those comparisons in which one individual has more of X than another, the former has more of Y 80 percent of the time. Ties on X must be eliminated, ties on Y count against the 80 percent figure. Tau doesn't admit ties or counts a tie half for and half against the 80 percent figure. Gamma excludes ties; Somer's dxy counts tied cases but does not count them against the 80 percent figure.

Hypotheses involving intervally measured properties are expressed in shorthand using difference equations: $\triangle Y = a\triangle x$ or $\triangle Y = a(\triangle X)^2$, etc. One should not be seduced by the equal sign. The expression of a hypothesis is almost always asymmetrical. "If X changes by one unit, then Y changes by a units," is the verbal counterpart of the first equation. The most commonly used measure of association for intervally measured properties is the correlation coefficient. Since the correlation coefficient is functionally related to the coefficient of the independent variable in a simple linear regression, let us consider this harder case.[6] Given intervally measured independent (X) and dependent (Y) variables, a unique equation of the form $y = ax + b$ can be found which satisfies the following, slightly redundant, *definitional* criteria: Given the observed values of X and Y, $y = ax + b$ passes through the mean values of x and y. Given observed values of X, the equation gives calculated values of Y which on average differ minimally from the observed Y's. Given X, the sum of the squares of the differences between the calculated and observed values of Y is minimized. Two points need be made. First, one will almost never find a zero coefficient in front of the

---

[6]Just about everyone agrees that the value of the correlation coefficient has no bearing on testing guesses about laws; they are "population dependent." At issue though is whether linear regressions have any bearing on this process.

independent variable; this simply reflects the fact that two properties are almost never randomly associated in populations of any size. Second, it is not at all clear that the definitional criteria employed to determine the linear equation need to have any bearing on testing a hypothesis involving the variables included. One would expect a regression to be useful in testing a hypothesis only under the most rigorously controlled conditions. In fact, the conditions would have to be those stated in the antecedent clause of the hypothesis.

Consider, for example, Riker's least minimal winning coalition hypothesis.[7] Crudely this asserts that under a specified set of initial conditions the smallest *in size* (*resources used to win*) of those coalitions that are minimal winning coalitions will form. Unfortunately, the hypothesis is not true—or better—the proofs offered are not valid because they assume empirical counterparts not named in the antecedent conditions. What is used to win or lose (say, voted) is not necessarily the same as what is won or lost. If we augment the antecedent conditions of the hypothesis with the specification that what an individual has to lose is a monotonically increasing function of his resources of the kind necessary to win, the proofs follow. This hypothesis must be tested under such conditions that all other theoretically significant antecedent variables can be absented or set at other (always the same) fixed value. The latter is explicitly given as among the boundary conditions for the hypothesis (i.e., zero air resistance, standard temperature and pressure, etc. in the case of some physical laws). In this context we care little about statements of an approximate-size principle for the "real world." While some pictorial relevancy may help one keep one's credentials as a political scientist, that is, as required by the profession if one is to be read widely enough to have impact, the picture is not a test of the hypothesis.

We should point out that just because a hypothesis is "analytically proved" does not mean it need not be tested. If only logic proper is used to derive theorems from a set of premises, we would not be so insistent on testing. However, the additional axioms of real analysis (or a game theory, etc.) often employed do not necessarily reflect

[7]William Riker, *The Theory of Political Coalitions* (New Haven: Yale University Press), pp. 32–33.

the way the world is in all applications. While analytic truths are produced, when content is given the empirical coordination does not always lead from empirically true statements to empirically true statements. (Think for example of the *one way* implications of laws, the *symmetry* of operations about the equal sign and the coordination of the two we employed earlier.)

An instance of the use of the axioms of real analysis in an "empirical proof" is the Hinich-Ordeshook spatial analysis of candidate strategies and voting behavior.[8] Some assumptions in these analyses may not be consistent with the way things are in most elections (i.e., all citizens weight the issues in an identical fashion). This does not matter; the theorems may still be proved and may give true empirical conclusions regardless of the assumptions made. This must be shown, though, for again more than logic proper (and definitions) has been used in the derivations. Further, to be fairly tested, any hypothesis must be tested under the conditions named in the antecedent clause. The Hinich-Ordeshook theorem, then, is most fairly tested in circumstances (controlled if possible) in which all citizens weight issues in an identical fashion. One may object that this is irrelevant to the political world as we know it—to which there are two responses: (1) The task of a science is not to replicate the world, but to discover and state *lawful* relations among properties (not facts, proper names, events, etc.). These laws may or may not be useful for any particular purpose. (2) One may possibly be helped to know what is the case when individual weightings of issues are the same before one can vary weighting. The situation is actually a little better than that surrounding gravity following Galileo and Newton. Air-resistance must be the same at zero in $S = \frac{1}{2}gt^2$ but weightings of issues must be the same at any value in a particular instance in the Hinich-Ordeshook hypothesis as posed.

The works of Riker, Hinich, Ordeshook, and others represents

[8]Melvin J. Hinich and Peter G. Ordeshook, "Plurality Maximization vs. Vote Maximization: A Spacial Analysis with Variable Participation," *American Political Science Review* 64, no. 3 (September 1970): 772–91; also Melvin J. Hinich, John O. Ledyard, and Peter C. Ordeshook, "A Theory of Electoral Equilibrium: A Spatial Analysis Based on the Theory of Games," School of Urban and Public Affairs, Carnegie-Melon University, 1970.

that portion of the profession which is concerned with the use of analytic methods in political analysis. Like others, those with this interest must be concerned with one of the most serious methodological problems encountered in the social sciences: that of false quantification. An illustration from the literature of interaction in groups illustrates the issue. Simon states that the intensity of interaction (in a social group) depends upon and increases with the level of friendliness and the amount of activity carried on within the group: restated, $I(t) = a_1 F(t) + a_2 A(t)$, $a_1, a_2 > 0$. This is false quantification. Friendliness and activity are not defined, and if they were, they need be only comparative properties for the "postulate" to make sense. Further, as soon as we are given some referent to friendliness, activity and intensity of interaction we need not regard the statement as a postulate but as two empirical hypotheses. The equation does not state the same thing the postulate (a comparative one) does, and the latter could be correct, while the former had no meaning or were wrong.

The advantages to be gained by symbolic expression are presumedly comparability and deducibility with and from other statements. Words and sentences, though, are symbolic expressions and one can do deductions without additive symbolization. The real advantage of stating things about intervally measured properties in difference equations is that one can use the axioms of real analysis for other derivations with coordinated empirical referents (whether or not empirically true). The advantage of coordination to nonverbal symbolism is increased as the symbolism has a richer axiomatic structure beyond statements of logic proper.

Given such a system, two types of confusions can arise. As in Simon's case, one can actually use some of the axioms (of real analysis) to derive other statements, but have both mistranslated one's verbal hypothesis and given no referent or coordination to the symbols. One simply cannot say what the resulting equations *say* about the variables involved (conditions of equilibrium) if one can even say what one would see if one had the variable present. In "A Theory of the Calculus of Voting," Riker and Ordeshook, following in a tradition begun with Anthony Downs, state the calculus of the individual voting act as $R + PB - C + D$ where $R > O$ for the individual to vote.[9]   We have no interval measures for C, D, and probably for B on an individual level.   Derivations using the real analysis are not critical to the sorts of hypotheses that Riker and Ordeshook wanted to test.   *Comparisons* on means of probabilities characterizing groups of individuals (say, percent that vote) are used to confirm hypotheses that must be of a more-less variety.   Strictly, if even the comparative hypotheses are about individuals, use of measures characterizing groups is not an adequate test.   Further, the comparisons made are so under conditions of assumed *ceteris paribus* or "equal amounts of" [vague] other variables in the "model."

One point made to justify the use of such models is that the hypothesis stated by an equation like $Y = a_1x_1 + a_2x_2$ is really about the sign of a.   If the hypothesis is not a universal one: some a_i can be positive (negative) when the majority of paired comparisons are in the opposite direction.   Further, the sign and value of a_i may not even be important to testing any hypothesis, if the former are given by normal MLE techniques.   Lastly, the preceding points have presumed X_i, Y to be intervally measured properties; what are we to do when we only have chapter heading words and (probably insignificant) comparative scores?

The preceding arguments have not been directed at suggesting that the scientific study of human behavior is not possible.   In fact, the reader may have gleaned some notion of what sorts (forms) of assertions and procedures would be involved in bringing about greater scientific knowledge of this sort.   We have only pointed out that much that passes for scientific political science is fraught with overlooked methodological traps and that the sort of statistical analysis that claims to embody scientific political science is at best unrelated to it.

---

[9]William H. Riker and Peter C. Ordeshook, "A Theory of the Calculus of Voting," *American Political Science Review* 62, no. 1 (March 1968): 25–42.

R = reward for voting
P = probability individual makes a difference by voting
B = utility of the difference in the outcome to the actor
C = cost of voting
D = other (socialized) benefits from voting at all

THE ADVOCACY AND INVESTIGATION OF VALUES

Fortunately, some political scientists have always been interested in the classical political questions: the appropriate relationship between man and his fellow citizens, the relation of man to the state of which he is a part, and those features of men that circumscribe his possible modes of social and political existence. The author is not experienced at proposing answers to these questions, but, following Duncan MacRae,[10] we can not only indicate what some desired characteristics of such answers would be, but we can join the advocacy of those that will consider systems with these arguable characteristics.

Any attempt to answer these basic questions inevitably includes some notion of the purposes of a political state, obligations of citizens to the state, the advantages of citizenship and the duties of each man to others. Also expressed but less basic are some rules, moral or ethical imperatives or injunctions, about how men ought to behave in various contexts. Ideally these rules should be logically consistent. Further, they should be derivable from the answers to the basic questions and matters of empirical fact and law. The basic questions should themselves be answered consistently. For one to be able to see whether all this is the case, or even to see what behavior is incumbent upon one, the words used must have reasonably exact, shared referent. Further, if the rules are to be of value, they should be relevant to more rather than fewer choice situations humans face.[11]

To advocate these norms for ethical discourse, however, is not to engage in it. And in a systematic way such discourse is rare among political scientists. Unsystematic discourse is frequent; it is engaged in predominantly to justify choices made in the public arena and to justify the preservation of private privilege. In this context ethical discourse is used partitively and almost always in a manner that

---

[10] Duncan MacRae, "Scientific Communication, Ethical Argument, and Public Policy," *American Political Science Review* 65, no. 1 (March 1971): 38–50.

[11] MacRae would probably add that the rules should obtain when the role of individuals is interchanged. This, though, is not necessary to give us the other features and would exclude some of Plato and possibly others we might not wish to dismiss so easily. We will not here prescribe a view of the politically relevant properties of humans which leads to interchangability.

serves to justify particulars; this is an inversion of the criteria advocated by MacRae in which the particular is not terminally justified, but is valued as an instrument to more generally valued ends.

These two streams of discourse mingle little. Advocates of particular interests are little interested in having their arguments shown inconsistent or bankrupt. Worse still, their arguments, if forced into a consistent mold, might be shown to lead to some undesirable policies as well. Such would be the case if we forced general consistency on economic and social conservatives who would wish generally unrestrained choice behavior and competition among adults. Some principles underlying this position are that individuals should succeed in obtaining what they value only to the extent that they can employ their own talents and efforts in competition with others, and that opportunity to employ one's talents and efforts should be initially equal on the margin. In particular, then, one should not be arbitrarily handicapped as a result of choices others make for one. If this is to be the case, massive educational and economic intervention on the behalf of disadvantaged *minors* would have to occur. There is no justification for punishing them for parental choices, before they enter the competitive arena, unless of course one prefers to view the relation between parents and children to be like Aristotle's view of the relation between master and slave. Then, of course, the obligations and prerogatives of the parents do not cease and we are again at some point left with a system in which all the premises of the "laissez-faire" argument cannot simultaneously obtain.

On the other hand, the academic has little interest in serious political attempts to force some consistency to value argumentation. His reward structure is based upon the readings and the recognition of fellow academics. No benefits accrue from sullying his life style and intellectual comfort by trying to force his work or arguments into a wider arena. Even MacRae's article is directed toward the profession.

We have suggested that there is a need of advocacy not just of norms for ethical discourse, but of particular ethical systems as well. This latter enterprise is more what we think of when describing the activities of modern political philosophers. Unfortunately, those involved in this enterprise are no more involved in wordly ethical discourse than are those proposing norms for such discourse.

POLICY ANALYSIS AND POLICY ADVOCACY

Most generally, the disputes of politics concern matters of policy, not grand ethical principles. Most of us can agree that all men should be free, equal, should have an opportunity to develop their skills and talents, and so on. It is at the level of what these general assertions imply for ongoing political and economic arrangements and how these ends are to be obtained that disagreement occurs. Several methods exist for clarifying these disagreements: If we insist that the referent for such words as "freedom" or better, "freedom from" and "freedom for" be exact and known, and if values are expressed in proper sentences, we will see that the advocates of freedom, equality, etc., are not advocating the same things.

If, however, we all agreed we wanted to do X better, whatever X may be, we are still confronted with the task of deciding how to do X better. Questions of means can be critical, particularly when we pose values that cannot be completely and/or immediately realized. Two features of means are commonly overlooked: their desirability in the short run to those who must live with them and their merit as means. Surely the Dahl-Key analysis of American democracy[12] falls short on both counts. Large numbers of individuals don't like these democratic means. What ends do they lead to? Possibly general acquiescence to the system has as much to do with lack of alternatives, alternative channels of information, and alternative foci for organization. While the result might be described as stable, the question of what values are served is still not answered.

The best circumstance in which to respond to this question would be one in which ends were clear, internally consistent, and means were *lawfully* related to ends. Of course, political scientists do not have laws to offer (the question is: Do they have talents to offer?). One must then resort to unobscured common sense, and some sort of decision about how to behave under uncertainty. The latter is necessary because there will always be other, ill-founded claims made in the policy arena. The response of the professional politician to uncertainty is to do what will maximize benefit to the ongoing political system in the short and intermediate run in the sense of keeping the system going. As Lipset and Rokkan[13] point out in their discussion

[12] Robert Dahl, *A Preface to Democratic Theory* (Chicago: University of Chicago Press, 1956).

[13] Seymour M. Lipset and Stein Rokkan, *Party Systems and Voter Alignment* (New York: Free Press, 1967), pp. 1–64.

of nation building, the politician often has the necessary information and incentive in terms of material and psychological payoff to bring peripheral areas and interests into the political system. However, grand schemes and systems to the contrary, we can count many instances in which politicians have not succeeded.

The political scientist might decide to act as one who poses values or who criticizes value systems offered by others. If he wishes either to offer means for obtaining valued ends or to point out the ends served by currently pursued means, the best sort of relevant knowledge he could have is of a scientific sort. Failing enough science, he must rely on sophisticated common sense, strategies for handling uncertainty, and, hopefully to a far lesser extent, accumulated professional approaches and techniques. There are some easy and systematic errors to fall prey to, however. The first is to extend analysis of or description of the present state of affairs into a proxy for value analysis. Pluralistic studies of American politics tend in this direction. Concomitant to this is the elevation of ideologies used to justify particular short-run interests into general values to be served. Such occurs in the argumentation over community control of urban public schools. The elevated ideologies are that education is intended to serve the particular interests of those partaking it and that education in a democracy is best when it is uniform and in the hands of experts. Neither argument makes the particular goals to be served clear; means are given. Above all else, schools teach children to read, write, and do math. How best to do this is open to speculation. There is no evidence that can be brought forward by the universalists that current experts know some "best" method of instruction for all or even subclasses of children. These are questions that revolve around matters of fact and law and the evidence is out. One can also point out that community participation in the schools without undercutting the basic aims of education mentioned seems to work best when it confines itself to peripheral cultural issues and does not infuse lower class cognitive habits into the classroom. This is possible, it seems, only when more than two ethnic or racial groups are involved, none is in a majority, and administrators are not responsible to professionals directly.[14]

A second trap is to fall in the habit of providing information

---

[14] Rhody A. McCoy, "The Formation of a Community-Controlled School District," in *Community Control of Schools*, ed. Henry M. Levin (New York: Simon and Schuster, 1970), pp. 169–90.

about means-ends relationships in terms of a professional framework for analysis or listing of variables. Donald Matthews and
James S. Coleman illustrate these pitfalls respectively in their recent
reports in *Race and the Social Sciences*.[15] Matthews simply lists research that has been done under the rubric provided by Easton's
input and output functions. Coleman uses tables in which "... an
X in a cell indicates that resources of the two types specified by the
row and column appear to interact with the result of a joint effect
on the level of operation of the relevant arena of action."[16] What is
the relevant arena of action? What is the interaction talked about?
In fact, what does the quoted section mean?

One can suspect that in Coleman's article the notion of an "effect"
is statistically based. He is not the only one to make that mistake.
Arthur Jensen makes the same error in the now infamous Jensen
Report.[17] The partitioning of differences in scores on a dependent
variable over several independent variables through use of analysis
of variance, multiple regression, and the like, is confused with obtaining lawful knowledge about the causes of the dependent variable.
Extensions of arguments in the second section of this paper would
show the basis of the confusion.[18]

At a time in which we are just beginning to learn about the causes
of kinds of human abilities and behavior, it would be an error to
allow the incapacity and lack of interest trained into political scientists to stall us. For example, the spatial structuring of the world
and organization of lexicon in children as differently formed in the
differing early environments associated with racial and class differences are just becoming known. The effect of organization of lexicon on later IQ scores, the preferences of teachers for certain cognitive styles (even when performance is equalized), the artificial as well
as real educational barriers to entry into occupations,[19] and the en-

---

[15] Reports found in Irwin Katz and Patricia Gurin, eds., *Race and the Social
Sciences* (New York: Basic Books, 1969), pp. 113–44, 274–341.

[16] James S. Coleman, "Race Relations and Social Change," in *Race and the Social
Sciences*, p. 323.

[17] Arthur Jensen, "How Much Can We Boost I.Q. and Scholastic Achievement,"
Harvard Educational Review 39, no. 1 (Winter 1969): 1–123, especially 20–37, 42–48.

[18] E. W. Kelley, *Race, Class and Educational Opportunity*, in preparation.

[19] B. C. Rosen et al., eds., *Achievement in American Society* (Cambridge, Mass.:
Schenkman, 1969).

joyment of systematically different discount rates for economic and social benefits as a response to the reward structure of the environment[20] are matters worth pursuing. To know if and how these things occur is necessary before one can sensibly talk about a program for providing "equal opportunity" for almost anything important. There is no reason to believe that, if political scientists will leave their frameworks and tools of analysis temporarily behind, they cannot be as useful as any other group of interested citizens at providing the needed answers.

[20] Ibid.; Kelley, *Race, Class and Educational Opportunity*.

Part Three: Political Science and Political Philosophy

Introduction

POLITICAL PHILOSOPHY perspectives on the discipline have those advantages, and disadvantages, inherent to a long-distance view. All of the essays in the preceding sections have been argued, at least implicitly, from an identifiable philosophical perspective. Nevertheless, the arguments focused on specific, usually direct, implications of their perspectives rather than an overview of political science itself. In this section four critical stances are defended that prescribe or discuss more generally the proper philosophical position and its implications for political science. The differences with preceding essayists are of degree in comprehensiveness of attack since, though implicit, the preceding discussions of specific proposals are based on standards just as universal. The difference in degree does have a major impact. The relationship of political knowledge and normative concerns are more dramatically illustrated.

The unanimity of concern over making knowledge useful to understanding and choice in normative matters is placed into sharper focus by these essays because of their specific topic, political philosophy. A consensus emerges for the discipline's "going beyond" narrow empirical research toward the vista of more comprehensive philosophical understanding. The assumption that understanding is the key to human improvement leads to divergent but powerful critiques of the limitation of science-as-usual—one could say Newtonian science as usual. Also shared is the belief that understanding is an open-ended process, not susceptible to simple truths and im-

213

mediate non-enigmatic solutions. The diversity of these essays, given these common themes, awakens us to sources of criticisms that seem to pervade the entire anthology.

The differences among the authors in this section point to an additional commonality. The disagreements over what should be the means of improving science vary from the dialectic of ordinary existence presented by Leo Strauss to the acceptance of a new evolutionary perception of science and mind envisioned by Thomas Landon Thorson. The distinction of three levels of knowledge presented by Dante Germino differs (not in actuality, but in conception) greatly from Ellis Sandoz's integration of reason. The need for new direction is shared along with the belief that the new direction requires an extension of understanding beyond scientific theory to the establishment of our purpose. This need for establishing a purpose for political science looms behind the many forms of disaffection within the discipline.

Strauss's essay provides a summary of a major orientation toward political science which has long challenged behavioralism. Known as "the Teacher" because of his impact in establishing the school of Straussians, his arguments take on new force in the setting of post-behavioral discord. He traces the problems within political science to climates of opinion long preceding contemporary difficulties, to the point at which science and democracy merged into faith in earthly perfectibility. He sees the crises of our time as one affecting political science and society at once. The return to classical philosophy, not with blind acceptance but rather as a guide, is his prescription. Aristotle provides a guide to appropriate *searching* for understanding. The role of common existence is fully recognized.

Political philosophy, political theory, and ideology are distinguished by Germino in order to specify the role each can and should play in the development of knowledge and in human existence. Focusing most extensively on political philosophy, he contrasts Eric Voegelin's philosophy for the few with Hegel's universalism to describe the inevitable tension in political philosophy which must somehow be reconciled. Political philosophy is described as the contemplative interpretation of the knowledge captured in political theory. Ideology is action-related political thought. The justification for pursuing any of these options is *tout court*, their eventual applicability in terms of human guidance.

In striking contrast to these positions is Thorson's excursion into biopolitics. His essay focuses on the physical development of man and its implications for political and moral learning. His positive perspective on the future reflects the effort to reinforce the potential of again treating political science as the master science. This new science is based on Thorson's view that man is a rule-making, deliberating animal who can—who must—replace instinct with reason. As the master science, this new political science must be an integrative, interdisciplinary one. The improvement now possible over the work of Aristotle and later theorists grows from the fact that man's present perspective—his place in the evolutionary process and his ability to observe nature from a larger perspective—makes it possible for him to develop a new logic of recommendation, employing reason in determining normative goals, developing a new philosophy and political philosophy as the new political science. Out of this serious evolutionary approach comes a merger of the two cultures of the sciences and the humanities and, what is more, a sociogenetic approach to thought which permits man to see and to use natural laws in a new perspective.

The thrust of Sandoz's essay is toward a general redevelopment of political theory, heavily adapting the conceptions of Eric Voegelin to fill the gap generally left by behavioralism. He marks the need for such theory with the words of those who led the behavioral revolution, arguing that those who dismissed Voegelin at the commencement of the behavioral revolution could do no better than concentrate on his arguments now that the revolution has come full circle. He is disturbed, however, by the fact that the new post-behavioral stance of the behavioralists seems to discount and even continually attack all but a special few normative theorists. The position of Voegelin is presented as compatible with science. Its advantage is its capacity to permit the pursuit of many divergent approaches to political analysis in the search for political knowledge. It is an "approach" with many approaches, interested in grounding all knowledge in reality while remaining unwilling to limit its sources to any single prevailing method. The position is developed from Voegelin's expansive notion of human reason.

.11. Political Philosophy and the Crisis of Our Time*

LEO STRAUSS

THE CRISIS of our time has its core in the doubt of what we can call "the modern project." That modern project was successful to a considerable extent. It has created a new kind of society, a kind of society that never was before. But the inadequacy of the modern project, which has now become a matter of general knowledge and of general concern, compels us to entertain the thought that this new kind of society, our kind of society, must be animated by a spirit other than that which has animated it from the beginning. Now this modern project was originated by modern political philosophy, by the kind of political philosophy which emerged in the sixteenth and seventeenth centuries. The end result of modern political philosophy is the disintegration of the very idea of political philosophy. For most political scientists today, political philosophy is not more than ideology or myth.

We have to think of the restoration of political philosophy. We have to go back to the point where the destruction of political philosophy began, to the beginnings of modern political philosophy, when modern philosophy still had to fight against the older kind of political philosophy, classical political philosophy, the political philosophy originated by Socrates and elaborated above all by Aristotle. At that time, the quarrel of the ancients and the moderns took

*Adapted from Howard Spaeth, ed., *The Predicament of Modern Politics* (Detroit: University of Detroit Press, 1964). Reprinted with permission from the publisher and the author.

place, which is generally known only as a purely literary quarrel in France and in England, the most famous document in England being Swift's *Battle of the Books*. It was, in fact, not merely a literary quarrel. It was fundamentally a quarrel between modern philosophy, or science, and the older philosophy, or science. The quarrel was completed only with the work of Newton, which seemed to settle the issue entirely in favor of the moderns. Our task is to reawaken that quarrel, now that the modern answer has been given the opportunity to reveal its virtues and to do its worst to the old answer for more than three centuries.

I

The assertion that we are in the grip of a crisis is hardly in need of proof. Every day's newspapers tell us of another crisis, and all these little daily crises can easily be seen to be parts, or ingredients, of the one great crisis, the crisis of our time. The core of that crisis, I submit, consists in the fact that what was originally a political philosophy has turned into an ideology. That crisis was diagnosed at the end of World War I by Spengler as a going down or decline of the West. Spengler understood by the West one culture among a small number of high cultures. But the West was for him more than one high culture among a number of them. It was for him the comprehensive culture, the only culture which had conquered the earth. Above all, it was the only culture which was open to all cultures, which did not reject the other cultures as forms of barbarism, or tolerate them condescendingly as underdeveloped. It is the only culture which has acquired full consciousness of culture as such. Whereas culture originally meant the culture of the human mind, the derivative and modern notion of culture necessarily implies that there is a variety of equally high cultures. But, precisely since the West is the culture in which culture reaches full self-consciousness, it is the final culture; the owl of Minerva begins its flight in the dusk. The decline of the West is identical with the exhaustion of the very possibility of high culture. The highest possibilities of man are exhausted. But men's highest possibilities cannot be exhausted as long as there are still high human tasks, as long as the fundamental riddles which confront man have not been solved to the extent to which they can be solved. We may, therefore, say—appealing to the authority of science in our age—that Spengler's analysis and prediction is wrong. Our highest authority, natural science, considers itself susceptible of infinite progress. And this claim does not make sense, it seems, if the fundamental riddles are solved. If science is susceptible of infinite progress, there cannot be a meaningful end or completion of history. There can only be a brutal stopping of man's onward march through natural forces acting by themselves or directed by human brains and hands.

The crisis of the West consists in the West having become uncertain of its purpose. The West was once certain of its purpose, of a purpose in which all men could be united. Hence, it had a clear vision of its future as the future of mankind. We no longer have that certainty and that clarity. Some of us even despair of the future. This despair explains many forms of contemporary Western degradation. This is not meant to imply that no society can be healthy unless it is dedicated to a universal purpose, to a purpose in which all men can be united. A society may be tribal and yet healthy. But a society which was accustomed to understand itself in terms of a universal purpose cannot lose faith in that purpose without becoming completely bewildered. We find such a universal purpose expressly stated in our immediate past; for instance, in famous official declarations made during the two world wars. These declarations merely restate the purpose stated originally by the most successful form of modern political philosophy: a kind of that political philosophy which aspired to build on the foundation laid by classical political philosophy, but in opposition to the structure erected by classical political philosophy, a society superior in truth and justice to the society toward which the classics aspired.

According to that modern project, philosophy or science was no longer to be understood as essentially contemplative, but as active. It was to be in the service of the relief of man's estate, to use Bacon's beautiful phrase. It was to be cultivated for the sake of human power. It was to enable man to become the master and the owner of nature through the intellectual conquest of nature. Philosophy or science, which was originally the same thing, should make possible progress toward an ever greater prosperity. Thus, everyone would share in all the advantages of society or life, and therewith make true the full meaning of the natural right of everyone to comfortable self-preservation (Locke's phrase) and all that that right entails, and the natural right of everyone to develop all his faculties fully, in concert with everyone else's doing the same. The progress toward an ever greater prosperity would thus become, or render possible, progress toward an ever greater freedom and justice. This progress would necessarily be progress toward a society embracing equally all human beings, a universal league of free and equal nations, each nation consisting of free and equal men and women. For it had come to be believed that the prosperous, free, and just society in a single country, or in a few countries, is not possible in the long run. To make the world safe for the Western democracies, one must make the whole globe democratic, each country in itself, as well as the society of nations. Good order in one country, it was thought, presupposes good order in all countries and among all countries. The movement toward the universal society, or the universal state, was thought to be guaranteed not only by the rationality, the universal validity of the goal, but also because the movement toward that goal seemed to be the movement of the large majority of men, on behalf of the large majority of men. Only those small groups of men, who hold in thrall many millions of their fellow human beings and who defend their own antiquated interests, resist that movement.

The experience of Communism has provided the Western movement with a twofold lesson: a political lesson, a lesson regarding what to expect and what to do in the foreseeable future, and a lesson regarding the principle of politics. For the foreseeable future, there cannot be a universal state, unitary or federative. Apart from the fact that there does not exist now a universal federation of nations, but only one of those nations which are called peace-loving, the federation that does exist masks the fundamental cleavage. If that federation is taken too seriously, as a milestone of man's onward march toward the perfect and, hence, universal society, one is bound to take great risks, supported by nothing but an inherited and perhaps antiquated hope, and thus endanger the very progress one endeavors to bring about. It is imaginable that in the face of the danger of thermonuclear destruction, a federation of nations, however incomplete, would outlaw wars. That is to say, wars of aggression. But this means that it acts on the assumption that all present boundaries are just, in accordance with the self-determination of nations. This assumption is a pious fraud, the fraudulence of which is more evident than its piety. In fact, the only changes of the present boundaries which are provided for are those not disagreeable to the Communists. One must also not forget the glaring disproportion between the legal equality and the factual inequality of the confederates. This factual inequality is recognized in the expression "underdeveloped nations," an expression, I have been told, coined by Stalin. The expression implies the resolve to develop them fully. That is to say, to make them either Communist or Western. And this despite the fact that the West claims to stand for cultural pluralism. Even if one could still contend that the Western purpose is as universal as the Communist, one must rest satisfied for the foreseeable future with a practical particularism. The situation resembles the one, as has often been said, which existed during those centuries when both Christianity and Islam each raised its claim, but each had to be satisfied with uneasily coexisting with its antagonist. All this amounts to saying that for the foreseeable future political society remains what it always has been: a partial or particular society whose most urgent and primary task is its self-preservation and whose highest task is its self-improvement. As for the meaning of self-improvement, we may observe that the same experience which has made the West doubtful of the viability of a world society has made it doubtful of the belief that affluence is a sufficient and even necessary condition of happiness and justice. Affluence does not cure the deepest evils.

I must say a few words about another ingredient of the modern project, and this needs a somewhat more detailed discussion. Very briefly, we can say that the modern project was distinguished from the earlier view by the fact that it implied that the improvement of society depends decisively on institutions, political or economic, as distinguished from the formation of character. An implication of this view was the simple separation—as distinguished from a distinction—of law from morality. Beyond positive law, there is a sphere of enlightenment indeed; that is to say, of a purely theoretical education as distinguished from moral education or formation of character. We may illustrate this by the example of one of the heroes of that modern project, by the example of Hobbes. Hobbes was, of course, not a simple absolutist who was charmed by Nero and such people. Hobbes wanted to have enlightened absolute sovereigns, "enlightened despots," as they came to be called. But his whole construction was of such a kind that he guaranteed only the possibility and necessity of despotism. The enlightened character of the despot remained a mere matter of hope.

Now this situation is repeated in a different way in the development of modern liberal democracy. Liberal democracy claims to be responsible government, a political order in which the government is responsible to the governed. The governed, of course, also have some responsibility to the government; the governed are supposed to obey the laws. But the key point is this: in order to be responsible, the government must have no secrets from the governed. "Open covenants openly arrived at"—the famous formula of President Wilson expresses this thought most clearly. Of course, liberal democracy also means limited government, the distinction between the public and the private. Not only must the private sphere be protected by the law, but it must also be understood to be impervious to the law. The laws must protect the sphere in which everyone may act and think as he pleases, in which he may be as arbitrary and prejudiced as he likes. "My home is my castle." But this is not simply true. My home is not simply my castle; it may be entered with a search warrant. The true place of secrecy is not the home but the voting booth. We can say the voting booth is the home of homes, the seat of sovereignty, the seat of secrecy. The sovereign consists of the individuals who are in no way responsible, who can in no way be held responsible: the irresponsible individual. This was not simply the original notion of liberal democracy. The original notion was that this sovereign individual was a conscientious individual, the individual limited and guided by his conscience.

It is perfectly clear that the conscientious individual creates the same difficulty as Hobbes's enlightened despot. You cannot give a legal definition of what constitutes the conscientious individual. You cannot limit voting rights to conscientious people as you can limit voting rights by property qualifications, literacy tests, and the like. Conscientiousness can only be fostered by nonlegal means, by moral education. For this no proper provision is made, and the change in this respect is well known to all. This change which has taken place and is still taking place may be called the decline of liberal democracy into permissive egalitarianism. Whereas the core of liberal democracy is the conscientious individual, the core of permissive egalitarianism is the individual with his urges. We only have to take the case of the conscientious objector; whatever you may think of conscientious objectors, there is no doubt that they are people who are perfectly willing to lay down their lives for something which they regard as right. The man who wants to indulge his urges does not have the slightest intention to sacrifice his life, and hence also his urges, to the satisfaction of his urges. This is the moral decline which has taken place.

Let me illustrate this great change by another example, the concept of culture. In its original meaning, it meant *the* culture of the human mind. By virture of a change which took place in the nineteenth century, it became possible to speak of culture in the plural (the cultures). What has been done on a grand scale, especially by Spengler, has been repeated on a somewhat lower level, but with at least as great effect, by such anthropologists as Ruth Benedict. What, then, does culture mean today? In anthropology, and in certain parts of sociology and political science, "culture" is, of course, always used in the plural, and in such a way that you have a culture of suburbia, a culture of juvenile gangs, nondelinquent and even delinquent. And you can say, according to this recent notion of culture, there is not a single human being who is not cultured because he belongs to a culture.

Looking forward to the end of the road, one can say that according to the view now prevailing in the social sciences every human being who is not an inmate of a lunatic asylum is a cultured human being. At the frontiers of research, of which we hear so much today, we find the interesting question whether the inmates of lunatic asylums also do not have a culture of their own.

Let me now return to my argument. The doubt of the modern project, which is today quite widespread, is not merely a strong but vague feeling. It has acquired the status of scientific exactitude. One may wonder whether there is a single social scientist left who would assert that the universal and prosperous society constitutes the rational solution of the human problem. For present-day social science admits and even proclaims its inability to validate any value judgments proper. The teaching originated by modern political philosophy, those heroes of the seventeenth century, in favor of the universal and prosperous society has admittedly become an ideology. That is to say, a teaching not superior in truth and justice to any other among the innumerable ideologies. Social science which studies all ideologies is itself free from all ideological biases. Through this Olympian freedom it overcomes the crisis of our time. That crisis may destroy the conditions of social science; it cannot affect the validity of its findings. Social science has not always been as skeptical or as restrained as it has become during the last two generations. The change in the character of social science is not unconnected with the change in the status of the modern project. The modern project was originated by philosophers, and it was originated as something required by nature, by natural rights. The project was meant to satisfy, in the most perfect manner, the most powerful and natural needs of men. Nature was to be conquered for the sake of man, who was supposed to possess a nature, an unchangeable nature. The originators of the project took it for granted that philosophy and science are identical. After some time, it appeared that the conquest of nature requires the conquest of human nature too and, in the first place, the questioning of the unchangeability of human nature. After all, an unchangeable human nature might set absolute limits to progress. Accordingly, the natural needs of men could no longer direct the conquest of nature. The direction had to come from reason as distinguished from nature, from the rational "Ought" as distinguished from the neutral "Is." Thus, philosophy, logic, ethics, aesthetics, as the study of the "Ought" or the norms, became separated from science as the study of the "Is." While the study of the "Is," or science, succeeded ever more in increasing man's power, the ensuing discredit of reason precluded distinction between the wise, or right, and the foolish, or wrong, use of power. Science, separated from philosophy, cannot teach wisdom. There are still some people who believe that this predicament will disappear as soon as social science and psychology have caught up with physics and chemistry. This belief is wholly unreasonable. For social science and psychology, however perfected, being sciences, can only bring about a still further increase of man's power. They will enable man to manipulate men still better than ever before. They will as little teach man how to use his power over men or non-men as physics and chemistry do. The people who indulge this hope have not grasped the bearing of the distinction between facts and values, which they preach all the time. This is, indeed, the core of modern science, of modern social science as it has finally developed in the last two generations: the distinction between facts and values, with the understanding that no distinction between good or bad values is rationally possible. Any end is as defensible as any other. From the point of view of reason, all values are equal. The task with which academic teachers in the social sciences are concerned is primarily to face this issue posed by the fact-value distinction. I believe that one can show that this fundamental premise of the present-day social sciences is untenable, and that one can show it on a variety of grounds. But I am now concerned with a somewhat broader issue.

When we reflect on the fact-value distinction, we see one element of it that is quite striking. The citizen does not make the fact-value distinction. He is as sure that he can reasonably distinguish between good and bad, just and unjust, as he can distinguish between true and false, or as he can judge so-called factual statements. The distinction between facts and values is alien to the citizen's understanding of political things. The distinction between facts and values becomes necessary, it seems, only when the citizen's understanding of political things is replaced by the specifically scientific understanding. The scientific understanding implies, then, a break with the pre-scientific understanding. Yet, at the same time, it remains dependent on the pre-scientific understanding. I may illustrate this by a most simple example. If someone is sent out by a sociology department to interview people, he is taught all kinds of things; he is given very detailed instructions. But one thing he is not told: address your questions to people, to human beings, and not to dogs, trees, cats, and so on. Furthermore, he is not even told how to tell human beings from dogs. This knowledge is presupposed. It is never changed, never refined, never affected by anything he learns in social science classes. This is only the most massive example of how much allegedly self-sufficient scientific knowledge presupposes of "a priori" knowledge, of pre-scientific knowledge which is not questioned for one moment in the whole process of science. Now, regardless of whether the superiority of the scientific understanding to the pre-scientific understanding can be demonstrated or not, the scientific understanding is surely secondary or derivative. Hence, social science cannot reach clarity about its doings if it does not dispose of a coherent and comprehensive understanding of what one may call the common sense understanding of political things which precedes all scientific understanding; in other words, if we do not primarily understand political things as they are experienced by the citizen or statesman. Only if it disposes of such a coherent and comprehensive understanding of its basis or matrix can it possibly show the legitimacy and make intelligible the character of that peculiar modification of the primary understanding of political things which is the scientific understanding. This, I believe, is an evident necessity if social science or political science is to be or to become a rational enterprise. Being a modification of the primary understanding of political things, it must be understood as such a modification. We must understand the pre-scientific, the common-sense understanding, the citizen's understanding of political things before we can truly understand what the modification effected by scientific understanding means.

But how can we get that understanding? How can our poor powers be sufficient for an elaboration of the pre-scientific primary citizens' understanding of political things? Fortunately for us, this terrific burden, the most basic work which can be done and must be done in order to make political science and, therefore, also the other social sciences truly sciences, rational enterprises, has been done. It has been done by Aristotle in his *Politics*. That work supplies us with the classic and unforgettable analysis of the primary understanding of political phenomena.

II

This assertion is exposed to a very great variety of seemingly devastating objections. But, before presenting in the next section what this enterprise, Aristotelian political science, means, I would like to introduce a strict *ad hominem* argument in order to lead, as it were, the now preponderant part in the profession, the so-called behavioralists, if they are willing to listen to an argument, to a somewhat better understanding of what they would do if they were well advised. When you look around, I think you can say with very few exceptions political philosophy has disappeared. Political philosophy, the decay of political philosophy into ideology, reveals itself today most obviously in the fact that in both research and teaching political philosophy has been replaced by the history of political philosophy. Many of you have read or used the famous work by Sabine, and you only have to read the preface of Sabine to see that what I am going to say is simply correct. Now, what does this substitution of the history of political philosophy for political philosophy mean? It is, strictly speaking, absurd to replace political philosophy by the history of political philosophy. It means to replace a doctrine which claims to be true by a survey of errors, and that is exactly what Sabine, for example, does. So, political philosophy cannot be replaced by the history of political philosophy.

The discipline which takes the place of political philosophy is the one which shows the impossibility of political philosophy, and that discipline is, of course, logic. What, for the time being, is still tolerated under the name, "history of political philosophy," will find its place within a rational scheme of research and teaching in footnotes to the chapters in logic textbooks which deal with the distinction between factual judgments and value judgments. These footnotes will supply slow learners with examples of the faulty transition by which political philosophy stands or falls, from factual judgments to value judgments. They will give examples from Plato, Aristotle, Locke, Hume, or Rousseau and will show when and where these famous men committed a blunder every ten-year-old child now knows how to avoid. Yet, it would be wrong to believe that in the new dispensation, according to the demands of logical positivism or behavioral science, the place once occupied by political philosophy is filled entirely by logic, however enlarged. A considerable part of the matter formerly treated by political philosophy is now treated by non-philosophic political science, which forms part of social science. This new political science is concerned with discovering laws of political behavior and, ultimately, universal laws of political behavior. Lest it mistake the peculiarities of the politics of the times and the places in which social science is at home for the character of all politics, it must study also the politics of other climes and other ages. The new political science thus becomes dependent upon a kind of study which belongs to the comprehensive enterprise called universal history. Now, it is controversial whether history can be modeled on the natural sciences or not, and, therefore, whether the aspiration of the new political science to become scientific in the sense of the natural sciences is sound.

At any rate, the historical studies in which the new political science must engage must become concerned not only with the workings of institutions, but with the ideologies informing these institutions as well. Within the context of these studies, the meaning of an ideology is primarily the meaning in which its adherents understand it. In some cases, the ideologies are known to have been originated by outstanding men. In these cases, it becomes necessary to consider whether and how the ideology as conceived by the originator was modified by its adherents. For, precisely, if only the crude understanding of ideologies can be politically effective, it is necessary to grasp the characteristics of crude understanding. If what they call the routinization of charisma is a permitted theme, the vulgarization of thought ought to be a permitted theme also. One kind of ideology consists of the teachings of the political philosophers. These teachings may have played only a minor political role, but one cannot know this before one knows these doctrines solidly. This solid knowledge consists primarily in understanding the teachings of the political philosophers as they themselves meant them. Surely, every one of them was mistaken in believing that his teaching was a sound teaching regarding political things. Through a reliable tradition we know that this belief forms part of a rationalization, but the process of rationalization is not so thoroughly understood that it would not be worthwhile to study it in the case of the greatest minds. For all we know, there may be various kinds of rationalizations, etc. It is, then, necessary to study the political philosophies, not only as they were understood by their originators, in contradistinction to the way in which they were understood by their adherents and various kinds of their adherents, but also by their adversaries and even by detached or indifferent bystanders or historians. For indifference does not offer a sufficient guarantee against the danger that one identifies the view of the originator with a compromise between the views of his adherents and those of his adversaries. The general understanding of the political philosophies which is then absolutely necessary on the basis of behavioral political science may be said to have been rendered possible today by the shaking of all traditions; the crisis of our time may have the accidental advantage of enabling us to understand in an untraditional, a fresh manner what was hitherto understood only in a traditional, derivative manner.

To the extent to which the social scientist succeeds in this kind of study, which is required of him by the demands of his own science, he not only enlarges the horizon of present-day social science; he even transcends the limitations of that social science.

For he learns to look at things in a manner which is, as it were, forbidden to the social scientist. He will have learned from his logic that his science rests on certain hypotheses, certainties, or assumptions. He learns now to suspend these assumptions because, as long as he maintains them, he has no access to his subject matter. He is thus compelled to make the assumptions of social science his theme. Far from being merely one of the innumerable themes of social science, history of political philosophy, and not logic, proves to be the pursuit concerned with the presuppositions of social science. These presuppositions prove to be modifications of the principles of modern political philosophy, which, in their turn, prove to be modifications of the principles of classical political philosophy. To the extent to which a behavioral political scientist takes his science and its requirements seriously, he is compelled to engage in such a study, in such a historical study of his own discipline, and he cannot conduct that study without questioning the dogmatic premises of his own science. Therewith, his horizon is enlarged. He must at least consider the possibility that the older political science was sounder and truer than what is regarded as political science today.

Such a return to classical political philosophy is both necessary and tentative or experimental. Not in spite, but because it is tentative, it must be carried out seriously; that is to say, without squinting at our present-day predicament. There is no danger that we can ever become oblivious of this predicament, since that predicament is the incentive to our whole concern with the classics. We cannot reasonably expect that a fresh understanding of classical political philosophy will supply us with recipes for today's use. The relative success of modern political philosophy has brought into being a kind of society wholly unknown to the classics, a kind of society in which the classical principles as stated and elaborated by the classics are not immediately applicable. Only we living today can possibly find a solution to the problems of today. An adequate understanding of the principles, as elaborated by the classics, may be the indispensable starting point for an adequate analysis, to be achieved by us, of present-day society in its peculiar character, and for the wise application, to be achieved by us, of these principles to our tasks.

III

Let us look at the specific grounds on which it is claimed that Aristotle's political philosophy has been refuted. The most common reason is that modern natural science, or modern cosmology, having refuted Aristotelian cosmology (e.g., by demonstrating "evolution"), has therewith refuted the principle or the basis of Aristotelian political philosophy. Aristotle took for granted the permanence of the species, and we "know" that the species are not permanent. But even granting that evolution is an established fact, that man has come into being out of another species, man is still essentially different from non-man. The fact of essential differences—the fact that there are "forms"—has in no way been refuted by evolutionism. The starting point of Aristotle, as well as of Plato, is that the whole consists of heterogeneous beings; that there is a noetic heterogeneity of beings, this common sensible notion on which we fall back all the time and this has in no way been refuted. I remind you of the famous seventeenth-century criticism of formal causes, a criticism, which was properly presented in its most impressive form by a comic poet, Molière, of the famous scholastic question, "Why does opium make men sleep?," and the answer, "*Quia est in eo virtus dormitiva, cujus est natura sensus assoupire*" (Because it has a dormitive power, a sleep-making power, the nature of which consists in putting the senses to sleep). This has been a famous joke repeated in this or that form innumerably often. It amounts to saying that reference to formal causes is in no way an explanation. But the joke is not so good as it appears at first hearing: if opium did not have sleep-making power, we would not be interested in it, if the ingredients of opium did not as such have this power; when you put together the elements out of which opium consists, then this whole has a character which the elements do not have, and this character is what makes opium opium. What is true of opium is true of man, as well as of any other being. It is, then, the notion of essence, of essential difference, which distinguishes the Aristotelian and the Platonic teaching from that of the characteristically modern philosophy, and especially modern science. If there are essential differences, there can be essential differences between the common good and the private good. However far the defeat of Aristotle's cosmology may extend, it does not go to the length of having destroyed the evidence of the concept of essential differences and, therefore, of essences.

The second argument, which is very common, is that Aristotle has been refuted because he was anti-democratic. I admit the fact, for I do not believe that the premises upon which some of our contemporaries seem to act—democracy is good and Aristotle is good—lead validly to the conclusion that Aristotle was a democrat. He was not a democrat. But on what grounds? Democracy meant at all times, in Greek times as well as today, the rule of all. But this is too abstract, because there is never unanimity, or hardly ever. In fact, in a democracy the majority rules. Yet, if there are stable majorities, then this stable majority will be in control in a democracy. What is that stable majority? Aristotle, in his great clarity and simplicity, said that in every *polis*, in every political society, there are two groups of people, the rich and the poor, and whatever may be the reason, the majority are the poor. Therefore, democracy is the rule of the poor. "Poor" does not mean "beggars." The poor are the people who have to earn their living, who cannot live as gentlemen. Because they are poor, they do not have the leisure for acquiring education, both sufficient theoretical and practical education, neither in maturity nor as children. They have no time for it; hence they are uneducated. And no man in his senses would say that the political community should be ruled by the uneducated. This simple argument is in no way vicious. What is our argument against it?

Aristotle took something for granted which we can no longer take for granted. He took for granted that every economy would be an economy of scarcity where the majority of men do not have leisure. We have discovered an economy of plenty and, in an economy of plenty, it is no longer true that the majority of people have to be uneducated. This is a perfectly legitimate reply to Aristotle as far as it goes. But we must see what precisely has changed. Not the principles of justice, they are the same. What has changed are the circumstances. On the very principle of justice, as Aristotle understood it, one would have to say that the argument regarding democracy as he stated it has to be modified because we have an economy of plenty. Yet this difference of circumstances is due to the modern economy, which in its turn is based on modern technology, which in its turn is based on modern science. Here we touch again on the fundamental difference between Aristotle and modern thought. A new interpretation of science, opposed to the Aristotelian interpretation, came to the fore in the seventeenth century in the works of Bacon, Descartes, and Hobbes. According to that new interpretation, science exists for the sake of human power and is not for the sake of understanding, as understanding, or of contemplation. As for this notion of science which is underlying the modern development, we have become doubtful whether it is as sound as it appeared for many generations. At the very latest, the explosion of the first atomic bomb made people doubtful whether the unlimited progress of science and technology is something unqualifiedly good. Not more than this is needed in order to see that Aristotle might have had a point when he denied that science is essentially in the service of the increase of human power.

Aristotle's non-democratic or anti-democratic view has apparently still another basis. This is his assumption, which he thought to be a fact, that men are by nature unequal in politically relevant respects. That they are unequal in regard to beauty would not be important, because we do not ordinarily elect officials on the ground of their being very handsome. But that there is a natural inequality regarding understanding is politically relevant. This kind of natural inequality can hardly be denied. It is, of course, recognized by modern democracy, as is shown by our speaking of equality of opportunity, which implies that differently gifted people are supposed to do very different things with the opportunity offered. Differently stated, modern democracy is representative democracy, meaning a democracy which elects the people whom it believes are above the average. Modern democracy as representative democracy is opposed to direct democracy.

Another objection to Aristotle—and we come somewhat closer to the key issues—is that Aristotle's whole political philosophy is narrow, or provincial. After all, he was a Greek, and the subject matter of his work is the Greek city-state, one particular form of human organization which was as important historically as any other, but which is just one among very many. This view is very common today, but it is not correct. Aristotle is not concerned with the Greek city-state. When you read the second book of the *Politics*, you see that he regarded a city like Carthage, which was a Phoenician city, as roughly equal to Sparta and definitely superior to Athens. The city-state is, then, not essentially Greek. This, however, is a minor difficulty. A more serious difficulty is this:

When we speak of the city-state, we imply that there is such a thing called the "state," of which there are *n* various forms, one of them being the city-state. This thought cannot be translated into Greek; that is, Aristotle's Greek. This concept of "state" is wholly alien to his thought. When we speak of "state" today, we ordinarily understand state in contradistinction to society. You will find it asserted in all textbooks that the Greek city—or let me now use the Greek word, "*polis*"—is not a state distinguished from a society. The *polis*, we may say, antedates the distinction of state and society. Aristotle does make a distinction between the *polis* and other associations or partnerships, but he does not bundle them all together under the title, "society," in contradistinction to the *polis*. His thought can be understood easily if you only look at the right place for the modern equivalent of the concept of *polis*. That equivalent is our modern term, "the country." When you say the country is in danger, you do not make a distinction between the state and society. The country is the modern equivalent to what Aristotle understood by the city. Or look at another saying of somewhat questionable morality which still has a certain reasonableness, "my country right or wrong." You cannot possibly say, "my state right or wrong," or "my society right or wrong"; it does not sound right. "Country" is, then, truly the modern equivalent of "city." The difference is by no means unimportant. The difference indicates that the city is an urban association. The country, as the word indicates, is not necessarily urban, and this is surely due to the feudal past of modern nations. We are separated from Aristotle by a gulf which we must somehow bridge if we wish to understand him. Therefore, we must look for equivalents in our experience in order to understand, to get the experiential analogue to what Aristotle means when he speaks of the *polis*.

Let me now turn to Aristotle's own analysis of the *polis*. What is the character of the *polis*? What is the essential difference between the *polis* and all other associations? Aristotle answers: The end of the *polis* is happiness. All other associations serve a special purpose. The political society is the only association which is directed toward the complete human good, and that is called happiness. Happiness means the practice of moral virtue above everything else, the doing of noble deeds. Aristotle assumes something which is today absolutely controversial, especially in scientific circles, but which he assumes is not controversial at all among reasonable people; namely, what happiness is. To develop this point fully, we would have to discuss the chapter of his *Rhetoric* where he speaks so clearly and beautifully about what happiness is. When reading that chapter, you will see that our ordinary notion of happiness is not different from the ordinary notion analyzed by Aristotle. What do we mean when calling a man happy? A man who has friends, who has good friends, who has many friends, who has children, and good children, who is healthy, reasonably wealthy, and so on. There is nothing particularly Greek about this. When we call a man happy, we mean, in the first place, that he is a contented man. But, we see from time to time people who are of a very low grade of understanding, perhaps moronic, who smile all the time. They are contented; yet no one would say that they are happy. We mean, then, by happiness a contentedness which is enviable, a reasonable contentedness. This is what all men understand by happiness, and, therefore, it is a good enough beginning for political philosophy, moral philosophy, to speak of happiness thus understood.

Yet, in modern times, surely from the seventeenth century onward, this beginning was questioned on a ground which, in present-day parlance, would be stated as follows:

Happiness is entirely subjective. What *A* understands by happiness differs from what *B* understands by happiness, and even what *A* understands by happiness is very different before he has had his dinner and after he has had his dinner. If happiness is entirely subjective, it can no longer be relevant for determining the common good. How then shall we find our bearing politically? The answer given by the founders of modern political philosophy was this: While happiness is radically subjective, the conditions of happiness are not. Whatever you may understand by happiness, in order to be happy you must be alive; second, you must be able to circulate; third, you must be able to pursue happiness as you understand happiness, and perhaps even as you understand happiness at the moment. So life, liberty, pursuit of happiness are the conditions of happiness, however you understand happiness. They constitute the objective conditions of happiness. They possess that objectivity, that universality, which happiness lacks. Therefore, the function of political society is not to take care that the citizens are happy, that they become doers of noble deeds, as Aristotle called it, but to create the conditions of happiness, to protect them, or to use a technical term, to protect the natural rights of man; for the natural rights of man in the modern sense of the meaning are the conditions of happiness in the sense indicated. Under no circumstance may political society impose any notion of happiness upon the citizenry, for any notion of happiness would be subjective and therefore arbitrary. People will then pursue happiness; each one as he understands happiness. They all strive for happiness. This striving is partly cooperative, but also partly competitive. This striving produces something like a web. This, I believe, is what is meant primarily by society, in contradistinction to the state.

If this analysis is in principle correct, we arrive at the following conclusion: the state is superior to society because its aim or end— the securing of the conditions of happiness, however happiness may be understood—is objective, that is, the same for all. On the other hand, society is superior to the state because only as members of society, as distinguished from the state, are we concerned with the end, with happiness itself, and not with the conditions of happiness or the means of happiness. From this point of view, the public, the political, is in the service of the essentially private, of happiness, however one may understand happiness. But this fact that from one point of view the state is superior to society, from another point of view that society is superior to the state, creates a great theoretical difficulty. The solution favored by modern social thought consists in postulating another basis, distinguished from state and society, a kind of matrix for both state and society; this, I believe, is the function of the modern concept of culture or civilization as terms susceptible of being used in the plural.

I have referred to these conditions of happiness, and I have indicated that what they meant were the natural rights, the rights of man. This doctrine, which was developed in the seventeenth and eighteenth centuries, reminds us, of course, of the traditional natural law teaching, the Thomistic teaching. Outside of Catholic circles, it is rarely admitted, although it is so obvious, that there is a radical difference between the natural law teaching of the seventeenth and eighteenth century, and the medieval and classic ancient teaching. To illustrate the difference very briefly by a simple formula, the name which came into use in the eighteenth century for natural law was the rights of man, whereas the traditional name was natural law.

First, "law" was replaced by "rights." When people spoke of law, they always meant the duties primarily, and the rights only derivatively. When Aristotle says that what the law does not command it forbids, he gives us a notion of what law originally meant. Second, "nature" is replaced by "man." In the older notion, natural law is part of a larger order, of a hierarchic order indicated by the word, "nature." In the modern view, nature has been replaced by man. Man, taken entirely by himself, is, as it were, the origin of the rights belonging to him. The term "rights of man" is the moral equivalent to that famous beginning of modern philosophy: Descartes' *ego cogitans*, the thinking ego. In Descartes' moral work, *The Passions of the Soul*, the word "duty" never occurs; but in the key passage the word "right" occurs, which I believe is very characteristic.

Let me return to the general reflection about the *polis*. We are frequently misled today by a kind of learning which, if kept in its place, is highly valuable. I mean what the historians and philologists tell us about the Greeks; yet this is not sufficient for understanding what men like Aristotle and Plato meant. We must make a distinction between the prephilosophic concept of the *polis* and the philosophic concept. I am concerned here only with the philosophic concept as developed by Aristotle especially. The philosophical concept of the *polis* is that the *polis* is the natural society, the society corresponding to the nature of man, society neither too small nor too large for man's reaching his perfection. Man's natural powers, especially his powers of knowing his fellow men and caring for them, are limited. Very roughly said, a *polis* is a society which is not too large for man, for the individual's power of knowing and actively caring. The *polis* is an association in which every man can know not every other—that would be a village—but an acquaintance of every other, so that he is in a position to find out for whom he votes; that is, to whom he entrusts his life and fortune. The present discussions about metropolitan areas rediscover to some extent what Aristotle meant by the *polis* as the natural association.

But is it sufficient to say that Aristotle's political philosophy is concerned with the *polis*? You would only have to read the beginning of every book of the *Politics*, except the first, in order to see that it is not sufficient. The *polis* is only a provisional indication. The proper subject of the *Politics* is called in Greek, "*politeia*," a derivative from the word, *polis*. The ordinary English translation is "constitution," which is a somewhat misleading translation because, when we speak of a constitution, we do not mean something like the constitution of an animal; we mean something like the law of the land, the fundamental law of the land. Incidentally, the historical origin of our concept of the constitution is the fundamental law. The *politeia*, as Aristotle meant it, has nothing to do with law; it is distinguished from all laws. One can render its meaning by words like the "political order" or the "political order which originates the laws including the so-called constitutional law," or perhaps more simply as the "regime." Examples are democracy, oligarchy, tyranny, etc. These phenomena originate law rather than being constituted by law. The character of the society is formed by the regime. Since there is a variety of regimes today, as well as at all times, the question inevitably arises: Which is the preferable regime? Or to state it with the proper simplicity, which is the best regime? This is, one can say, the most important question for Aristotle. He surely is greatly concerned with discovering the order of rank of the various regimes. One cannot know the truth about any regime if one does not know how good or bad it is. For example, you do not know anything, to speak of, about democracy if you do not know its virtues and defects. This simple fact points theoretically to the thought of the regime which has no defects, the best regime, and this is indeed the highest theme for Aristotle.

Let us return to the more practical level, to the variety of regimes. This is the subject of Aristotle; not the state, as the subject of political philosophy came to be called in the nineteenth century. The state as understood in these Victorian doctrines was something politically neutral, whereas the regime as Aristotle understands it is something politically divisive. It does not have to be divisive within a given society because all may be fully satisfied with the established regime. But it is in principle divisive because there will be other regimes elsewhere, and the claims of each of these regimes to be the best necessarily clash. Aristotle's political philosophy is political not only because of its subject matter, but because Aristotle is animated by the political passion, the concern for the best regime.

There is a certain difficulty here, a grave practical and moral problem, which Aristotle indicates in a way that seems to be quite academic. He says, citizen is relative to the regime; that is, a citizen in a democracy is not necessarily a citizen in an oligarchy, etc. But if citizen is relative to the regime, then surely good citizen is also relative to the regime. Here we see the great difference between the good citizen and the good man. The good man is not relative to a regime, whereas the good citizen necessarily is. This creates some difficulties for many modern readers, although if we look around us we can easily recognize present-day parallels. For example, a good Communist cannot be a good citizen in a democracy, and vice versa. The relation of the regime to what is not the regime, to "society," corresponds to the general metaphysical distinction used by Aristotle between form and matter. Metaphysical means the same as common sensible here. The regime gives to the city its form. What, then, is the matter? All kinds of things, but the most important are the people, or more simply, the inhabitants of the city considered as not affected and molded by the regime. Not the citizens as citizens, for who is and who is not a citizen is already determined by the regime. The form is higher in dignity than matter; for only the form is directly connected with the end. Therefore, the regime, and not the people on the subpolitical level, are connected with the end of civil society.

Again speaking empirically, or common sensibly, every society is characterized by the fact that it looks up to something. Even the society which is wholly materialistic looks up to materialism. Every human being is what he is by the fact that he looks up to something. Even if he does not look up to anything because he is a slave of his belly, for example, this is only a deficient mode of looking up to something. If we take a simple view of democracy, it looks up to equality, and this gives it its character. I have been told that the travelers of old China—a thousand years ago or more—when they came to a foreign country, to barbarians as they probably called them, they asked them first, "How do you greet or bow to your prince or king?" They were wiser than many present-day anthropologists, because their question was only a too-special form of the question of what do you look up to. Every society, or civilization as they say today, has its unity due to the fact that there is a certain *order* to the things which they cherish, to their values, to what they esteem. There would not be a unity if there were not one, and only one, thing which is at the top. This gives a society its character. Aristotle adds that there must be a harmony between that to which a society looks up and the preponderant part of a society, the part of society which sets its tone; that is, the regime. This, then, is the connection between the "end" and regime, the "form," the preponderant part, which may be the majority but need not be. There were societies in which a small part of the population was the preponderant or authoritative part. There is an essential connection between the *eidos*, the form, the character of a city, and the end to which the city is dedicated. This is an empirical proposition. Here we have come to the difficulty which even very good scholars sometimes fail to solve properly.

From his notion of the regime as *the* central and key political phenomenon, Aristotle apparently drew the conclusion that a change of regime transforms a given city into another city, and this seems to be abstruse. How can you say that Athens, when she became oligarchic, was no longer the same city as she was before that change? Aristotle's assertion seems to deny the obvious continuity of a city in spite of all changes of regime. Is it obviously not better to say that the same France which was first an absolute monarchy became thereafter a democracy, than to say that democratic France is a different country from monarchic France? Or generally stated, is it not better to say that the same substance of France takes on successively different forms, which, compared with the substance, are mere forms? Is this not the common-sensible way of saying it, as shown by the way in which people write a history of the French constitution, or of the English constitution: the one thing, the same substance, the English constitution, undergoes these and those changes. It goes without saying that Aristotle was not blind to the continuity of the "matter," as distinguished from the discontinuity of the forms. He did not say that the sameness of a city depends exclusively on the sameness of the regime. For, in that case, there would not be, for instance, more than one democratic city. If the form alone establishes the identity, then there can be only one democratic city. He said that the sameness of the city depends above all on the sameness of the regime, but not exclusively. Nevertheless, what he says runs counter to our notions. It does not run counter to our experience.

In order to see this, we must follow his presentation more closely than is usually done. Aristotle starts from an experience. Immediately after a city has become democratic, the democrats sometimes say of a certain act, such as a certain contractual obligation, debt, etc., that it is not an action of the city, but of the deposed oligarchs, or the deposed tyrant. The democrat, the partisan of democracy, implies that when there is no democracy there is no city which can act. It is, of course, no accident that Aristotle refers to a statement made by democrats as distinguished from oligarchs; Aristotle is always concrete. The oligarchs would not say that when there is a democracy there is no city. But they would say that the city has gone to pieces. This, however, leaves us wondering whether the city which is going to pieces can still be said simply to be. Let us say, then, that for the partisan of any regime, the city *is* only if it is informed by the regime which he favors. The moderate and sober people reject this extreme view and, therefore, say that the change of regime is a surface event which does not affect the being of the city at all. Those people will say that however relative the citizen may be to the regime, the good citizen is a man who serves his city well under any regime. We are very familiar with this, especially in countries where there have been changes of regime. Let us call these men the patriots, who say the fatherland is first, with the regime a strictly expediential and secondary consideration. The partisans will call the patriots turncoats, because if the regime changes the patriot changes his allegiance. Aristotle is neither a patriot in that simple sense, nor a partisan in that simple sense. He would disagree with both the partisans and the patriots. He says that a change of regime is much more radical than the patriots admit, but less radical than the partisans contend. Through a change of regime the city does not cease to be; the partisans go much too far. But the city becomes another city in a certain respect, in the most important respect. For with a change of regime, the political community becomes dedicated to an end radically different from its earlier end, and, therefore, it is the greatest and most fundamental change which a city can undergo. In making his apparently strange assertion, Aristotle thinks of the highest end to which a city can be dedicated; namely, human excellence. Is any change, he as it were asks us, which a city can undergo comparable in importance to its turning from nobility to baseness, or vice versa? We may say that his point of view is not that of the patriot, nor of the ordinary partisan, but that of the partisan of excellence. He does not say that through a change of regimes a city becomes another city in every respect. For instance, it will remain the same city with regard to obligations which the preceding regime has undertaken.

He fails to answer the question regarding treaty obligations not because he cannot answer it, as some people believe, but because it is not a political question strictly speaking, but rather, as he says, a legal question. Because he was a reasonable man, it is very easy to discern the principle which he would have followed in answering this legal question. If the deposed tyrant undertook obligations which are beneficial to the city, the city ought to honor these obligations. But if the tyrant undertook the obligations merely to feather his own nest or to pay for his bodyguard, then the city, of course, should not pay them.

In order to understand Aristotle's thesis regarding the supremacy of the regime, one has only to consider the phenomenon, which we all know, and of which we have heard so much, known by the name of loyalty. The loyalty demanded from every citizen is not mere loyalty to the bare country, to the country irrespective of the regime, but to the country *informed* by the regime, by the constitution. A fascist or Communist might claim that he undermines the Constitution of the United States out of loyalty to the United States. For, in his opinion, the Constitution is bad for the people of the United States. But his claim to be a loyal citizen will not be recognized. Someone might say that the Constitution could be changed constitutionally so that the regime would cease to be a liberal democracy and become either fascist or Communist, and that every citizen of the United States is then expected to be a loyal fascist or Communist. But no one loyal to liberal democracy, who knows what he is doing, would teach this doctrine, precisely because it is apt to undermine loyalty to liberal democracy. Only when a regime is in the state of complete decay can its transformation into another regime become publicly defensible.

We have come to distinguish between legality and legitimacy. Whatever is legal in a given society derives its ultimate legitimation from something which is the source of all law, ordinary or constitutional, from the legitimating principle—be it the sovereignty of the people, the divine right of kings, or whatever else. The legitimating principle is not simply justice, for there is a variety of principles of legitimacy. The legitimating principle is not natural law, for natural law is, as such, neutral as between democracy, aristocracy, and monarchy. The principle of legitimacy is in each case a specific notion of justice: justice democratically understood, justice oligarchically understood, justice aristocratically understood, etc. This is to say, every political society derives its character from a specific public or political morality, from what it regards as publicly defensible; and this means from what the preponderant part of society, not necessarily the majority, regards as just. A given society may be characterized by extreme permissiveness, but this very permissiveness is in need of being established and defended, and it necessarily has its limits. A permissive society which permits its members every sort of non-permissiveness will soon cease to be permissive. It will vanish from the face of the earth. Not to see the city in the light of the variety of regimes means not to look at the city as a political man; that is to say, as a man concerned with a specific public morality. The variety of specific public moralities, or of regimes, necessarily gives rise to the question of the best regime, for every kind of regime claims to be the best and, therefore, forces one to face these claims, to meet them by wondering whether a given regime is best or not.

Let me conclude with a remark about a seeming self-contradiction of Aristotle regarding the highest theme of his *Politics*. He bases his thematic discussion of the best regime on the principle that the highest end of man, happiness, is the same for the individual and the city. As he makes clear, this principle would be accepted as such by everyone because it is a common-sensible principle. The difficulty arises from the fact—and this arises more for Aristotle than for the ordinary citizen—that the highest end of the individual is contemplation, and not the doing of noble deeds. Aristotle seems to solve the difficulty by asserting that the city is as capable of the contemplative life as the individual. Yet it is obvious that the city is capable, at best, only of an analogue to the contemplative life. Aristotle reaches this apparent result only by an explicit abstraction appropriate to a political inquiry, strictly and narrowly conceived, from the full meaning of the best life of the individual. In such an inquiry, the transpolitical life, the superpolitical, the life of the mind in contradistinction to the political life, comes to sight only as a limit of the political. Man is more than the citizen or the city. Man transcends the city, however, only by what is best in him. This is reflected in the fact that there are examples of men of the highest excellence, whereas Aristotle has no example of cities of the highest excellence, cities informed by the best regime. Man transcends the city only by pursuing true happiness, not by pursuing happiness, however happiness may be understood.

.12. Two Conceptions of Political Philosophy

DANTE GERMINO

ALTHOUGH I have argued elsewhere[1] for the virtual identity of the terms "political theory" and "political philosophy," I have more recently come to the conclusion that it may be better to distinguish them.[2] For example, in an article for the new interdisciplinary journal on literary interpretation at the University of Virginia I argued as follows:

Political philosophy I shall take to be the most comprehensive manner of self-conscious reflection discovered and utilized by man in the consideration of his existence in community with his fellows. Political theory aspires to the same level of understanding and critical awareness as does political philosophy, but it may confine itself to the explicit elaboration of only a "segment" or dimension of man's political existence and so only implicitly contains the comprehensive reflection discovered in political philosophy proper. Political thought I take to mean any form of human speech about politics that has attained to such a level of coherence as to be recognizable as serious thought. In distinguishing these three terms, we have moved from a specific and limited to a general category; there are few political philosophers, a somewhat greater number of political theorists, and an exceedingly great number of political thinkers. All political philosophers are also political theorists (with reference to a segment of their teaching), but

---

[1] Dante Germino, *Beyond Ideology* (New York: Harper & Row, Publishers, 1967), chaps. 1, 2, and passim.

[2] Dante Germino, "Modernity in Western Political Thought," *New Literary History* 1 (Winter 1970): 293–310 at 293–95.

not all political theorists are political philosophers in the full sense. Both political philosophers and political theorists are political thinkers, but by no means all political thinkers are either political theorists or political philosophers. Political thinkers may be preachers, partisans, publicists, behavioral scientists, institutional analysts, ideologues, utopian dreamers, etc., instead of political philosophers or theorists.[3]

Elaborating on the above passage, I would hold with Eric Voegelin that philosophy is a "radical" enterprise in the sense that the philosopher himself is clear and explicit about the "roots" (*radices*) of his thinking,[4] and furthermore that he presents an entire intellectual and spiritual (*geistliche*) orientation toward existence grounded on an epistemology or theory of the consciousness. The true philosopher is free, insofar as a man can be, to "follow the truth wherever it may lead" (Jefferson) and therefore does not exhibit arbitrary arrests in his analysis dictated by nonphilosophical considerations, such as the assumptions of the conventional wisdom, or the pressures of outside authority. Philosophy, the philosophy of man— *philosophia peri ta anthropina*[5]—commands our "ultimate concern"; it matters fundamentally to our personal existence whether the results of the philosopher's investigations into the highest good are valid or not. In this sense, but only in this sense, philosophy resembles theology. Where it parts company with theology is in its refusal to play any apologetic role for a specific revealed religion, for to play such a role would inhibit its character of untrammeled critical thought. Nor does philosophy, when true to itself, emerge as advocate for a specific type of regime; this is the area of political doctrine. However, every philosopher is the "son of his time" (Hegel), and as such he may either unconsciously or deliberately endorse specific policies or trends. Such endorsement, however, forms no part of his philosophical work as such, except insofar as his philosophical principles clearly rule out certain practices which militate against man's humanity. Affirmatively, every philosophical teaching about politics contains a vision of the good society, but such teaching is presented with the full knowledge of the difficulties involved in fully or even substantially realizing this vision in history.

[3] Ibid., p. 294.
[4] Eric Voegelin, "In Memoriam Alfred Schutz," in *Anamnesis: Zur Theorie de Geschichte und Politik* (Munich: R. Piper & Co., 1966), p. 25.
[5] Aristotle, *Nichomachean Ethics*, 1181 b 15.

Political philosophy—and the masterworks of Plato, Aristotle, Machiavelli, Hobbes, Rousseau, and Hegel immediately come to mind here—is characterized by a remarkable sense of tension between the good, or "natural," and the practicable. The tension is difficult to maintain, however, and can easily collapse in favor either of status quo accommodation to the merely existent with all of its irrationality, contingency, and error, or of advocacy for the use of unlimited means to establish the philosophical city of God here and now. The question as to the area of maneuverability man's historical condition affords for the realization of the good society in time, is one of the cardinal questions explored by political philosophers.

Political *theory* is a relatively more bloodless affair than political philosophy, which commands, as Plato expressed so well, the involvement of the whole person insofar as he engages in critical self-conscious reflection on his condition. Philosophy, then, is the poetry, and theory and prose of man's inquiry into his world. *Theoria* originally meant the "beholding" or "observing" of a given segment of experience. The term implies the mood of the spectator rather than of the participant; detachment from the enterprise being observed is the key attitude of the "theorist." Thus, for example, Gaetano Mosca can offer up a "theory" of the ruling class without at the same time providing us with an explicit political philosophy, James Harrington may suggest a theory of the economic basis of political change; or more recently, theories of political development, setting forth the conditions for modernization, may be put forward by political scientists. "Theory," of course, has different connotations today for different practitioners of political science, depending on one's epistemology. A logical positivist will demand different tests of verification than will more broadly based followers of phenomenological philosophy or of psychoanalysis or of some form of the *philosophia perennis*. Nonetheless, all tend to agree that theories are designed to "explain" political behavior and events; theorists take as their problems relatively manageable chunks of political reality rather than that reality in its entirety. In the works of political philosophers political "theories" may be found (e.g., Aristotle's theory of "revolution"—really *stasis* or disintegration—or Rousseau's propositions about the relation of the size of a community to its form of government), but such works are not primarily given over to the elaboration of theories. Rather, it is the task of the political philosopher to supply the missing dimension of the work of the theorist by sketching in the contours of political reality apprehended as a *Gestalt*. The "arbitrary arrests" (Michael Oakeshott) in experience—resulting in the abstraction of certain elements from and the bracketing out of other aspects of reality for purposes of clarity and simplicity—characteristic of theory can be fruitful, but must be measured against the larger view. Of course, the philosopher is open to the charge of arrogance for implying that only he "sees life steady and sees it whole" (Matthew Arnold); if he made such a claim as a private privilege he would not be worth our attention. However, many of us return to Plato, Hegel, and others time and again, not because we find in their writings some precious, esoteric wisdom to be kept from the uninitiated, but because, whatever their relative deficiencies, we encounter explorations of political experience which surpass in depth, conceptual luminosity, and imaginative symbolic reconstruction anything we encounter elsewhere. Philosophy is not a private solipsistic enterprise. It must speak to the totality of our experience, or it will die.

In the remaining part of this paper, I propose to compare two conceptions of the role philosophy should play in relation to politics. One view is that of Hegel, whose relevance for our time is perhaps becoming increasingly evident. The other appears in the writings of Eric Voegelin, one of the most creative contemporary political philosophers.

According to Heinrich Heine, Hegel once elaborated on his famous dictum that "what is rational is real and what is real, rational" by adding that "what is rational must be."[6] Even if Heine's account of this conversation with Hegel were regarded as apocryphal, the addition is well in keeping with the general tenor of Hegel's account of history as the unfolding of reason and freedom in the modern state, which he understands in a special sense as the organized political community and culture which makes possible the synthesis of universality and particularity, of both individual aspirations and the requirements of the public interest.[7]

---

[6] "Was ist vernünftig, muss sein." From Dolf Starnberger, "Heine and Hegel," paper delivered to the 1970 Annual Meeting of the *Institut International de Philosophie Politique*, at the University of Heidelberg.

[7] See Dante Germino, "Hegel as a Political Theorist," *Journal of Politics* 31 (November 1969): 885–912 for references to Hegel's *Philosophy of Right* pertinent to this point.

Against this Hegelian "political rationalism,"[8] Voegelin uncompromisingly maintains opposition to the view that reality in the historical sense can conceivably become "rational." Indeed, he rejects on principle the Hegelian view of "rationality," finding it misconceived. For Voegelin, Hegel was driven by a monstrous intellectual lust for power to make the world over in his own image; the Hegelian *Weltgeist* is really Hegel's own *Geist*, he argues. As he expressed the matter in a recent manuscript entitled "On Hegel—A Study in Sorcery":

... Hegel ... wanted to become, not a man, but a Great Man ... Moreover, he did not want to become just any Great Man in history ... but the greatest of them all; and this position he could secure only by becoming the Great Man who abolishes history, ages, and epochs through his evocation of the Last Age that will forever after bear his imprint.... To gain power over history, by putting an end to history with its dire motion and boredom was the driving force of Hegel's sorcery.[9]

Eric Voegelin explicitly contrasts his own conception of philosophy—or, better, the conception of philosophy he discovers Plato and Aristotle to have articulated in a paradigmatic way—with that found in Hegel. Philosophy is, quite literally, the "*love* of wisdom"; wisdom (*sophia*) is not "vain and perishing curiosity" about things in this world but the rightly ordered orientation of the psyche toward the transcendent ground of Being. True "philosophy" for Voegelin presupposes the experience of openness of the soul toward transcendence. As a result, he concludes that the greater part of modern "political philosophy" is not philosophy at all but *gnosis*, or the bogus claim to have gained systematic "knowledge" of essential reality.

The "knowledge" of the authentic philosopher is for Voegelin, then, a knowledge of our ignorance (*ein Wissen vom Nicht-Wissen*).[10] What the political philosopher learns above all is *not* to make utopian and messianic demands upon the historical political commu-

---

[8]Z. A. Pelczynski stresses the rationalism of Hegel's approach to politics in his lengthy introduction to T. M. Knox, *Hegel's Political Writings* (Oxford: Oxford University Press, 1964).

[9]Eric Voegelin, "On Hegel—A Study in Sorcery," p. 28. An unpublished monograph scheduled to appear in *Studium Generale*. I am grateful to Professor Voegelin for sharing this monograph with me.

[10]Eric Voegelin, "Was ist Politische Realität?" in *Anamnesis: Zur Theorie der Geschichte and Politik*, p. 289.

nity. He recognizes the limitations upon man as a political actor and acknowledges the impossibility of achieving the perfect social order within time and the world.

Beyond that, the political philosopher can diagnose the intellectual and spiritual diseases which periodically threaten to overwhelm mankind. He can expose fallacious ideologies for the deceptions that they attempt to put over on men. His role in history is modest, however, and such influence as he may have is indirect and limited:

> Nobody can heal the spiritual disorder of an "age." A philosopher can do no more than work himself free from the rubble of idols which, under the name of an "age," threatens to cripple and bury him; and he can hope that the example of his effort will be of help to others who find themselves in the same situation and experience the same desire to gain their humanity under God.[11]

As a political philosopher, Voegelin defies classification according to the language of the political struggle: he is not left, right, or center, but is engaged in the critical study of politics. However, a philosopher's thought does have implications for the practical politics of his time. In Voegelin's case, it is particularly difficult to ascertain how much room for maneuver he regards political reality—and specifically contemporary political reality—as affording for the creation of a relatively more decent and humane world. Granting Voegelin's elimination of a "qualitative" transformation of human existence from consideration,[12] what does he have to say about the possibilities of concrete political reforms or changes in foreign or domestic policy in a given community such as the United States? To my knowledge he remains silent on the burning questions of our time, such as American participation in the Indochina war, the arms race, the struggle for racial equality, the "inverted welfare state," and tendencies toward the repression of radical dissent. Given such silence, his philosophical orientation is frequently

[11] Voegelin, "On Hegel—A Study in Sorcery," p. 28.

[12] The question of what constitutes a "qualitative" transformation of existence—*metastasis* in Voegelin's vocabulary—is a difficult one to answer, however. If a society were to be erected on the basis of the Platonic *metanoia* (conversion), would it not mark a qualitative breakthrough for man? Does not the advance from the "compactness" of the myth to the "differentiation" of philosophy amount to a change in the "quality of life" for those who engage in it? For explication of these terms in Voegelin's political philosophy, see Germino, *Beyond Ideology*, chap. 8, and "Eric Voegelin's *Anamnesis*," *Southern Review* 7 (January 1971): 68–88.

claimed to imply a conservative position, for example, the acceptance of inequalities within existing society or reliance on military force to resolve disputes between societies. While his profound understanding of the magnitude of the spiritual and intellectual crisis in which we find ourselves speaks to us with utmost relevance, Voegelin leaves himself open to a mainly traditionalist or conservative interpretation of his work through his failure to explore the question of the "best practicable" political order, given current conditions.

To interpret Voegelin as essentially a partisan of conservatism is surely to misinterpret him, however. One cannot ignore that fact that he denounces not only "utopian" thought, which preaches a politics of salvation, but also the entire range of contemporary "secondary ideologies" which he holds to be merely reactive in nature.[13] The recovery of a philosophy of order (and by "order," Voegelin intends something far more profound and liberating than the current reactive cry of "law and order") is seen by him to be the essential *preparatio* for a practical politics which assists rather than hinders the full development of personality.

There is no question that Voegelin wishes to replace a politics of "ideology" with a politics of humanism, and that he believes philosophy has a role to play in achieving such a consummation. For one thing, philosophy can indicate the noetic basis for the political virtue of "common sense." For another, it can indicate the route of maximal psychic development for the minority of the population which chooses to lead the life of reason. Beyond this, however, we learn little from Voegelin about how philosophy can contribute to a better world. His one attempt to devise a paradigm for the good society appropriate to our time is extremely general and offers little to the majority of the people more fully preoccupied with mundane tasks of living.[14]

[13] See Voegelin's *Anamnesis*, pp. 329 ff. for a discussion of Christian democracy, neo-liberalism, etc., as "secondary ideologies."

[14] The good society is to be: (1) as large and prosperous as is necessary to make possible the life of reason for the minority choosing to lead it; and (2) organized in such a way that the "life of reason becomes a soul force in the culture and political affairs of the society." Furthermore, it should be remembered that the good society is in no sense to be confused with eternal paradise on earth. Eric Voegelin, "La Societé industrielle a la recherche de la raison," in *Colloques de Rheinfelden*, ed. R. Aron (Paris, 1960), pp. 44 ff.

It is at this point that the value of the Hegelian paradigm becomes evident, not as a replacement for, but as a supplement to, the approach of Voegelin. To take a distinction from the development of Buddhism, we may describe Voegelin's conception of the role of philosophy as that of the Hinayana school, while Hegel espouses that of the Mahayana. The truth of the Voegelinian—or Hinayanic—conception is that philosophy will die without its saving remnant and if its primary objective becomes to communicate its insights to all men, irrespective of their preparation for them, it is almost certain to be corrupted and debased. The lesson of the Mahayana school, represented by Hegel in our typology, is that the universalism implicit in philosophy, with its understanding that not one, or a few, but *all* men are free, does not permit it to remain the affair of the happy few but points the way to a transformed existence in reason and freedom for all men.

It has been observed by Leo Strauss, in his famous debate with Alexandre Kojève, that Hegel's philosophy supports the creation of a "homogeneous world state." While it was (characteristically) perceptive of Strauss to detect the universalism implicit in Hegel's theory of the state[15]—even though the German philosopher as a "son of his time" accepts for the present the plurality of competing nation-states—it is surely incorrect to describe the theory as implicitly calling for a "*homogeneous*" world state. On the contrary, the greatness of the Hegelian conception of the "state" consists precisely in its discovery that the full development of man as person can come only through the synthesis of the particular needs of individuals and groups with the universal needs of man as such. This is surely the meaning of Hegel's conclusion in the *Philosophy of Right*—that the state is the "actuality of concrete freedom," which consists in a situation where "personal individuality and its particular interests" are maintained and preserved by "the passing over of their own accord into the interest of the universal.... The result is that the universal does not prevail ... except along with particular interests and through the cooperation of particular knowing and willing."[16]

[15] I have tried to elaborate on this point in the final pages of my paper, "Hegel's Theory of the State: Humanist or Totalitarian?" delivered to the IPSA World Congress, September 1970, and published in the *Statsvetenskoplig Tidskrift* (*Swedish Journal of Political Science*), December 1970.

[16] *Hegel's Philosophy of Right*, trans. T. M. Knox (Oxford: Oxford University Press, 1967), pp. 160–61.

Just as in the nation-state the particular interests of individuals and groups in civil society would be preserved and given a rational framework for their expression, so in any world-state true to Hegelian principles the rich diversity of customs, traditions, and life styles found throughout the world would be preserved. "Homogenization" is thus out of the question.

For Hegel the very Idea of the state precludes the destruction of individuality and particularity. When he observes, in the *Lectures on the Philosophy of World History*, that it is in the state where one finds *Selbstständigkeit* (autonomy and independence) of the individual protected,[17] he could not be more emphatic in rejecting a "totalitarian" construction of the relationship between the individual and the state. The great advance made by the modern state over the Greek *polis* had to do precisely with the fact that although a philosopher like Plato had a profound sense of the need for unity and the demands of the common good, he was relatively insensitive to the needs of individuality and particularity to find free play.

Hegel's political philosophy is grounded on the dignity of human personality. To "be a person and respect others as persons"[18] is the goal of human development. Personality is something "inherently infinite and universal."[19] As a person, man is free. Freedom for man as such and not only for one or a few is the goal of world history. Whatever their empirical differences, men are essentially equal by virtue of their capacity for thought, self-consciousness, and awareness of rights and duties in organized community with their fellows. "A man counts as a man by virtue of his manhood alone, not because he is a Jew, Catholic, Protestant, German, Italian, etc.," Hegel wrote in the *Philosophy of Right* in one of the most eloquent expressions of his humanism.[20]

As noted earlier, Hegel frequently observed that every man, including the philosopher, is the "son of his time." Far from assuming that he was the last of the philosophers and the "Great, Great Man" of history (Voegelin), he regarded his own teaching as embodying only the "present standpoint" of philosophy. The limita-

---

[17] G. W. F. Hegel, *Die Vernunft in der Geschichte*, ed. J. Hoffmeister (Hamburg: Meiner, 1955), p. 120.

[18] *Hegel's Philosophy of Right*, p. 37.

[19] Ibid., p. 38.

[20] Ibid., p. 134.

tions of that standpoint did not permit him to draw out the full implications of his political philosophy by concluding that reason calls for the emergence of a world political community capable of maintaining peace in a framework of mutual respect and cultural diversity. As he himself pointed out toward the end of the *Philosophy of Right*, the system of competing sovereign nation-states leads ineluctably to war, and in war all rights of personality are effectively suspended. In war, the nation-state thus acquires "absolute power against everything individual and particular, against life, property, their rights, even against Societies and associations."[21] Thus, the very goal of world history—the full development of all men as persons in reason and freedom—is constantly in jeopardy through the irrationality of the competitive state system.

Hegel was a thinker of integrity, and as such could abandon neither the "idealism" of his philosophy of history nor the "realism" of his highly concrete understanding of the contradictions inherent in the modern nation-state. His political philosophy is thus a blend of rationalism and conservatism, of activism and resignation. In his analysis of "civil society," he brooded prophetically over the creation of an alienated "rabble" (*Pobel*) of the poor and unemployed in the midst of the affluent modern society, as well as over the imperialistic tendency of such a society to "push beyond its own limits and to seek markets ... in other lands which are either deficient in the goods it has overproduced, or else generally backward in industry, etc."[22]

Despite his wholly realistic assessment of the difficulties in the path of creating a newer, more human political world, Hegel never lost his confidence in the capacity of the human spirit to create such a world. This confidence, he was convinced, was not the result of blind faith or desperate hope, but was grounded on mankind's growing awareness of its responsibility for shaping its own condition. As he wrote in his *Philosophy of World History*:

This is the goal of world history: that the spirit create a world in accord with its own nature, a world that is suitable for it to inhabit. . . .[23]

[21] Ibid., p. 209.
[22] Ibid., p. 151.
[23] Hegel, *Die Vernunft in der Geschichte*, pp. 256–57.

Such a goal is not messianic, in the sense that it represents a qualitative transformation of existence (or *metastasis* in the Voegelinian sense). Rather the spirit's creation of a "world suitable for it to inhabit" is perceived as a logical culmination of the centuries-old struggle by man to comprehend his condition. That condition remains *human*, and transcending the state—or the "appearance of the spiritual dimension" (*die Erscheinung des Geistigen*) in history through the articulation of the people into an authentic community —is the realm of art, religion, and philosophy. The state makes possible and nourishes these activities, which in turn find in the state (or political culture) their roots.[24]

It would appear that the two conceptions of political philosophy we have been discussing in this essay—the Hegelian and the Voegelinian (the Hinayanic and the Mahayanic)—serve as correctives of each other. Political philosophy at its best exhibits a marvelous tension which is always in danger of collapsing in favor of one or the other alternative. If the Hegelian conception prevailed alone, we should run the risk of philosophy's ultimately ceasing to play the role of critic and gadfly it has supposedly done since Socrates. This is because, for all his expressions of doubt and resignation, Hegel was clearly convinced that the social and political "reality" of history would become increasingly permeated with the truth of philosophy. (The more philosophical existing reality becomes, the less critical work there is left for philosophy to do.) We could even foresee the possibility of an eventual disappearance of philosophy, and its absorption into social *praxis*, after the manner conceived by Karl Marx. If on the other hand, only the Voegelinian view of philosophy prevails, we might expect precious little guidance from political philosophers as to how one might advance the prospects for a relatively more humane, less brutal and degrading political world, not only for some but for all. Political philosophy would carefully keep its distance from the cave, where from experience it knows itself to be misunderstood and even hated and despised. It would serve as a consolation to those who are committed to a life of reason

[24] As I argue in my paper, "Hegel's Theory of the State," we cannot begin to do justice to Hegel's understanding of the term "state," unless we distinguish it from its conventional connotations. The state for Hegel is not an alien force or power machinery operating upon a subjugated mass of individuals.

and of the spirit, but who find the majority of men hostile and alien to this experience. The ugly and banal realities of practical politics would continue to be perpetrated over the heads of subjects, philosophical and nonphilosophical alike.

The above summation of the two perspectives considered has been deliberately heightened to draw out the conflicting emphases in each. It should be recalled that withdrawal and involvement, particularism and universalism, and "elitism" and egalitarianism are present in the thinking of all political philosophers, none of whom can be neatly categorized in terms of either end of the pole. What all political philosophers share is an overriding humanism which, despite all the horrors that men and nations can inflict upon each other, retains an unconquerable faith in man as such. "Existence is good to the good man," Aristotle wrote. Our wisest and most profound minds do not cease to proclaim this even in the face of innumerable examples of obtuseness, viciousness, and irrationality. Philosophy, then, *is* a consolation, but need not imply withdrawal, or at least not always.

Thus far, as you may have noticed, I have failed to say anything about the third term in the trilogy: ideology. I do not suppose that I can use as an excuse for avoiding the term that I have been trying to get as far as possible "beyond" it. I do not want to trespass excessively on Richard Cox's territory, but let me conclude with a word or two about ideology.

As Cox's excellent reader, *Ideology, Politics, and Political Theory,*[25] demonstrates, the word "ideology" is today employed in myriad ways and is in desperate need of conceptual clarification if it is to be of value to political science. Indeed, it seems at present to be for many social scientists a kind of intellectual dumping ground to which every type of political thinking from party programs and tracts to treatises in political philosophy are consigned.

I think it important to note that the word ideology was unknown until the time of the French Revolution when it is coined by the political reformer Destutt de Tracy. Tracy meant by ideology the "science of ideas." By means of this science, the origin of men's thoughts could allegedly be determined through tracing them to

[25] Belmont, Calif.: Wadsworth Press, 1969.

their roots in sense experience, which was itself claimed to be the whole of experience. Such knowledge was believed to be of immense practical value because it would serve to guide statesmen in the most effective ways to reform political and social institutions and achieve as a result a new, "enlightened" political consciousness.[26] Although ideology has in the main been employed in a pejorative way to stand for the interest-related and practical political ideas of a given individual or group, rather than as the scientific study of those ideas themselves, perhaps there is something to Tracy's original formulation to which we should hold fast in discussing the concept. If this were so we would not use the term ideology to apply loosely to every conceivable type of political thought. Rather, we should restrict it to a comprehensive set of action-related political ideas that: (1) claims the support and prestige of (phenomenal) science and (2) systematically excludes whole dimensions of political reality on the basis of a reductionist epistemology. Thus, Comtean positivism, Nazi racist "science," and a good deal of "Marxist"[27] political thought and social science, for example, could be accurately characterized as "ideology."

Such a restricted use of the term would not, however, imply that all other types of political thought were somehow "non-ideological" in the sense of being devoid of special interest pleading, parochial perspectives, or intellectual naiveté. Far from it. Voegelin's distinction between "noetic" (or philosophical) and "non-noetic" modes of political thought is important here.[28] Most political thought is non-noetic in the sense that it is not self-consciously critical of its basic assumptions and goals. Non-noetic thought fails consciously to ground itself in a multidimensional analysis of the person in his political existence. It is not eager to receive new evidence which may cause it to revise its conclusions. Non-noetic thought is relatively (although not absolutely) unreflective and uncritical. Political doc-

---

[26] See Germino, *Beyond Ideology*, pp. 48–51, for an elaboration of these observations.

[27] Marx himself said there could not be any Marxists.

[28] Voegelin, *Anamnesis*, pp. 284ff. The adjective "noetic" is derived from the Greek *nous* (mind or intellect) and *noesis* (thinking or cognition). Voegelin describes political science as a "noetic interpretation of man, society and history claiming a critical knowledge of order *vis-à-vis* the non-noetic conception of order prevailing in society itself." Ibid., p. 284.

trines of all "persuasions," civil theologies, mythologies, utopias, behavioralist programs, messianic creeds, etc., are all examples of non-noetic thought, in addition to ideologies as used in the more restricted fashion I suggested. Ideologies, however, are particularly resistent to permeation by the noetic, or philosophical, spirit because they dogmatically exclude the kinds of questions raised by philosophy as a result of their "scientific" pretensions and their reductionist conception of reality. Ideologies may well be disastrous when literally applied to the realm of practice (and, fortunately, the basic humanity of some practitioners succeeds in blunting this pernicious effect), because they have a way of substituting abstractions for living, concrete, individual men who may be sacrificed to these very abstractions. In this respect, the Nazi attempt to exterminate the Jews stands out as the most brutal and horrible example of ideological politics in history. By comparison, even vulgar "Marxism" has at least a formal commitment to humanism, although this is dangerously diluted by the concept of the "enemies of the people."

I think it would be unfortunate, however, if such a concept of ideology as I am suggesting were used in such a way as to argue for the *identification* of ideology and totalitarian thought and practice. Hannah Arendt seems to take such a position in her article "Ideology and Terror," reprinted in the most recent edition of her *Origins of Totalitarianism.* Again harking back to Tracy, the word originally did not convey antihumanist implications, but was supportive of reforms of a "progressivist" type. Here, everything would depend on the pre-intellectual qualities (such as "common sense") of the *ideologues* as well as on the substance of the ideology (i.e., whether it advocates at its core universal human values, recognizes the essential equality of all men, etc.). Although I disagree with much of what B. F. Skinner proposes, for example, I doubt very much that we could call his ideology, expressed in *Walden II* and other writings, totalitarian because—among other reasons—his rejection of terror and physical coercion appears to disqualify him from such an appellation. In addition, it needs to be stressed that Nazism was totalitarian in practice not only because it was ideological but because of a host of other factors (sociological, psychological, historical) as well. As students of political philosophy and theory we must beware of the temptation to assume that *only* ideas matter in conditioning political behavior.

In commenting upon the dangers of reductionism, Voegelin points out that "neither an idealistic nor a materialistic metaphysics is tenable."[29] This is because either approach commits the fallacy of substituting the *pars pro toto*. "Idealism," whether in philosophy or in politics, neglects the "bodily foundation" of man's existence and is thereby led to spurious and unrealistic speculations based on some view of man as a wholly spiritualized essence. "Materialism," on the other hand, ignores man's capacity for the experience of transcendence and attunement with Being, thereby compressing man into an exclusively corporeal existence with a resulting loss of his humanity.

Voegelin cites the "bodily foundation" (*Leibfundament*) of existence as an admonition to greater realism and common sense in approaching questions of what is realizable in politics.[30] He is, of course, justified in offering this admonition to all who seek far-reaching transformations in present-day domestic and international political arrangements. Perhaps it may be in order here to suggest, however, that what we know about the body, its meta-rational drives, and its capability of responding to new environments and life styles has been rather considerably advanced in recent decades, in particular as a result of Sigmund Freud's discoveries and those of others following in the Freudian footsteps.[31] It is more appropriate to the open and critical spirit of a "philosophy of man," therefore, to be receptive to new possibilities for a life of fulfillment in and through the body than to continue to espouse the dualistic doctrine of soul and body found in the books of the old philosophers. For the *philosophia perennis* is perennially young.[32]

[29] Ibid., p. 57. From his essay, "Zur Theorie des Bewusstseins." I do not, incidentally, regard Hegel's "metaphysics" as idealistic in the subjectivist sense that Voegelin has in mind. Hegel conceived of *Geist* as both "objective" and "subjective."

[30] Ibid., pp. 340 ff.

[31] See, for example, Norman O. Brown's creative and provocative work, *Life Against Death* (Middletown, Conn.: Wesleyan University Press, 1970).

[32] Carl J. Friedrich's *Man and His Government: An Empirical Theory of Politics* (Boston: Little, Brown and Co., 1963), among his many important contributions to political philosophy and theory, serves as an example for us all to follow in its openness to all available evidence and its generous estimation of the contributions of writers embodying diverse perspectives.

.13. The Biological Foundations of Political Science: Reflections on the Post-Behavioral Era

THOMAS LANDON THORSON

I

A WHILE ago I heard a story about a lawyer addressing a county medical association in Texas. "At the same time that members of your profession were bleeding George Washington with leeches in order to cure him of a fever," he said, "members of mine were writing the Constitution of the United States." The oft-repeated claim that while man has made great technological and scientific progress he has made none whatever with respect to human relations is not fully accurate.

The exponential rise in the curve of scientific advance over the past two or three decades makes things look out of phase, but the Texas lawyer has a point. The Constitution written in Philadelphia nearly two hundred years ago has proved to be a remarkably successful piece of social engineering. The American continent north of the Rio Grande has seen no major disruption since the 1860s. Upward of 200 million people live on this vast piece of land in a remarkable condition of peace. Furthermore, another 200 or 300 million on the European continent may very well be finished with major war through the influence of the North Atlantic Treaty Organization, the European Economic Community, and the Warsaw Pact.

In a strange way the most pessimistic of the modern interpretations of man is the one that suggests he is innately peaceful. The

258

threat of nuclear annihilation and the conflict that accompanies increasing prosperity and urbanization can from this point of view only be understood as a mass insanity. Civilization and technology are the evils, and the antidote is some sort of return to the state of nature. Advocates of this perspective seem curiously unaware that it was in the name of the restoration of simple tribal values that Hitler struck out against what Stalin called, in a not altogether dissimilar context, the rootless cosmopolitans who operated the institutions of finance and mass communication. If nature equips man only for peace, and if war is somehow the product of civilization, how can we be expected to handle the threat of a war that will destroy us all? Surely if this is the case, we are docile and weak and we are doomed to be overwhelmed by the inexorable march of weapons technology. Such an analysis is pessimistic indeed.

Fortunately it is belied by the facts. Man is far from docile. He is fierce, aggressive, with a powerful urge for self-preservation and the courage and determination to carry it through. One has only to watch a Vietnamese peasant, buffeted by years of war, hammer beer cans with a stone into a wall for a new shack to know that man is no weakling riding on the froth of the wave of history.

Recent writers have revived the old debate about man's essential nature. Some say that deep "subhuman" urges to kill have evolved with man from the remote man-ape of the African savannas, *Australopithecus Africanus*. Others deny any such urges or instincts and stress human cooperation. This debate misses the crucial point. Whether the urge to aggress is present or not, what undoubtedly has evolved is the human brain itself. The brain of modern man is roughly three times the size of that of the average australopithecine. Exactly how much more capable this brain is of weighing and considering, of learning and reasoning, we can only guess. There is no doubt, however, that men can outreason and outlearn smaller-brained apes. What is equally certain is that in the hominid line of descent— from australopithecine to *Homo erectus* to Neanderthal man to Cro-Magnon man to contemporary man—there has been a general tendency to increase brain size. If as a matter of natural history man has developed a progressively larger brain, what does this suggest for the future of the species now that the real threat of species suicide is upon us?

Sigmund Freud once suggested that nature's production of man was a "careless and uneven piece of work." What he meant to suggest is that nature did not provide man with basic equipment fitted precisely to his needs. Freud being Freud we can be sure that he was particularly struck by the fact that the human sex drive was far more powerful and pervasive than it needed to be for the task of reproduction. The whole of Freudian analysis follows from this premise and who can deny that he was in some measure correct.

The distinguished German student of animal behavior, Konrad Lorenz, makes a similar point with respect to aggression. Animals, Lorenz argues, whom nature has provided with powerful weapons, have also developed inhibitory instincts which prevent destruction of the species by the species itself. Lorenz contrasts wolves and doves. Wolves, powerfully equipped for bloodletting, engage in frequent contests for dominance, but they almost never fight to the death. A dominance contest between two male wolves nearly always ends with a ritual. The loser positions himself in a certain way relative to the winner and deliberately exposes his throat, the most vulnerable spot on his body. The winner snarls and nudges, but *he does not bite.* Dominance contests among doves imprisoned by man so that the loser cannot retreat result in carnage of a most brutal and final sort.

Lorenz concludes that man has a special problem. Whatever inhibitory instincts he has do not and cannot mitigate man's aggression when that aggression is manifested through extensions of the human body, namely, weapons—whether they be bows and arrows or hydrogen bombs. Thus, again one might say that evolution's combining aggression with the big brain and the opposable thumb was an uneven and careless piece of work. Lorenz's suggestion that man is unique because he alone practices intraspecific aggression, that is, kills his own kind, is somewhat more dubious. It makes too much of the fact that man is biologically one species.

Given the dominance of the cultural component in human behavior, we should perhaps think in terms of cultural speciation (speciation by language and cultural group) in terms of which man probably does not act much differently than any other animal. If man's instincts are inadequate to restrain his ability through weaponry to kill at a distance, then our only hope lies in his intelligence. And here the paradox of the human condition begins to reveal itself at least in outline. Our hope for the restraint of aggression lies in the big brain and yet it seems likely that the big brain is the biological product of hundreds of thousands of years of warfare, of men slaughtering other men. Can we suppose anything other than that we are children of the winners in the struggle for existence not only against nature, but also against other men eliminated too early to have progeny?

Zoologist Robert Bigelow suggests that the only plausible way to explain the biologically extraordinary fact of the trebling of size (the measure of increased complexity would, of course, be many times three) of the human brain in a relatively short period of time (by evolutionary standards) is the continued presence of an unusually powerful selective force. This force, he suggests, must have worked on man alone, for nothing comparable has happened to the brains of other primates over the same period. Since the brain is a social instrument, the force must be related to social life and, finally, the force must have eliminated those men with the smallest brains. Moreover, it continued to eliminate them even after their brains had increased to size double that of any other primate.

It is only intergroup fighting to the death, in short, warfare, that meets all these requirements. The brain grew because of the high premium nature put on social cooperation in the life-and-death struggle with other human groups. One might expect, Bigelow suggests, some brain growth and development given pressures of adaptation to a changing climate or food supply, but nothing like so rapid a growth as has been the fact.

This theory [Bigelow concludes] is based on several basic assumptions and if any one of these is unsound, so is the theory. It assumes that warfare—defined as inter-group conflict with intent to kill on both sides—began with australopithecines, if not sooner. It assumes that communication and efficient social organization require brains, that brains are the products of the interactions of sets of genes, and thus that the threefold increase in brain size was a biological event produced by biological forces like brains directing hands in the wielding of clubs or spears or machine guns. It assumes that, on the average, the winners have produced more offspring than the losers of wars, that not all the best men are killed in battle, and that the victorious survivors are very generous with their genes. It assumes also, of course, that good soldiers are not only ferocious killers, but also intelligent men who are willing to risk their lives to protect their families and friends from massacre or starvation or satanic foreign ideas.[1]

If the brain has grown according to the formula cooperation-for-conflict, we now face the problem of changing cooperation-for-conflict into cooperation-for-survival. And the evidence seems to suggest that our instincts cannot solve the problem because they are not good enough. It is our brains that have evolved to greater power, not our instincts to restraint. What we need then—the honest convictions of many notwithstanding—is not love-power or flower-power but brain-power.

Today, when so many challenge so loudly what they call the system, and the American system in particular, we need desperately to see not the inadequacies of Madison's machinery but the acuteness of his vision for the future of man. For Madison and his colleagues, while they knew little of biology and nothing whatsoever of evolution or of australopithecines, knew well that if one wishes to organize peace over large territories and populations, one must create a framework of rules built not so much on the principle of "love thy neighbor" as on the principle of "minimize thy neighbor's capacity and inclination to do serious harm." This is not sentiment or instinct, but intelligence—and the men of Philadelphia make us sure that the brain's increase in size has not simply been a matter of weight.

The question for today is whether there will be a tomorrow fit for human life. The problem has arisen rapidly after more than twenty million years of hominid evolution, after the development of a clever ape into a dome-skulled creature with unprecedented and unforseen powers to create and destroy. The crisis man faces is the first to involve the fate of the entire species. We are all that is left of the family of man, and the question of our survival will almost certainly be decided in the next hundred years. And it is just now and in just this context that political science, properly understood, re-emerges as what Aristotle said it was: the master science.

The history of international relations has been a matter of unstable peace with islands of stable peace. If we use our heads, those

[1] Robert Bigelow, *The Dawn Warriors* (Boston: Little Brown and Co., 1969), pp. 57–58.

islands will become larger and, ultimately, the pattern will reverse itself, creating a world with islands of unstable peace in a general framework of stable peace. The answer lies not in self-righteous breast-beating or walking interminably in circles, but in synthesizing the vast quantities of information which our sciences, both natural and social, and our humanistic studies are producing. Only in this way can we transcend NATO, the EEC, the Warsaw Pact, the Organization of American States, the British Commonwealth, the Organization of African Unity, the Arab League, the Southeast Asian Treaty Organization, the United Nations—even though each of these is in some sense a step in the right direction. The future, if there is to be a future, belongs to the constitution makers. And political science in its classical sense is at heart constitution making.

II

What I have just said about synthesizing the vast quantities of new knowledge sounds, I am sure, like another pious call for interdisciplinary studies. But I intend something far more presumptuous and imperialistic. I mean to say that political science to emerge again as the master science must become the interdisciplinary science par excellence.

If it is indeed the case that the question of survival will be decided in the next hundred years there is no excuse not to be presumptuous. If man's long, violent history points to the overwhelming necessity of brain power, of the creative use of intelligence; then man's most important animal task, that task which is fundamental to biological survival, is what Aristotle said it was long ago: reasoning about political and social organization, that enterprise we have come to call political science.

Time and experience have made it difficult to assent to the notion that the *polis* is natural to man, but we can perhaps say in Aristotle's spirit that, along with several other characteristics that differentiate the human species, "Man is by nature a political-scientizing animal." Given the growth of the brain, the decline of instinct, the necessity of cooperation for survival, man as a biological matter has become the animal that deliberates, argues, and plans his social organization.

The distinguished British embryologist C. H. Waddington has argued that man is the animal that "goes in for ethicizing" and his suggestions have much to teach us.[2]   The core of Waddington's argument is his description of what he calls the sociogenetic system of information transmission in men.   Evolution works through a process of information transmission; the genetic system is nature's way of passing adaptive information from generation to generation. Viewed from this perspective man is unique because in man nature has found a way of transmitting adaptive information *outside* the genes.   A system of information transmission is, thus, from an evolutionary point of view what culture is, and Waddington refers to it as a "sociogenetic system."

Thus, it is a part of man's fundamental biology that he should be a rule-making and rule-deliberating animal.

To summarize the argument very briefly [Waddington says in his preface], I shall try to support the following four points: Firstly, that the human system of social communication functions as such an efficient means of transmitting information from one generation to the next that it has become the mechanism on which human evolution mainly depends. Secondly, that this system of "socio-genetic" transmission can operate only because the psychological development of man is such that the new born baby becomes moulded into a creature which is ready to accept transmitted information; and, I shall suggest, it is an empirically observed fact that this acceptance is founded on the formation of "authority-bearing" systems within the mind which also result in the human individual becoming a creature which goes in for having beliefs of the particular tone that we call ethical. Thirdly, I argue that observation of the world of living things reveals a general evolutionary direction, which has a philosophical status similar to that of healthy growth, in that both are manifestations of the immanent properties of the objective world. Finally, I conclude that any particular set of ethical beliefs, which some individual man may advance, can be meaningfully judged according to their efficacy in furthering this general evolutionary direction.[3]

No one, I suspect, would quite want to argue that political science understood even in its classical sense as an "experiential science of right order" (in Professor Voegelin's phrase) is identical with ethics. Without laboring the point, however, it is easy enough to see that Waddington could as easily be discussing the biological foundations

[2]C. H. Waddington, *The Ethical Animal* (London: George Allen and Unwin, 1960).
[3]Waddington, *Ethical Animal*, U.S. ed. (New York: Atheneum Publishers, 1961), p. 7.

of "political-scientizing." Indeed his argument might even be more appropriate to "political-scientizing" than it is to "ethicizing." What is perfectly clear is that, viewed from a biological, evolutionary standpoint, political science is very much a part of man's "species business." Rule making and rule deliberating are fundamental to the human animal and thus political science has a biological foundation in a way that sociology, psychology, or anthropology do not. Men have always made and deliberated rules, long before a few Western men created academic departments of political science.

III

It has become increasingly possible, since Waddington's discussion in 1961, to speak precisely about the relationship between the genetic system of information transmission and the extragenetic or sociogenetic system of information transmission which is the core of human culture. This is so because biologists, on the one hand, have exposed the mechanism of genetic information transmission. They have, as they so significantly put it, literally "cracked the genetic code." Linguists and information theorists are, on the other hand, breaking open the structure of human symbolic communication and in so doing they may be exposing the mechanism of cultural evolution.

The importance of developing an adequate understanding of cultural evolution and its mechanism cannot be overestimated. It is only through such an understanding that political change and political development, that is, politics in its important senses, can be penetrated. To ignore cultural evolution as an aspect of evolution in the broader sense is to run the risk in political studies of a biological reductionism, of turning the biological investigation of politics into nothing more than the urine sample school of behavioralism.

What is striking are the extraordinary similarities between the mechanism of genetic information transfer and the mechanism of symbolic information transfer.[4] A number of social scientists, mostly

[4]Professor Roger D. Masters of Dartmouth College, whose discussion I here summarize, has presented a remarkable and lucid account of these matters in "Genes, Language, and Evolution," *Semiotica* 12, no. 4 (1970): 295–319. For a more thorough discussion than I can provide here and for the full panoply of references I urge you to consult Masters' article.

anthropologists, have over the last decade or so begun to take more seriously the obvious analogies between organic and sociocultural evolution. Modern evolutionary theory makes it no longer possible to regard these analogies as mere metaphor or as residual Social Darwinism. The modern biologist teaches that common biological needs or ecological situations can be met by parallel or analogous but nonetheless different physical features or behavioral patterns.

These analogies are not, from the biological point of view, to be confused with "homologies"—i.e., somewhat differentiated forms of the same mechanism in phylogenetically related species. Human binocular vision, as has often been observed, survived originally because it provided good depth perception for our tree-dwelling primate ancestors. Thus, our binocular vision is the "same" as that of a chimpanzee and most other primates in the sense that they are homologous structures.

The now famous Galapagos finch that uses a thorn as a tool to get at insects under bark is not *homologous* but *analogous* to a woodpecker. Likewise the different kinds of eyes or wings of bats, flies, and birds are parallel developments in different evolutionary lines, and are, thus, in the strict sense of the term "analogous" structures. There is no metaphor here, only the recognition of the empirical reality of evolutionary selection meeting a· similar problem with a similar solution.

At the broadest level it is possible to argue that all biological systems or structures exhibit both repetitive patterns of functioning and non-repetitive or developmental patterns of change or evolution. It is obvious enough that human sociocultural systems are biological systems in this sense. They certainly do provide a means for transmitting adaptive information from one generation to another with sufficient repetition so that relevant adaptive experience is not lost (when they are successful at least) and with enough flexibility so that innovations can be adopted (again, of course, when they are successful). There is surely some sort of analogy here, but can it be said to be genuinely biological in the sense just described or is it merely metaphorical?

It is clear enough that man's language allows the formation of symbols which can be repeated and modified. Thus, the more precise question is "Are verbal symbols in some meaningful sense analogous to the mechanisms of repetition and innovation in organic evolution?

If genes and mutation were the great inventions for speeding change at the molecular level, and gamete formation and fusion at the cellular level, so were the nervous system and the engram at the individual level, and language and other information flow—and the cerebral mechanisms that mediate this—at the social level.[5]

And further,

Most social behavior of insects is genetically determined, while most social behavior of man is culturally determined through symbolic communication. . . . Although this great difference in the basic mechanisms of social evolution lies at the root of the uniqueness of man as contrasted to the social insects, symbols have many functional attributes of genes. Variation, isolation, and selection are operative factors in the evolution of both genetic and symbolic systems.[6]

If there is anything genuinely biological to these suggestions, one might hypothesize that nature in developing a parallel and analogous means of transmitting adaptive information would rely upon the techniques that make genetic transmission of information so successful. One might suppose that basic structures might be similar and that patterns or rules of functioning would also be parallel. The extraordinary fact is that a variety of independent lines of research are demonstrating that such is in fact the case. There is, first of all, a strikingly similar triadic structural patterning in both genetic material and human languages. As Masters puts it:

One characteristic of human languages that sets them apart from animal languages has been called "duality of patterning" (Hockett, 1958, 1959): human speech is composed of meaningless units (phonemes) which are combined into symbols that convey meaning (morphemes). The genetic code, based on a "genetic alphabet" of four nucleotides, has this same duality of patterning (Beadle and Beadle, 1966). Moreover, like words in a human

[5]R. Gerard, "Becoming: the Residue of Change," in *Evolution of Man*, ed. S. Tax (Chicago: The University of Chicago Press, 1960), p. 264, quoted in Masters, "Genes, Language and Evolution," p. 300.

[6]A. E. Emerson, "The Evolution of Behavior Among Insects," in *Behavior and Evolution*, ed. A. Roe and G. Simpson (New Haven: Yale University Press, 1958), p. 331, quoted in Masters, "Genes, Language and Evolution," p. 300.

language, genes are transmitted not in isolation but in sequences whose structure (chromosomes) could be compared to the structure of utterances or sentences. Since the meaning of a word, like the phenotypical expression of a gene, depends in part on the context in which it appears, it is evident that Hockett should have spoken of three-fold patterning. . . . Hence one could say that both genes and linguistic symbols have the same structural attributes: discrete, meaningless components (phonemes or nucleotides), structured into "binary opposition" by means of "distinctive features," are combined into meaningful units that form longer, functional "strings" or messages.[7]

But more than this the two languages *function* along strikingly similar lines. Genetic language like verbal language has a definite syntax. Masters quotes the distinguished linguist Roman Jakobson:

The transition from lexical to syntactical units of different grades [in human languages] is paralleled by the ascent from codons to "cistrons" and "operons," and the latter two ranks of genetic sequences are equated by biologists with ascending syntactic constructions, and the constraints on the distribution of codons within such constructions have been called "the syntax of the DNA chain." In the genetic message the "words" are not separated from each other, whereas specific signals indicate the start and end of the operon and the limits between the cistrons within the operon, and are metaphorically described as "punctuation marks" or "commas." They actually correspond to the delimitative devices used in the phonological division of the utterance into sentences. . . .[8]

Because it is the case that in normal circumstances each cell of a complex organism has the same collection of chromosomes in its nucleus, biologists conclude that cell growth and differentiation must be a consequence of the capacity of a particular mass of genetic material to produce different messages at different times in different cells. Thus, there must be a regulatory device, a set of processes that serve as rules in the genetic language.

Recent research in linguistics has led to the powerful suggestion that speech is properly to be understood as the formation of "well-formed" strings of symbols under the direction of largely unconscious or preconscious grammatical rules. Just as a universal DNA structure has been discovered to underlie the enormous variety

[7] Masters, "Genes, Language and Evolution," pp. 300–302.
[8] Ibid., p. 304.

of organic forms, so linguists have identified transformational pat- terns that appear to be common to all human speech. The universal features in both cases can, it appears, best be understood as gram- matical or syntactical rules; in particular as rules of transformation that regulate the formation of well-formed strings of coded symbols.[9]

Thus, increasing evidence suggests that linking culture and genetics under the general category of information transmission as Wadding- ton does cannot be dismissed as fancy or as mere word-play. On the contrary it may very well be that through its relationship with

[9]I do not mean to suggest with this discussion that anything like the final word has been spoken on these matters. What I do intend to point up is an extraordinarily exciting area of frontier research, one which may have profound implications for the future of political understanding. In this connection Roger Masters' con- cluding remarks are worth quoting at some length:" ... a theory of socio-cultural behavior and change that emphasizes the role of language as a functional and evolutionary analogue of genetic material has great promise. Such a theory would fully reflect the uniqueness of *homo sapiens*, since no other known animal has a fully developed capacity for verbal language; at the same time, this approach would be compatible with the biological sciences. By utilizing fundamental concepts derived from recent evolutionary theory, it should become possible to take into consideration the extent to which instincts or biological functions influence human behavior without either assuming that man is MERELY an animal or that man is in NO WAY an animal. The study of the biological evolution of *homo sapiens* and of his cultural evolution could then be distinguished for practical purposes, since the processes are parallel, without ignoring the necessary interactions between culture and biology.

The resulting theory of human behavior could well claim to be synthetic, in the same sense that modern biology is said to rest on a "synthetic" theory of evolution. In recent years, various forms of structural and functional analysis have become increasingly prominent in sociology, anthropology, and political science; such theoret- ical approaches have been opposed both from a more traditional standpoint, which emphasizes the importance of historical development and uniqueness, and from a behavioral standpoint, which emphasizes the need for experimental or quantitative analysis of behavior. All of these approaches have validity if utilized appropriately, but at present the proliferation of models and theories gives the impression of chaos since the social sciences lack a common frame of reference.

In biology, the concepts of structure or "being," function or "behaving," and evolution or "becoming" have been integrated thanks to the modern, synthetic theory. On the hypothesis that human speech is an evolutionary analogue or parallel to genetic material, providing a mechanism that is structurally and func- tionally similar to inheritance yet a product of social learning, perhaps the concepts of structure, function, and evolution—and the correlative approaches of systemic, behavioral, and historical analysis—can be integrated in social science as they have been in biology. Hence a general theory of human behavior, based on the primary role of language as the means by which human individuals and societies transmit and create adaptations to their environment, offers the promise of unifying the social sciences while linking them with biology," pp. 312–13.

teacher-learner authority factors in information transmission "ethic-izing" and/or "political-scientizing" is in a profound sense rooted in the biology of the human animal.

IV

Twentieth-century insights into the nature of human biology may say something useful and informative about the essential humanness of "political-scientizing," but they do not, on their face at least, tell us much about what political science should be concerned with in this latter third of the twentieth century. I suggested a few moments ago that political science was re-emerging as the master science and that in so doing it must become *the* interdisciplinary science. I think that this assertion is true and that it is probably much more impor-tant than we realize. But to see the full sense in which it is true we must look further at the twentieth-century's insights into human biology. The notion that I hope to get across is that the intellectual situation for political science, and for that matter for science in gen-eral, during the last 100 to 150 years has been utterly unique. I stretch the period to 150 years because, retrospectively, one can see the trends forming that long ago. In the important sense, however, this utterly new philosophical perspective could only be fully grasped by twentieth-century man. Students of political philosophy in the twentieth century have, however, almost entirely failed to under-stand this fact and have argued for some sort of restoration to the classics. Likewise, they are inclined to reduce whatever they find ap-pealing in contemporary writings to identity with the teachings of a classical writer. Thus, what we have said here might be understood simply as a sort of recapturing of the man-in-nature perspective of Aristotle. There is, of course, truth in this, but I should like to stress the important difference.

Only in the last hundred years or so could any man have possibly known: (1) that man is the product of an evolutionary process stretching back some six billion years; and (2) that man was capable of establishing the detached observer position, of devising modern science and technology, and of creating modern society. Plato, Aristotle, Augustine, and Thomas Aquinas—masters though they were—could not possibly have known of these parameters. Des-cartes, Hobbes, Locke could see the position of detachment and some of its implications, but by the same token man's connection with the rest of nature had to be rejected and the significance of time could not have been grasped. They were, moreover, too busy creating modern science and modern society to step back and reflect on the implications of the possibility.

Twentieth-century man, however, can see the vastness of time and its overriding significance, man's connection with the natural world through evolution, and the fact of modern culture, its intellectual style, and its material product. The recognition of these factors—all of them together—provides a standard, a perspective, utterly unique in human history in terms of which man can decide what he *ought* to do. In this sense a new standard for philosophy and for political philosophy *cum* political science in particular becomes possible. What arises from this perspective is a new understanding of recommendation and justification, a new logic of recommendation and justification, which can only make full sense in the twentieth century.

V

Whether he satisfies our inclination for neatness or not, whether we understand him as an uneven and careless piece of work or not, from the point of view of evolution the human animal has "worked," that is, he has survived, which from evolution's point of view is the only thing that counts. What about the intellectual faculty itself? Do we really want to subscribe to the notion that this piece of equipment is some sort of ethereal spirit unattached to nature? What plausible reason could there be for such a bizarre conclusion?

Claude Lévi-Strauss begins his book *The Savage Mind*[10] with an extensive cataloging of the inclination of primitive peoples to engage in the most elaborate classification of the world around them. He cites the reports of a wide variety of observers in different parts of the world. Lévi-Strauss, by way of example, quotes the observations of a prominent ethnologist studying the Indians of the northeastern United States and Canada who emphasizes the wealth and accuracy of the Indians' zoological and biological knowledge and then continues:

Such knowledge, of course, is to be expected with respect to the habits of the larger animals which furnish food and materials of industry to primi-

[10]Chicago: University of Chicago Press, 1967.

tive man. We expect, for instance, that the Penobscot hunter of Maine will have a somewhat more practical knowledge of the habits and character of the moose than even the expert zoologist. But when we realize how the Indians have taken pains to observe and systematize facts of science in the realm of lower animal life, we may perhaps be pardoned a little surprise.

The whole class of reptiles . . . affords no economic benefit to these Indians; they do not eat the flesh of any snakes or batrachians, nor do they make use of other parts except in a very few cases where they serve in the preparation of charms against sickness or sorcery.[11]

And yet, "the northeastern Indians have developed a positive herpetology, with distinct terms for each genus of reptile and other terms applying to particular species and varieties."[12]

Lévi-Strauss, after listing a variety of examples comparable to the one just quoted, goes on to present an extensive list of cures and remedies developed by primitive peoples. He then concludes:

Examples like these could be drawn from all parts of the world and one may readily conclude that animals and plants are not known as a result of their usefulness; they are deemed to be useful or interesting because they are first of all known.

It may be objected that science of this kind can scarcely be of much practical effect. The answer to this is that its main purpose is not a practical one. It meets intellectual requirements rather than or instead of satisfying needs.

The real question is not whether the touch of a woodpecker's beak does in fact cure toothache. It is rather whether there is a point of view from which a woodpecker's beak and a man's tooth can be seen as "going together" (the use of this congruity for therapeutic purposes being only one of its possible uses), and whether some initial order can be introduced into the universe by means of these groupings. Classifying, as opposed to not classifying, has a value of its own, whatever form the classification made takes. . . . The thought we call primitive is founded on this demand for order. This is equally true of all thought but it is through the properties common to all thought that we can most easily begin to understand forms of thought which seem very strange to us.[13]

VI

The sociogenetic system of information transmission seems then to have not only its "genes," its individual ideas and pieces of infor-

[11] F. G. Speck, "Reptile Lore of the Northern Indians," *Journal of American Folklore* 36, no. 141 (Boston–New York, 1923): 273.

[12] Lévi-Strauss, *Savage Mind*, p. 8.

[13] Ibid., pp. 9–10.

mation, but also its "chromosomes," its vehicles for the carrying of groups of ideas and pieces of information. The inclination to order, to classify—Lévi-Strauss suggests—is built in. It is an important part of the way that the big brain operates in dealing with its environment. We have no reason to be surprised by the fact that nature would select for the capacity to learn and to teach when confronted with the peculiar characteristics of the human animal. And the capacity to learn and to teach involves the ability to organize information, to generalize it, and thus to pass it on efficiently. We have, further, no reason to be surprised when Thomas S. Kuhn and Stephen Toulmin call attention to the importance of paradigms and ideals of natural order[14] or to be surprised at Aristotle's acceptance of the premise of order. For Aristotle is a man like those we have come to call primitive, and so even are modern scientists.

We all know, when we reflect on it, that uncertainty and inconsistency fills us with the same sort of vague anxiety induced by failure in achieving status or rejection by the opposite sex. Reflect on the universality of religion or on the easily observed fact of contemporary American life that frustration breeds the fanatical, consistency-at-all-costs political understanding of the senile Old Right and the infantile New Left. The inclination to "put things together," to achieve a consistent, universal view is part of man's natural state, and when it comes to seeing the world as it is we may perhaps note another aspect of Freud's notion of the "uneven and careless piece of work."

Ashley Montagu describes nonliterate man and his intellectual processes:

> What happens is reality to the non-literate. If ceremonies calculated to increase the birth of animals and the yield of plants are followed by such increases, then the ceremonies are not only connected with them but are part of them; for without the ceremonies the increase of animals and plants would not have occurred—so the non-literate reasons. It is not that the non-literate is characterized by an illogical mind; his mind is perfectly logical, and he uses it very well, indeed. An educated white man finding himself suddenly deposited in the Central Australian desert would be unlikely to last very long. Yet the Australian aboriginal manages very well. The

[14]Thomas S. Kuhn, *The Structure of Scientific Revolutions* (Chicago: University of Chicago Press, 1962); and Stephen Toulmin, *Foresight and Understanding: An Enquiry into the Aims of Science* (Bloomington: Indiana University Press, 1961).

aboriginals of all lands have made adjustments to their environments which indicate beyond any doubt that their intelligence is of high order. The trouble with the non-literate is not that he isn't logical, but that he applies logic too often, many times on the basis of insufficient premises. He generally assumes that events which are associated together are causally connected. But this is a fallacy which the majority of civilized people commit most of the time, and it has been known to happen among trained scientists! Non-literates tend to adhere too rigidly to the rule of association as causation, but most of the time it works . . . [15]

VII

We ought now to be able to see that the scientific culture we in the contemporary West take so much for granted, which in fact we take to be the intellectual standard of the universe, is an abnormal and unusual state of affairs, a special case, when viewed against the sixteen thousand or so years of distinctly human development. The method of science is a set of rules built up over time as a way of checking our natural tendency to overgeneralize. The substance of scientific achievement is intellectual creation (but so are art and metaphysics and story-telling intellectual creation), but it is intellectual creation limited and checked by rules designed to discover error. Accounts of science which stress verification and those which stress creative imagination are both partly right. They become wrong only when they attempt general characterizations that purport to define science and when they fail to notice that science occurs in time.

We are faced with the fact—not the speculation—that scientific culture, industrial society, and modern politics have developed in the West since A. D. 1500. These phenomena are to be found nowhere else (save by transplantation) and never before. Why? This is the question that must be faced—no matter how complex and how difficult—even if we do not know enough to give a complete answer. Many signs of caution and an equal number of uncertainties warn us to set ourselves a meaner question; but no less a question will do, and we are obliged, therefore, to be bold.

It has already been suggested in a variety of ways and from a variety of angles that cultural evolution is a matter of information

[15] Ashley Montagu, *Man: His First Two Million Years* (New York: Columbia University Press, 1969), p. 200.

transmission, a sociogenetic system we have called it (following Waddington). Let us take our bold leap at the questions before us from this piece of solid ground. If, then, cultural evolution is a matter of information transmission, then what information is transmitted and in what form it is transmitted ought to be crucially important for cultural change. I mention "what information" is transmitted and "in what form" the information is transmitted as if there were two distinct things involved. The fact, however, is that the content and the form in which it is presented and received are inseparable parts of any transmission of information. If I wish to transmit to you a notion of the bird I now see at my window, it will make a great deal of difference if I present the printed words "the red cardinal," a photograph, a painting, a sketch, or if I am able to say the words to you or even sing them.

Let me compare two quite different kinds of "information receiving" experiences. Imagine yourself, first of all, attending a church service, preferably one of the more ceremonial sort, say, Roman Catholic, Episcopalian, or Lutheran. I have something in mind here like the state funeral of Sir Winston Churchill at the moment of the singing of "The Battle Hymn of the Republic." Put yourself, for the second situation, in a classroom taking an introductory course in symbolic logic. If you have missed that experience, an algebra class will probably do just as well. In the first case you are virtually surrounded by the communication. The complex of tones that makes up the music rings in your ears. The pew is hard and smooth and it vibrates with the thunder of the organ. The light plays on the stained glass, the golden candlesticks, and is absorbed by the black vestments. You sense the congregation, its breathing, its occasional cough. All of your senses are involved and you are in touch with your ancestors and their practices in a hundred ways at once.

But the situation in the logic class is precisely focused. All that counts are the marks on the blackboard and the way in which they represent a theoretical reality. There is no smell, no feel, no taste, and the sound of the instructor's voice is profoundly subordinate to the marks on the slate. We may like to say that pure reason is working here, but notice that reason is working through the visual sense, and to all intents and purposes the visual sense alone, isolated from all the other senses. Is it, perhaps, that this is what makes us incline to regard the latter case as one of *pure* reason and the former as mixed, even inundated, with emotion? What after all do we mean by "pure" in this context? If it occurs to you, as it did to me when I began to write these examples down, that it is rather peculiar to call the church service an instance of information transmission, reflect on the possibility that our modern minds have given the term "information" a bias toward situations of the logic-class type. Did "knowledge" or "wisdom" mean the same thing to Plato or Aristotle that "knowledge" means to a twentieth-century Logical Positivist? If not, why not?

We have talked about the social transmission of information as the core of cultural evolution. There must, we have said, be a teacher-learner relationship. Prolonged infancy and the big brain make possible a sociogenetic system for information transmission. All of this is hard to deny and yet it does not touch the question of how culture evolves. For it is significant not only that culture moves through time, is passed on from generation to generation, but also that its content has changed radically, especially in the last few thousand years.

The question, of course, is: How are we to explain the changes? A great many answers to this question or to ones quite like it have been offered. For Huntington it was climate, for Hegel the march of the Absolute Spirit, and most plausibly perhaps, for Marx the relationship of man to the means of production. We are all, I am sure, familiar with the kinds of criticism advanced against these various proposals. Because, however, answers have typically been overstated—in terms of *the* key to history—this does not detract from the overriding importance of the question. Notice that the typical explanation tends to lay stress on changes in the environment to which men react in a new way. But culture is not something that occurs in the physical environment—a climatic disturbance is not culture—it is something that occurs in the process of communication between men and between generations. There can be little doubt that the invention of the steam engine made a great deal of difference to the modern West, but saying this does not speak to the question of what circumstances would make a man want to invent a steam engine, know what he had done, and want to communicate this information to others. And even more importantly, what circumstances allow or persuade a man to want to invent anything at all? So far as we know, Buddhist monks have never been interested in inventing anything whatsoever.

VIII

Lately we have begun to hear a line of argument which stresses the impact of changes in the form and style of the cultural communication process itself.[16] An alteration in the physical environment cannot become culturally significant unless it is in fact reacted to, grasped, and communicated by man—and any understanding and communication of that understanding can only be done through the means of communication available. If we look back over the development of Western man we can discern stages in the development of means of communication. They overlap and merge in various ways, but stages are recognizable nonetheless.

Earliest communication was undoubtedly almost entirely oral, supplemented, of course, by gestures. This oral period is by far the longest, constituting by definition the whole of human prehistory. Then pictographic or ideographic writing developed, first on stone and clay and later on more portable substances. This was presumably an extension of early graphic representations like those which have been discovered in the caves of Spain. For the West the next important step was the development of a phonetic alphabet by the ancient Semites. This, it is interesting to note and may indeed be profoundly significant, is a step which the Chinese never took. The Greeks grasped the phonetic alphabet, adapted it to their fertile oral tradition, and the West has never been the same since. There follows an extended period in which culture was carried by the copying, recopying, and reading aloud of manuscripts. The portability of written messages and regulations literally made the Roman Empire possible. The fact that Christianity not only survived but conquered the barbarians is closely related to Christianity's control of information through its nearly exclusive possession of the ability to deal with manuscript. And then, at the dawn of the modern era

---

[16]See especially Harold A. Innis, *Empire and Communication* (Oxford: Clarendon Press, 1950), *The Bias of Communication* (Toronto: University of Toronto Press, 1951); and Marshall McLuhan, *The Gutenberg Galaxy* (Toronto: University of Toronto Press, 1962).

came Gutenberg and the printing press. I shall, for the moment at least, leave the development of radio and television to Marshall McLuhan who deals with it so imaginatively.

That the printing press created the public and the possibility of mass politics is, I think, so obvious that in one sense it scarcely needs discussion. And it certainly has not been discussed at least by social scientists. Western society and its politics—and preeminently that of the United States—grew up with the printed word; but because we have not taken time and cultural evolution seriously, we have built up elaborate accounts of Western politics and then been shocked to discover that they did not apply to the essentially oral cultures of Africa or the manuscript cultures of Asia.

IX

The insights of twentieth-century biology lead us to the notion of information transmission. If the genetic system is one of information transmission, then so also is the sociogenetic system one of information transmission. And if this is the case then the mode and manner of information transmission ought to be of central importance in cultural evolution. From the post-modern twentieth century, armed with a comprehensive evolutionary view, we can look back on the classical and the modern in political science and philosophy.

When we talk in broad categories such as classical and modern, we are, as our earlier discussion has clearly indicated, dealing with all-encompassing matters of perspective, with fundamental modes of thought. My contention, which follows upon the insights of Harold Innis and McLuhan, is simply that the dominant means of information transmission conditions, primarily by its form, the dominant mode of thought. A good many writers on epistemology have accepted the notion of Kant that the human world is defined and delimited by the structure of human thought. What they have not typically noticed, however, is that the structure of human thought has not always been the same, that the very structure of thought is affected by the way in which information moves from person to person.

The culture of the Athens of Socrates, Plato, and Aristotle was essentially oral, or more broadly what McLuhan calls audile-tactile. From the point of view of political theory the center of attention was the *polis* and the *polis* was understood as a natural and an oral phenomenon. It was speech (not writing), according to Plato and Aristotle, that opened the possibility of fullest human development. Socrates wrote nothing, Plato presented his ideas as speech transferred to writing (the dialogue form), and Aristotle's "writings" are said to be notes taken by his students.

Aristotle did not receive information by poring over the printed pages of an *Encyclopaedia Britannica*. He was not, and could not have been, the detached observer *looking* out at the world through the medium of the printed, and thus wholly visual, proposition. The world was all around him—he heard it, he felt it, he saw it, he smelled it, and all of these at once. Ethnologists of almost every description and opinion stress the unity of nature in the primitive mind, the lack of distinction between subject and object. We quoted Lévi-Strauss a few moments ago, noting that the important thing from a primitive point of view was whether or not there was a perspective from which a woodpecker's beak and a human tooth could be seen as "going together." We must recognize that Plato and Aristotle for all their towering achievement were from an evolutionary point of view just a step or two from the primitive. Should we then be surprised that Plato assumed that because there was a noun "justice" that there must be something in reality that corresponded to it.

You may very well be thinking something like this: "Aristotle was not the only one who had the world all around him. I smell, feel, hear, and touch things as well!" But think a little further. Our whole culture is built upon seeing behind the appearances. We are *taught* and we *learn* to realize that the roar of the automobile is incidental to the chemistry of gasoline combustion and to the physics of the piston rod. Aristotle did not think by holding a printed proposition before his mind and seeing how it relates to reality, but we do. Learning for us simply *is* a matter of mentally taking something apart and seeing how it "works." This does not encompass all that we learn and know, but it is its core. Print and all that goes with it is the dominant form of information transmission for us and it creates the dominant mode of our thinking. This was not so for Aristotle. Suppose that all of your experiences were like church services and none of them like classes in symbolic logic. Would you think differently or not?

Descartes and Hobbes were men of genius and they caught early the implications of the new way of thinking implicit in the printed, visually dominant, method of information transmission. Descartes and Hobbes responded quickly and began to think *objectively* in a way that only makes sense in the modern world. How can I prove that I exist? What kind of weird question would this be to a man swallowed up in nature? What would man be like in a completely pregovernmental situation, in a state of nature? What sort of strange question would this be for a man to whom man was by nature a political animal?

In this sort of context summation is dangerous, but let me nonetheless attempt a crystallization that will allow us to proceed. Modern society and modern culture—that which began in Europe around A.D. 1500—is built around the detached observer. It is only the detached observer who can attempt to conceive natural processes as a whole, who can consider a manufacturing-marketing process as a whole with the interworking of all of its parts, and who can conceive the governing of a large number of people over a large territory as a whole problem. Conceiving a political system as a whole and attempting to build one in the style of Hobbes or Madison requires a position of detachment like a man observing an ant colony.

Print, which concentrates information transmission into the visual sense, creates this position of detachment. Consider the forest-fire sequence in Walt Disney's *Bambi*. What would it be like if this had to be transmitted to us through the sense of touch or smell? I defy you to be detached from a forest fire communicated by the sense of touch, but because *Bambi* comes to us visually, we can be detached, we can consider the action from the outside.

Aristotle operating as a man in nature is not bothered by the jump from "some" to "all" involved in the proposition, "Man is by nature a political animal." He hears it, he feels it, he sees it, all at once and thus he *knows* it. We, however, in our detached position hold the *words* before our "mind's eye" and we immediately see the difficulty in moving from "some" to "all." Aristotle was not a fool—he knew the difference between "some" and "all"—but because he understood the world from another perspective the difference did not dominate his whole mode of thinking.

The phenomenon of politics, then, is not something for which we can provide an anytime-anyplace definition. It occurs in time. It is rooted in our biological nature and it has evolved as culture has evolved. It involves instinct and natural human inclination, but it also involves creative thought and thought has not always been the same. Neither is it the same throughout the world. In 1972 we can be conscious of print-culture politics rubbing against oral-culture and manuscript-culture politics. We can perhaps begin to make sense of our politics—that is, the politics of we humans and not simply we Westerners—if we tear ourselves loose from print-culture science and begin to look at man in the whole sweep of nature.

X

Teilhard de Chardin once remarked that evolution was not simply a theory, it was an epistemological condition, "a curve that all lines must follow" as he says in another place. This is the spirit of the argument I am attempting to make here. From the perspective of the late twentieth century we can see the biological foundations of political science, not only as the product of an animal who is by nature political-scientizing but as itself an evolving phenomenon moving and changing through time with the development of man's sociogenetic system. In Sir Julian Huxley's phrase man since Darwin has become "evolution become conscious of itself." It is increasingly clear that behavioralism as we know it in political studies, far from being the wave of the future that some contend, is in fact the last gasp of the detached observer perspective. The heavy stress on the separation of "is" and "ought" and the narrowly verifiable proposition, while unexceptionable detached-observer science, is being pushed aside by a generation of students avowedly interested in "values." It is true enough that this interest in "values" often amounts to little more than an acting out of the emotive theory of values, beloved of the behavioralists and the Logical Positivists, in the language of a shallow neo-Marxism, but it is nonetheless symptomatic of the dawning of a post-behavioral era. It is the form that the post-behavioral era ought to take that we are discussing here.

The problem of behavioralism in political studies has not been one of the application of scientific method where it did not belong; it has been one of the imperialism of a scientific culture which defines itself in terms of nineteenth-century physics.[17]   The push for empirically verifiable generations on the model of nineteenth-century physics labels all other investigatory activity "sub-scientific" and intellectually second-class.   Political studies has developed its own microcosmic variation of C. P. Snow's two cultures.

Taking seriously evolution in general and the biological foundations of political science in particular, however, has a profound effect on the two-cultures problem. First, the notion of the evolution of society as an extension of natural evolution in its more ordinary sense inevitably sends scientists and humanists looking for one another. When, for example, Talcott Parsons, surely one of the principal inspirers of contemporary scientific social science, takes up the evolution of societies, the footnotes to distinguished humanists abound.[18]   Similarly, because they deal with the evolution of man, as Professor Piggott suggests, "archaeologists are among those least likely to feel that they find any essential dichotomy between Snow's *Two Cultures.*"[19]   For a man who deals one day with ancient verb forms and the next with carbon-14 dating the two-cultures problem begins to dissolve, and I suggest that it dissolves under a philosophical-scientific perspective that is evolutionary.

The second effect of taking evolution seriously in political science is the more important. We can now see in 1972—although I have no doubt that many will refuse to see—when we understand the implications of the sociogenetic system of information transmission that empiricism as we have known it, the radical is-ought separation, scientism, the two-cultures problem, and indeed behavioralism itself in its expansionist, chauvinistic form are not final truths but byproducts of a phase in the evolution of the sociogenetic system.   And it is this insight that makes the post-behavioral era not just a childish

[17]Cf. Thomas Landon Thorson, *Biopolitics* (New York: Holt, Rinehart, and Winston, 1970).

[18]See Talcott Parsons, *Societies: Evolutionary and Comparative Perspectives* (Englewood Cliffs, N.J.: Prentice-Hall, Inc., 1966).

[19]Stuart Piggott, *Ancient Europe* (Chicago: Aldine Publishing Co., 1965), p. 10.

fad or a set of neo-Marxist Tinker Toys for frustrated assistant professors, but the opening of a new intellectual era in which social science will pay less attention to aping the method and style of natural scientists and much more attention to the substantive teachings of natural science itself. Natural science has paved the way for the recovery of the idea of the natural law which has until recently been the core of the Western political tradition. But it is a natural law with a substantive difference. It is no longer the metaphysically teleological natural law of Aristotle and Thomas Aquinas, it is a statement of cosmic evolution supported by a wealth of empirical evidence which gives substance and detail to vague but powerful phrases like Cicero's "right reason." Contemporary natural law synthesizes the "conform to nature" directive of the classical tradition with the "manipulate nature to human ends" exhortation of the scientific and industrial revolution into a notion well expressed by Francis Bacon, "We cannot command nature except by obeying her."

Man is part of nature, subject to the laws of energy transfer, to the need for food and reproduction, and to the force of gravitation. Man is also apart from nature, and the discovery of the sense of apartness by René Descartes and others broke the chains of tradition and made the scientific revolution possible. But the detachment has been overdone, for from another point of view, as biologist Marston Bates suggests, "Mankind can be viewed as a new sort of geological force, reshaping the landscape, favoring some kinds of organisms and destroying others, changing the very composition of the atmosphere with the smoke of countless chimneys, starting new chains of radioactive decay with atomic explosions."[20]

Political order is not in some separate compartment from this "geological force." On the contrary it controls it, directs it, brings it into and out of being; and thus it is that the operators of political order must come to know what they are doing. We cannot, however, expect them to know unless the scientists of political order make an effort to know and to teach.

The legislators of tomorrow are in our hands, and political science

[20]Marston Bates, *Man in Nature* (Englewood Cliffs, N.J.: Prentice-Hall, Inc., 1964), p. 106.

is the master science in Aristotle's sense, namely, that without right order very little else is possible. As a distinguished Fellow of Trinity College, Cambridge, once remarked to me: a political science that teaches nothing more than the way the public order is manipulated by private interests teaches cynicism. It may just be that we have seen the fruits of that teaching of cynicism.

.14. *The Philosophical Science of Politics Beyond Behavioralism*

ELLIS SANDOZ

> *". . . whence the Soule*
> *Reason receives, and reason is her being,*
> *Discursive, or Intuitive; discourse*
> *Is oftest yours, the latter most is ours,*
> *Differing but in degree, of kind the same."*
> *Raphael to Adam,*
> *John Milton,* Paradise Lost

It is rumored that positivist-behavioral political science is moribund if not dead. It is said that we now live in the post-behavioral period of political science; and credence need not be placed exclusively in rumors among the disgruntled. For this is the talk not only of challengers outside the present "establishment" but, fascinatingly, the demise has been proclaimed by unimpeachable authority. That assertion constituted the thesis and central thread of David Easton's presidential address to the American Political Science Association in September 1969—which thereby took on the variegated, macabre hues of, at once, the usual funeral oration, a *mea culpa* confession Soviet-style, and an incumbent's concession statement. Modern political science therewith crossed over a watershed, to all appearances. Moreover, the passing of behavioralism was further confirmed two months later when the Southern Political Science Association held its annual meeting in Miami, and among the panels was one devoted to "Post-Positivist Methodology in Political

Science." It was little short of astonishing that *none* of the participants on the panel itself—and not one member of the audience—
challenged the proposition that the end of positivist-behavioralist
political science has been reached. The controlling "orthodoxy"
of the past decade or so—"the most distinctive advance overall in
American political science since World War II"—apparently has not
only been thrown into unseemly disarray but is slipping into oblivion
with scarcely a word to suggest that there may yet be left in it the
breath of life.[1]

METAMORPHOSIS OF THE CHRYSALIS OR
THE EMPEROR'S NEW CLOTHES?

It is, of course, well known that men's persuasions—including
scientistic and sectarian ones—die hard, and it has been asserted
on the good authority of the 1971 president of the American Political
Science Association, Professor Heinz Eulau, that behavioralism is
one such "persuasion."[2] Perhaps there is yet no need either to
wipe away the bitter tear of nostalgia or sufficient reason to dance
gloatingly over the grave of the late lamented, the reports of whose
death are perchance greatly exaggerated. Still, representative evidence suggests a good deal more than the scant possibility of the

[1] The sustained attack from within (i.e., from the Left) against the behavioralist
orthodoxy began in 1967 with the publication of Charles A. McCoy and John Playford, eds., *Apolitical Politics: A Critique of Behavioralism* (New York, Thomas Y.
Crowell Co., 1967) and with the formation of the Caucus for a New Political Science
at the American Political Science Association Meeting in Chicago the same year.
"Establishment" and "orthodoxy" are quoted in context from McCoy and Playford,
Apolitical Politics, pp. 2, 9–10; cf. David Apter, ed., *Ideology and Discontent* (New
York: Free Press of Glencoe, 1964), pp. 34–35. The designation of behavioralism as
the most "distinctive advance" since the Second World War is by Marian D. Irish,
"Introduction: Advance of the Discipline?" *Journal of Politics* 30 (May 1968): 300;
cf. 307. The entire Thirtieth Anniversary Issue of the *Journal* is largely devoted to
celebration of the "advance" of "'the revolution' which has occurred . . . since
1948." (Ibid.) The transformation of that revolutionary advance into a *caput
mortuum* through Easton's perception of the "New Revolution" of post-behavioralism
must mark the months between May 1968 and September 1969 as the period of most
colossal scientific progress since the apple fell on Newton.

[2] ". . . my understanding of the behavioral persuasion in politics rests on a premise that may be accepted or rejected but that cannot be proved or disproved"
because it "is a statement of value, and as such it cannot be scientifically demonstrated to be either true or false." The "value" specified is "man." Heinz Eulau,
The Behavioral Persuasion in Politics (New York: Random House, Inc., 1963), p. 133.

passing of behavioralism; and if it should be true (as we are told) that political science has entered a post-positivist and post-behavioral epoch, one may properly wonder what meaning this has. Some will have a lingering doubt that behavioralism as such was ever much more than a mindless mistake. George Feaver observes that "the revolt against traditional political theory may be conveniently traced to David Easton's 1951 *Journal of Politics* article on "The Decline of Political Theory." There and in his widely received *The Political System* (1953), Easton set out his case against the central preoccupation of political theorists up to that time with the history of political ideas."[3] The reference here is obviously to the recent rise of "behavioralism," the descendant (conditioned by empiricism and logical positivism) of the movement in psychology initiated in the second decade of this century by John B. Watson and called "behaviorism," not to the more distant origins of the movement. If Feaver is indeed correct that behavioralism takes its immediate rise from the 1951 and 1953 utterances of David Easton, a

---

[3] Feaver, "Beyond Positivism: Recent Developments in Political Philosophy," paper prepared for delivery at the 41st Annual Meeting of the Southern Political Science Association, Miami Beach, Florida, November 6–8, 1969, p. 5. Antecedents reach back into ninteenth-century American political science, of course, and even much before that, if a long perspective is taken. For a larger pedigree see Albert Somit and Joseph Tanenhaus, *The Development of American Political Science: From Burgess to Behavioralism* (Boston: Allyn and Bacon, 1967), chap. 12. For the behavioral indebtedness to David Hume see Eugene F. Miller, "Hume's Contribution to Behavioral Science," *Journal of the History of the Behavioral Sciences* 12 (1971): 154–68. For a sketch of the "long perspective," see Leszek Kolakowski, *The Alienation of Reason: A History of Positivist Thought*, trans. N. Guterman (Garden City, N.Y.: Doubleday & Co., Anchor Books, 1968).

The evidence must be noticed that suggests the possibility that charlatanism played some part in the rise of behavioralism, for the decisive motivation for launching the behavioral movement in political science apparently was—if not a fascination for modish gimmickry—interestedly monetary rather than dispassionately scientific: "Orthodoxy has it that the term 'behavioral science,' subsequently corrupted to 'behavioralism,' was coined by a group of quantitatively oriented, 'rigorously' inclined social scientists at The University of Chicago. Anxious to secure federal financing for social science research, but apprehensive that some unenlightened 'persons confound social science with socialism,' they conceived the term 'behavioral science.'" Somit and Tanenhaus then notice this still-prevalent prejudice: "On the federal level, access to public funds was largely limited to the social sciences deemed worthy of the appellation 'behavioral sciences.'" Somit and Tanenhaus, *Development of American Political Science*, pp. 183, 185. Cf. the reinforcing remarks in this connection of H. R. G. Greaves, "Political Theory Today," in McCoy and Playford, *Apolitical Politics*, pp. 235–36, 242–44.

view which would seem to express something of a consensus, then it might be argued that behavioralism as a positivist mutation was a stillbirth, since that approach to politics and the social sciences generally had received deft and fatal theoretical critique in Eric Voegelin's Walgreen Lectures at The University of Chicago in 1951. But better to blunder than to read Voegelin, and his book was placed on the Index of the New Orthodoxy.[4]

The immediate concern here is to trace the configuration of the newly opened horizon of the discipline now that the dogma of the past generation has at last effectively been broken, for whether to be dated from 1951 or 1969, and whether it is the butterfly so long promised or a radically new creation in the making, it is plain to see that a quickening of American political science is in progress. The directions to be taken by a revived science of politics may no doubt be suggested by invoking the clichéd tag "relevance." Whether one is attentive to an Easton, a McCoy, or a Strauss, there can be little doubt that the widespread demands for a "revolution" in political science in our generation have been spurred by the perceived irrelevance and, hence, radical deficiency of the received science. Easton himself articulated this conviction of irrelevance in his work of 1951 and 1953. He devoted *The Political System* to explaining "why [and in what sense] political theory should continue to be included as a central part of political science" and to expressing "the ground for thinking that the development of any theory is an urgent task confronting political science today...." He argued for "construction of a systematic theory, the name for the highest order of generalization. Clearly, if political science could arrive at such a general theory" which would provide an "understanding of political life that ... would be both profound and extensive." In short if political theory were "to carry out the promise implicit in its designation as the theoretical field within political science ... [then] it ought to devote itself to analysing and constructively formulating causal as well as moral theory."

4 Published as Eric Voegelin, *The New Science of Politics: An Introduction* (Chicago: University of Chicago Press, 1952); see pp. 3–26. Representative was the response to the book of another eventual president of the American Political Science Association (1967), Robert A. Dahl: Voegelin, he wrote, "has not only 'un-defined' science; he has un-scienced it." Dahl, "The Science of Politics: Old and New," *World Politics* 7 (April 1955): 489.

The impetus of these and subsequent formulations by Easton helped both to effect the breach with the "old" or "traditional" political science and to sustain the behavioral movement into the present. As promise failed of performance, however, McCoy and Playford struck home from the "liberal" viewpoint and condemned "... the behavioralists ... [for] conservatism, a fear of popular democracy, and an avoidance of vital political issues." Professor Leo Strauss already had raised his banner in defense of liberal democracy in 1962 and concluded a withering critique by himself and four other prominent philosophical scientists in this vein:

> The crisis of liberal democracy has become concealed by a ritual which calls itself methodology or logic. This almost willful blindness to the crisis of liberal democracy is a part of that crisis.... Only a great fool would call the new political science diabolic: it has no attributes peculiar to fallen angels. It is not even Machiavellian, for Machiavelli's teaching was graceful, subtle, and colorful. Nor is it Neronian. Nevertheless, one may say of it that it fiddles while Rome burns. It is excused by two facts: it does not know that it fiddles, and it does not know that Rome burns.

Against the backdrop of this last remark, one may say that Easton's presidential address provides a formal acknowledgment that the behavioralists have been fiddling and an admission that Rome has been burning. But he only answered the fire alarm seven years after Strauss sounded it.[5]

There is also to be noticed a substantial affinity between the efforts in the 1930s and thereafter by those who have since sought the revival of a philosophical political science and the more recent men

---

[5] David Easton, *The Political System: An Inquiry into the State of Political Science* (New York: Alfred A. Knopf, 1953), pp. ix, 4, 314, 320; cf. Easton, "Introduction: The Current Meaning of 'Behavioralism' in Political Science," in *The Limits of Behavioralism in Political Science*, ed. James C. Charlesworth (Philadelphia: The American Academy of Political and Social Science, 1962), pp. 18–25; reproduced in Easton, *A Framework for Political Analysis* (Englewood Cliffs, N.J.: Prentice-Hall, Inc., 1965), pp. 16–22. McCoy and Playford, *Apolitical Politics*, p. 3. Leo Strauss, "An Epilogue," in *Essays on the Scientific Study of Politics*, ed. Herbert J. Storing (New York: Holt, Rinehart, and Winston, 1962), p. 327. From a less polemical stance, Strauss wrote also as follows: " . . . political philosophy deals with political matters in a manner that is meant to be relevant for political life; therefore its subject must be identical with the goal, the ultimate goal of political action." Leo Strauss, *What is Political Philosophy? And other Studies* (Glencoe, Ill.: Free Press, 1959), p. 10.

of the Left who clamor for relevance, invoking in their variety existentialist philosophy as well as revolutionary praxis. Both exoduses from received doctrine originated in an awareness of inadequacy gained under pressure of pragmatic crises in the social and political order: the former through the crisis of European and world politics of the Nazi period, the latter through urban turmoil, collapse of the universities and, more distantly, the contemporary threats of extinction by nuclear holocaust, surging demographic pressures, and a toxic environment. This to observe that political experiences of fundamental proportions were decisive in both instances. And this is a fact of significance, for it correctly suggests political science to be intimately connected with political experience in the common-sense meaning of the term.

The 1969 Easton address can serve our illustrative analysis as a prime example of the texture of the newest "new revolution" in political science. A striking, largely unarticulated theme throughout is the traumatic awareness that the behavioral period has abruptly and irretrievably ended precisely because a significant fraction of the political science profession has belatedly, almost hysterically, reacted to the geometrically intensifying pragmatic problems of political existence. The pathos of desperation pervades the address. The decisive argument to which Easton responds is that, unless political science addresses itself to immediate action and to the solution of snowballing problems which cannot wait for answers through ordered research, catastrophe is likely to overtake the profession, the country, perhaps humanity itself. It is existential trauma rather than rational discourse which has broken the behavioral lockstep of American political science today (if it is broken), just as it compelled abandonment of post-Weberian positivism in Europe a long generation ago.[6]

In the very nature of the case, the politics of pathos and trauma poses delicate problems, both dangers and opportunities, and no doubt provides a moment to be assayed with care. The earlier and present situations are significantly analogous especially since the experiential urgency of both derives from the perception of imminent

[6] Easton, "The New Revolution in Political Science," *American Political Science Review* 63 (December 1969): 1052, 1055, 1057, 1061. The pathos of the address as delivered was greatly enhanced by the visual and auditory spectacle of the apostle of behavioralism declaiming as its undertaker.

danger of the dehumanization of man—formerly through totalitarian *Gleichschaltung*, racism, and genocide, presently through obliteration of identity and personality in anomic vulgarian societies of alienated mass men living under pressure of chronic crisis.

Professor Easton reflects a recognition of this portentous moment in his presidential address. A leading apostle of the behavioral movement since its inception at Chicago, he now wishes to identify himself with the continuing revolution of the new politics movement —not the new politics, of course, of Eric Voegelin, but that of the Caucus for a New Political Science and, more generally, of the New Left which he shrilly proclaims to be the next stage in the revolution he helped set in motion twenty years ago. This progressive attitude (that Voegelin once described as "expert surf-riding on the wave of the future") is reflected in the Address from first sentence to last, and finds especially pungent formulation in Section 5 of the published document as it climaxes in these two sentences:

Those philosophies that seek to revive classical natural law and that reject the possibility of a science of man have thereby forfeited their opportunity and put in question their fitness to undertake this creative task of theory. We require boldly speculative theorizing that is prepared to build upon rather than to reject the findings of contemporary behavioral science itself and that is prepared to contemplate the implications of these findings for political life, in the light of alternative, articulate value frameworks.[7]

The quotation is of interest in several respects. It expresses conciliatory goodwill toward certain insurgents within the discipline and profession and opportunistically seeks to make common cause with them against philosophical reactionaries who have "forfeited" their right to be heard. The gesture is demagogically obsequious. The familiar, self-righteous anathema of excommunication from the profession is hurled at those benighted wretches who "reject science," and they are dropped one dreary time more down the oblivion hole. But the old orthodoxy is splintered; and instead of efficacious pronouncement one hears the plaintive whine of whistling in the dark.

The first sentence quoted reflects an ingenuous and denigrating misapprehension of the substance of creative work of seminal importance published over the past two decades. It is filled with incomprehending animus which spoils the nobility of Easton's other-

[7] Ibid., p. 1058; cf. p. 1051.

wise rightly conciliatory purpose. And in so doing, it does a distinct disservice to distinguished colleagues and to political science itself. Moreover, it sets up a straw man since, empirically speaking, no political scientist can be found who supposes that a revival of classical natural law could suffice to create a viable science of politics in this or any other century. Nor does any political scientist who is a reputable scholar believe a "science of man" to be "impossible."

Easton's assertion is, at best, *argumentum ad populum*, a coarse and regrettable appeal to the gallery. But, taken together, the meaning of his several statements is clear enough: the olive branch is extended to "H. Marcuse, C. A. McCoy, J. Playford, and T. Roszak," and the door is once again resoundingly slammed on the philosophers.[8] One may well wonder whether this is an optimal response to a propitious moment. But, after all, Easton also believes that "contemplative science was a product of the nineteenth century when a broader moral agreement was shared."[9] Well, what is there left to say? Perhaps only that the new wine of the 1970s is likely to be too strong for the old behavioral bottles Mr. Easton apparently still has in mind.

A TARDY PREAMBLE

What are the consequences for the *scientific study of politics* (and it is only this question that can be addressed here), granted the fact of at least the eclipse and perhaps the end of positivist-behavioralism? Clearly there is a philosophical critique of positivism and behavioralism that has been urged over the past twenty years, especially by Eric Voegelin and Leo Strauss, which undermines its theoretical presuppositions in a way that is unanswerable. And, equally clearly, there is acute and widespread disenchantment with behavioralism from the Left as well as throughout the spectrum of political and theoretical orientations which deplores its irrelevance, triviality, and inability to come to grips with urgent pragmatic problems of personal and social existence. The convergence of these two lines of critical and pragmatic rejection of what is called "scien-

---

[8] Cf. ibid., pp. 1058–1059, where the persons named are approvingly cited.

[9] Ibid., p. 1052. The statement is made in the context of Easton's formulation of "a Credo of Relevance" of post-behavioralism.

tific politics" reaffirms the adage that politics does indeed make strange bedfellows, since both those labeled as "traditionalists" and as members of the "New Left" are, in a sense, making common cause against the latest orthodoxy which is, as a result, foundering. This current situation permits an auspicious new freedom in the discipline and supplies the footing for broad establishment of a new philosophical science of man whose outline will be attempted in succeeding pages.

Perhaps certain misconceptions can be avoided and misgivings allayed by some preliminary observations about the "philosophical science of politics." From Socrates to Hegel politics was a "philosophical science," and it is particularly to the classical meaning of *episteme politike* that modern political scientists must be attentive if we are to have a *science* at all. This concretely means that Aristotle's *Nicomachean Ethics* and *Politics* comprise the cornerstone of political science, and the teaching there must be taken to heart. That is the indispensable first step, although it cannot be the last. For it is obvious that the empirical horizon and the theoretical range of political thought have expanded since Aristotle, and both of these dimensions of achievement must be accommodated in a modern philosophical science. Many scholars in many fields have contributed to the exploration of the materials to be embraced as well as to the work of theoretical penetration, work so momentous as to make the half century since 1925 one of the most spectacular in modern intellectual history. While this has largely been an underground movement as far as political science is concerned, perhaps nowhere else has the whole of this mammoth enterprise been so comprehensively drawn together as a philosophical science as in the writings of Eric Voegelin. It is, therefore, his great creative synthesis—so strange and little known to the average professor and student of academic political science—that supplies the foundation for the new science of politics and the basis of the presentation to follow.[10]

---

[10] The following pages sketch key aspects of the theory of political science for the most part implicit and explicit in the work of Eric Voegelin whose principal published studies are, in addition to *The New Science of Politics, Order and History*, (3 vols. to date; Baton Rouge: Louisiana State University Press, 1956———); *Science, Politics and Gnosticism: Two Essays*, trans. W. J. Fitzpatrick and Gregor Sebba (Chicago: Henry Regnery Co., 1968); and *Anamnesis: zur Theorie der Geschichte und*

From working steadily in these materials for more than two decades, and from both actively participating in professional associations and teaching undergraduate and graduate students for half of that period, I am acutely aware that communication about a "philosophical science of politics" is a demanding task. The very term is nearly nonsensical to a generation steeped in the jargon of positivism and behavioralism and a climate of opinion dominated, in addition, by Marxism and Freudianism. One might as soon seek to speak meaningfully of round squares and square circles, so profound is the communication gap caused by destruction of the language of rational discourse common to Western civilization for over two millennia and the general deculturation of our Enlightened society—especially, one may say, among the more sophisticated intellectuals who comprise the university crowd where the deleterious effects of the ideologies of the day have run rampant as the "mainstream" of contemporary thought. Hence, the attempt to provide a terse and lucid statement of the principal features of the philosophical science of politics faces, at the outset, the formidable obstacle of lack of a common linguistic medium. Closely related to this difficulty is the more profound one, namely, that the deculturation process in the universities not only has eroded theoretical literacy, but it has so penetrated the intellectual and ethical substance of

---

Politik (Munich: R. Piper & Co., 1966). Forthcoming are two major works: *In Search of Order* and *The Drama of Humanity*. The new science is exhibited also in the monumental sixty-five-volume *Geschichte des politischen Denkens*, under the general editorship of Jürgen Gebhardt, Manfred Henningsen, Peter J. Opitz, and Eric Voegelin, which is being published in Munich by the List Verlag. Volumes published to date are: Voegelin, ed., *Zwischen Revolution und Restauration: Politisches Denken in England im 17. Jahrhundert* (1968); Arno Baruzzi, ed., *Aufklärung und Materialismus im Frankreich des 18. Jahrhunderts: La Mettrie—Helvetius—Diderot—Sade* (1968); Jürgen Gebhardt, ed., *Die Revolution des Geistes: Politisches Denken in Deutschland 1770–1830; Goethe—Kant—Fichte—Hegel—Humbolt* (1968); Peter J. Opitz, ed., *Chinesisches Altertum und Konfuzianische Klassik: Politisches Denken in China von der Chou-Zeit bis zum Han-Reich* (1968) and *Vom Konfuzianismus zum Kommunismus: Von der Taiping Rebellion bis zu Mao Tse-tung* (1969). Peter Weber-Schäfer, ed., *Das Politische Denken der Griechen* (1969); Peter von Sivers, ed., *Respublica Christiana* (1969); Manfred Henningsen, ed., *Vom Nationalstaat zum Empire* (1970).

The presentation is also generally indebted to the work of Leo Strauss and that of his students; to writings by Hans Jonas, Étienne Gilson, Bernard Crick, Arnold J. Toynbee, Mircea Eliade, Ernst Cassirer, Albert Camus, Henri Bergson, F. M. Dostoevsky, and to others in ways too intricate to be detailed in this note.

the populace of academia that the indispensable common ground of agreement presupposed by rational discussion has been deformed to the point of disintegration.   Deculturation abetted by narrow specialization of studies has created a vacuum and made a fiction of the "academic community," and this void bars attempts at existential communication with a brutal efficiency.

Perhaps some lifelines thrown across this void can assist the task of communication.   For purposes of generalization, one may say that those who pursue the philosophical science of politics share with David Easton the conviction that theory is the heart of political science, but they reject the view that restricts scientific theorizing to the sphere of reflections upon regularities in the data of sensory perception and in elaboration of systematic interpretive constructs; and, they, therewith, reject as specious the celebrated and correlative dichotomies of fact-value and objective-subjective.   The proponents of the philosophical science agree with at least some of the essayists who contributed to *Apolitical Politics* that the error basic to the positivist-behavioralist doctrine "lies in the misguided attempt to assimilate political studies to the natural sciences"; but they reject as ill-founded the contention that philosophical science denigrates "practical knowledge" or at all proposes to "substitute one orthodoxy for another."   The philosophical political scientists reject the orientation, shared by the behavioralists and the insurgents from the Left, that politics is preeminently the knowledge of opinion and praxis, although they cheerfully endorse the demands of the former for theoretical and empirical rigor as scientists, and applaud the latter for perceiving "methodology as a pathological condition and the 'establishment' of behavioralism as a restricting orthodoxy."[11]   Finally, philosophical political scientists are as appalled as everyone else—even as is Mr. Easton, even as are nonpolitical scientists—by the crisis of our times and just as stoutly convinced that we must "do something!"   And they believe that what we must do is seek to restore common sense to its rightful place in the classroom and in political inquiry, no less than in the councils of state, and to recover for science the full range of reason that is our birthright as men, the very mark of our humanity, and the core of all political deliberation, choice and action.

[11] McCoy and Playford, *Apolitical Politics*, pp. 235, 10.

CONTOURS OF A NEW SCIENCE

A clarification of the language of philosophical science can best serve to introduce it and sketch its dimensions; we shall address successively, therefore, the meaning of *philosophy, experience, science,* and *reason.* The presentation is purposefully terse and mention is made only of essentials, as befits a sketch; for a more discursive understanding, the literature cited in the bibliographic note above may be consulted (see note 10).

Philosophy

The most comprehensive knowledge of political reality is attained primarily through a *philosophical* investigation, not through one narrowly modeled on the supposed "methodology" of the natural sciences. This means that in contradistinction to the prevailing paradigm of American political science, there need be no preoccupation with phenomena, no naturalistic reduction, no restriction of "reason" to inferential reasoning, no juxtaposing of "traditional" and "behavioral" schools, no dogmatic postulation of assumptions or doctrine, no specious fact-value dichotomy, and no systems of political thought. This is of course *not* to say that the science of politics may neglect phenomena, or dispense with the inferential processes, or set aside the understanding of institutional operations and political processes, or the gains (N.B.) made through the development of behavioral techniques of investigation and analysis. It is to say, however, that present tendencies in political science *needlessly* contract the scope of the discipline, fragment the profession, and result in fallacious historicism, on the one hand, and vitiating reductionism of one kind or another, on the other hand.

It is not man the animal, nor much less man the sentient integer, but man the political living being in the fullness of his *humanity* that science seeks to know and to assist toward a well-ordered and happy existence. No arbitrarily exclusive consideration of merely phenomenal reality can attain these objectives; and it is to philosophy that political science must ineluctably turn if it is to suffice as "relevant" to human needs.

Philosophy is literally the love of wisdom, and it is not commensurate with the systematic possession of knowledge: only God is Wise. Philosophy denotes, on the existential side, an erotic tension to the Ground of reality (being, *ousia*), a passion of mind (*nous*) which mediates the distance between the seeking knower (*zetein*) and the reality sought and known. What is sought and appropriated as "known" is only a fragment of the truth that Is; the insights gained are partial and provisional, but they are within these limits nonetheless validated to the exhaustion of rationality and evidence. Knowledge (*episteme*) is, thereby, clearly distinguished from (uncritical) opinion (*doxa*); and it both carries conviction and claims to be true.

The articulation of true knowledge is the work of the scientific inquiry or investigation (*zetesis*). This is carried out from the inevitable starting point of *a* man's passionate involvement in existence as a self-reflective participant in the reality to be explored; thence the inquiry rises the arduous way (*methodos*) toward the dispassionate contemplation (*theoria*) of truth in the scientific attitude. A life devoted to such endeavor is that of the philosopher or scientist, the *bios theoretikos*, or contemplative life. The cumulus of symbolic expression whereby the investigation reflects through language the experiences that constitute the moments of encounter with the reality explored compose the sequence of propositions (and other symbolisms) which "fix" them in consciousness and communication; taken all together these form the body of settled knowledge called "philosophy" and "political science" as subject fields.

The scientific propositions advanced as true, therefore, are the more or less adequate expressions or representations of experienced reality; it is plain to the investigator that: (1) the reality experienced outruns propositional statements and can never be exhaustively expressed; and (2) alternative formulations are acceptable. The primary test of the validity of statements is just this adequacy— that is, their conformity with the facts, or more broadly, with the contents of experience. Logical coherence is no more than a secondary demand, a support of rigor, not a guarantee of truth. Truth, therefore, lies at the level of experience, not at the level of the ideational construct or the propositions which articulate the experience.

The objective of the kind of philosophical investigation called "political science" is not so much knowledge as "action"; but this should not be superficially construed. Knowledge of the nature of man, and of moral, intellectual, and existential virtue is (for example) the presupposition of any rational attempt either to live in order or to so educate and legislate as to foster order in the lives of a citizenry; and it is the steadfast endeavor to live well as a man and govern well as a ruler—and thereby to attain, sustain, and foster happiness—which alone is *action*. The good life is the existential realization (or actualization) of the known truth in the lives of single persons and in political societies. And it is for this reason that "happiness" is the highest good for persons and for polities and political science the master art and science.

Experience

The scope of the "experience" which forms the empirical basis of political science is dramatically expanded beyond the present "permissible" limits of sensory perception and reflections on phenomenal regularities. This means that in the new science of politics the entire range and all the modes of man's experience become resources from which may be drawn by way of rational inquiry the knowledge of reality and its order. And that implies an epistemological revolution worthy of the name. *Truth* lies at the level of experience, not at the level of the propositions and symbolisms which articulate its content.

The experiential foundation of the science of politics, and the very source of scientific *objectivity*, is man's pre-scientific participation in all of the realms of being from the somatic and simply sentient to moral, aesthetic and mystical levels of experience. This existential participation is the means whereby man attunes himself with reality and gains the primordial grip on the whole of being which is the foundation of all knowledge. Participation (Plato's *methexis*, Aristotle's *metalepsis*) forms the human consciousness (*psyche*) itself, the essence of man's nature and humanity.

For conciousness is the site of all experience and the sensorium through which experiences happen—from sensory perception to mystical encounter with the divine. By reflecting on one's consciousness as articulated through participation in levels of reality from the corporeal to the divine Ground, the insight is gained that the process of consciousness is the "In-Between" (*metaxy*) of the tension bounded by the polarities of immanent and transcendent being.

Consciousness is, thereby, seen to be neither a "thing" (or object) of the external world (*immanence*), nor yet the transspatial-temporal or eternal divine reality (*transcendence*). Yet it *is*; and so it may correctly be designated as the nonobjective (or nonexistent) reality, or as the metaleptic reality of the In-Between. Lastly, consciousness is self-luminous, the clearing in reality, this luminosity being called "knowing," and knowing being contrasted as a mode of consciousness with forgetting, on the one hand, and with remembering, on the other hand, as the two further modes of the process of consciousness. Among the gradations of "knowing," the scale runs from simple sentient awareness through the reflective intensity of the modalities of reasoning to the brilliance of intuitive illumination. Encompassing the luminous consciousness is the darkling subconsciousness with its latent knowing and the receding experienced reality that first outstrips articulation and, ultimately, coherent experience itself.

In Western thought the major modes of differentiated experience and its representation through the self-reflective consciousness are the pneumatic and the noetic modes: the former is called *revelation*, the latter *philosophy*. Behind these lie the compact, primary experience of the divine cosmos as symbolized in ancient myth. This is not, however, to minimize the significance of other modes of experience and symbolization of importance to man, including sensory perception. But the highest modes of experience control existential understanding and are decisive to the scientific enterprise as that fosters man's grasp of existence and of the human condition.

Man participates through his composite nature in all of the realms of being so that his nature is their epitome. Participation differentiates the polarities of being experienced as an existential tension symbolized by linguistic "indexes": the tension between the pole of world-immanent reality and the pole of divine reality, of the "beyond" (Plato's *epekeina*) of transcendent Being. The tension of existence expands itself horizontally as well as vertically, as it were, so to embrace the whole of reality as articulated by the universal ideas which represent its quaternarian structure: God, man, society, and the world (*to panton*). And, finally, participation as historically expressed from remotest antiquity into the present—through the symbolic forms of myth, revelation, history, and philosophy—centers on the apprehension that being is a community which envelopes a common bond of oneness or sameness experienced as consubstantial to the principal partners, underlying all distinctions.

Science

There is, then, the task of redefining science (*episteme*) itself as the knowledge of reality attained by the rational faculty in man through its self-reflective search of experience for truth throughout all the realms of being as this transaction occurs in the concrete consciousness of individual men. Verification or validation or authentication is through an appeal to empirical evidence. But (and perhaps the point must be stressed) it need not be *restricted* to appeal to the kind of "experience" typical of a political science which takes as its paradigm physical science and which especially commends the experimental torturing of nature, as Leo Strauss has it.

The exploration of experience, in order to gain universality, is made both through direct observation and reflection and through a sifting of the historiographic documents available to scholarship by which man's past experience comes to mind in recollection. The process reaches from the empirical present to all past generations and to all societies of which we have knowledge. For it is plainly imperative that, *if* there is to be a political *science*, it must aspire to universal validity. Such an aspiration is patently incongruous in an enterprise parochially based until recently almost exclusively upon American and modern Western experience.[12]

This is to underscore the centrality of experience to any scientific undertaking as its empirical foundation. Whereas an imaginative effort is to be commended in addressing oneself to the problems of political existence, this is not a license to speculate "freely" and "boldly" if by that is meant in disregard of the actual content of men's experience as vouchsafed through direct and documentary evidence. Aristotle's statement near the end of the *Nicomachean Ethics* has permanent validity in this respect: "So we must examine

---

[12]This is, for example, one of the most telling criticisms in Bernard Crick's study, *The American Science of Politics: Its Origins and Conditions* (Berkeley and Los Angeles: University of California Press, 1959), chap. 12 and passim. Cf. Albert Somit and Joseph Tanenhaus, *The Development of American Political Science: From Burgess to Behavioralism*, pp. 61–62, 201–202.

the conclusions we have reached so far by applying them to the actual facts of life: if they are in harmony with the facts we must accept them, and if they clash we must assume that they are mere words" (1179a20–23).

Reason

Reason in science is the counterpart of experience. The political inquiry is conducted in openness to the whole range of rationality and through all the modalities of intellection known to the classical thinkers who first coined the term. It is a matter of pivotal importance that the new science operates with the differentiated reason of classical philosophy, rather than with the truncated "reason" of the Enlightenment *philosophes* and their latter-day successors. Eric Voegelin has shown that the meaning of reason (*nous*) in classical philosophy, which he calls "noetic science," is at least tenfold.[13] It can be predicated as follows. *Reason is:*

1. the consciousness of existing from a Ground, an awareness filled with content and not empty. Reason is thereby the instrument for handling world-immanent reality. Rebellion against reason since the eighteenth century creates a void in this dimension that must then be filled by substitutes.
2. the transcendence of human existence, thereby establishing the poles of consciousness: immanent-transcendent.
3. the creative Ground of existence which attracts man to itself.
4. the sensorium whereby man understands himself to exist from a Ground.
5. the articulation of this understanding through universal ideas.
6. the perseverance through lifetime of concern about one's relation to the ground, generative of existential virtue: *phronesis* (wisdom, prudence), *philia* (friendship), and *athanatizein* (to immortalize human existence).

[13] The following analysis of *nous* was presented by Voegelin in "The Drama of Humanity," The Candler Lectures of 1967, given at Emory University, Atlanta, Georgia, in April 1967. See the related discussion in Voegelin, "Was ist Politische Realität?" in *Anamnesis*, pp. 283–354; also, "Immortality: Experience and Symbol," *Harvard Theological Review* 60 (1967): 272–74. Cf. Ellis Sandoz, "The Foundations of Voegelin's Political Theory," *The Political Science Reviewer* 1 (Fall 1971): 30–73; "Civil Theology of Liberal Democracy; Locke and His Predecessors," *Journal of Politics* 34, No. 1 (February 1972): 2–36.

7. the effort to order existence by the insight gained through understanding the self to be existentially linked to the Ground and attuned to it: the major intellectual operation of so translating consequences of this insight as to form daily habits in accordance with it.

8. the persuasive effort to induce conscious participation of the self, and other men's conscious participation, in transcendent reason (Plato's *peitho*). The problem of communicating and propagating the truth of being.

9. the constituent of man through his participation in [the reason of] the Ground; *or*, the constituent force in man qua human through participation in the divine Nous which is his specific essence.

10. the constituent of society as the *homonoia* or "like-mindedness" of Everyman in a community formed through recognition of the reason common to all men. In Aristotle, if love within the community is not based upon regard for the divinity of reason in the other man, then the political friendship (*philia politike*) on which a well-ordered community depends cannot exist. The source of the Christian notion of "human dignity" is the common divinity in all men. Nietzsche perceived that if that is surrendered then there is no reason to love anybody, one consequence of which is the loss of the sense and force of obligation in society and, hence, of its cohesiveness.

If any of the enumerated components of reason is lost, imbalanced constructions result which eventuate in psychological and social breakdowns and disintegrations. As is suggested by this listing of the meanings of reason in Plato and Aristotle, noetic reason *is* philosophic or scientific reason, an activity of the consciousness articulated out of experience in a variety of interrelated symbolisms and symbolic forms.

THE MODESTY OF NOETIC SCIENCE: CONCLUSION

It is important to notice that political science is only a part of science and not the whole of it. Moreover, scientific knowledge itself is only one type of knowledge. The implications of these propositions are vast and only certain central ones can be mentioned on this occasion by way of conclusion.

1. Science can go no further than formulation of the hypothesis of transcendent Being as the divine Ground. It cannot draw the transcendent into the immanent to express it discursively. This is to say that Wittgenstein is in a sense epistemologically correct in his refusal to speak and in his insistence that one remain silent about dimensions of reality beyond the immanent. The problem is, strictly speaking, an insuperable one. It derives from an awareness of the ineffability of the transcendent partner in being and leads to the crises of symbolization which affect communication of the highest experiences. Man's existential reach outdistances symbolization in that certain kinds of experience cannot be adequately represented. Yet because his existence is in the In-Between experience itself transcends immanence. The alternative to the mystic's silence is the employment of paradox, analogy, allegory, and myth out of the urgent need to communicate the most important truths, however inadequately.

2. Nonscientific knowledge cannot be directly incorporated into, or annexed by, science. But, as rooted in documented experience, it does support the hypothesis of transcendent Being and finds expression through music, poetry, and the fine arts generally as non-noetic contemplative and symbolic modes. And this includes, of course, revelation itself and other modes of so-called religious experience and representation of both the West and the East, although the noetic dimensions of these experiences are only now being discovered and the problem remains, therefore, in suspense.[14]

3. A pre-scientific kind of knowledge is common sense, the personal and social self-interpretation of reality. The classical philosophers began discussion with common-sense propositions and proceeded through the methodical refinement of these concepts to an analytical and dialectical formulation in the scientific mode of noetic reflection. Common sense is no more (but no less) than the essential starting point of all scientific reflection on politics.

4. Finally, in the twentieth century the claims of ideological "knowledge" must again be mentioned, since by its massive presence it supplies a pervasive vocabulary for the discussion of things politi-

---

[14]See the important paper by Voegelin, "The Gospel and Culture," in *Jesus and Man's Hope*, eds. Donald G. Miller and Dikran Y. Hadidian, vol. II of *Proceedings of the Pittsburgh Festival on the Gospels* (2 vols. to date; Pittsburgh, Pa.: Pittsburgh Theological Seminary, 1971): pp. 59–101.

cal. Ideologies, whether of the Right, Left, or Center, are opinions (*doxai*) vitiated by existential deformation. Hence, rather than illumining existence, as does common sense which is also doxic, they systematically obscure it. The scientist must, therefore, extricate himself from this mode of intellection if he is to arrive at the dispassionate gaze on reality which it is his purpose to achieve. The essential precondition to rational discussion of political reality is a readiness to pursue the questions to the originating point in the Ground of being. If this condition is not met, the discussion cannot be termed either scientific or rational.

By way of conclusion certain applications of the foregoing reflections may be mentioned. The new science of politics just sketched is maximalist in conception. It supplies a large enough umbrella for almost everyone to stand under. It certainly accommodates, and welcomes, both traditional and behavioral approaches to political study and activity. And it welcomes the insights of those who have broken with the behavioralist orthodoxy because of irrelevance and triviality.

It urges, however, a sense of caution and restraint upon those who espouse one approach to the study of political reality in preference to another; and that is the caution that each approach be understood to be partial and not exhaustive. Noetic reality no more exhausts being than does the reality of things. The attitude of the scientist is one of openness to the whole of being and a sensitivity for the distance between the truth one knows and the truth as it is. This essentially Socratic attitude is the permanent therapy against prideful dogmatism and the debilitating closure of existence against truth—the experience of which the contemporary generation has had ample opportunity vividly to know. This openness and restraint is the foundation for every revival of scientific thought from the time of Bacon to the present. Not least of all it is the foundation for rejecting "systems" as being inimical to the scientific enterprise on principle. A "system" of science would be possible only if the knower were omniscient, a condition men cannot fulfill. No less than methodologies, systems are pathological phenomena.

The philosophical science of politics asserts both that man can, has, and does *experience* truth—and that his knowledge of it is fragmentary, tentative, and never exhaustive. The ordering of existence in accordance with the truth insofar as men are given to know it in experience is the end of politics as both art and science. It is therefore equivalent to the obligation of Everyman to live justly within his powers.